Writing ar
Digital Gene..........

# Writing and the Digital Generation

*Essays on New Media Rhetoric*

*Edited by*
HEATHER URBANSKI

McFarland & Company, Inc., Publishers
*Jefferson, North Carolina, and London*

LIBRARY OF CONGRESS CATALOGUING-IN-PUBLICATION DATA

Writing and the digital generation : essays on new media rhetoric /
edited by Heather Urbanski.
    p.    cm.
Includes bibliographical references and index.

ISBN 978-0-7864-3720-7
softcover : 50# alkaline paper ∞

1. Mass media and language.   2. Language and culture.
3. English language — Discourse analysis.   4. English language —
Rhetoric.   I. Urbanski, Heather, 1975–
P96.L34W75    2010
302.2301'4 — dc22                          2009049385

British Library cataloguing data are available

Cover image ©2010 Brand X Pictures

Manufactured in the United States of America

*McFarland & Company, Inc., Publishers
Box 611, Jefferson, North Carolina 28640
www.mcfarlandpub.com*

This book began in science fiction and fantasy fandom
and so is dedicated to all those in that community.

# Table of Contents

## II. Re-Mix: Participating in Established Narratives

## III. Re-Create: Creating Narratives within Established Frames

## IV. Teaching the Digital Generation

# Preface

Like my first book, *Plagues, Apocalypses and Bug-Eyed Monsters: How Speculative Fiction Shows Us Our Nightmares* (McFarland, 2007), which I wrote alone, the idea for this collection came to me at a World Science Fiction Convention. In August 2006, two months after I had submitted the manuscript for *Plagues*, I was struck by all of the panels at that WorldCon in Anaheim where digital media was a key part of the fandom. Having just completed one project, and planning to take my doctoral exams in just a few months, I knew that it wasn't exactly the right time to start another major project. But the idea stuck. All through the Con — at parties, in the hallways, after panels — I found myself drawn into discussions of an evolving digital aspect to fandom, and when I returned to Pennsylvania, working on that idea actually became a welcome break from preparing for my exams.

Fast forward several months to April 2007: my exams were over, my dissertation proposal was moving along, and I was presenting the first iteration of my thoughts on participatory entertainment at the Popular Culture/American Culture Association's National Conference in Boston. By this point, I was convinced that this line of research had a lot of potential, and as I attended other panels, I came to believe that the time was right for a book about digital media and rhetoric. But I also knew that I was not in a position, either from an expertise perspective or from a time commitment one, to do it all myself. That's when I looked around and realized I didn't need to do it all myself— and the idea for an edited collection, calling on the expertise of those around me, was born.

So this collection is very much the product of the various communities to which I belong, both fan and scholarly. The ideas began and were fostered at conventions and conferences and the calls for proposals were circulated at such events as well as online. The history of the collection's creation mirrors its subject, with its roots in a "physical" fan community, and then its use of digital media (mostly email) to communicate and circulate information. Some of the contributors I know personally and asked to participate because I know

1

their work; others I met at conferences after having accepted their chapters; and still others I only know via email (but hope to meet in person someday).

Much has changed in my life and career since I conceived this project: I was a Ph.D. student at Lehigh University in Pennsylvania when it began and am now an assistant professor at Central Connecticut State University. Along the three-year journey from idea to project completion, my thinking has been influenced and adjusted in many small ways, some of which I may not even be consciously aware of yet. One thing that has not changed, however, is my belief that digital media is enabling an explosion of creative, rhetorical activities that occur in places and in media that do not fit conventional, traditional Humanities, or educational, definitions. But just because they look different from the texts at the foundation of our disciplines — literature especially — that is no reason to ignore, or at worst devalue, them. When I set out to capture those activities, I knew I wanted to gather as many perspectives as possible. With twenty-nine contributors in the pages that follow, I believe that I have succeeded.

Because this book is so firmly rooted in fan and scholarly communities, my first debt of gratitude is to both the individuals and those organizations that devote their time and energy to maintain fan sites, run conventions, and just generally keep everything going. In addition to expressing my thanks to all of my contributors for their work and their willingness to share their experiences, I also want to thank several others whose insights and advice were helpful to me as I conceived and developed the project: Jamie Bono; Scott Warnock; Marc Zicree; and Chris Garcia. I'd also like to single out one particular contributor, Diane Penrod, for her unflagging support and invaluable advice that has been a source of strength for me since she was my advisor when I was in graduate school at Rowan University.

And, of course, none of this would be possible without the support of my family, especially my "research assistant" (aka Mom), who proofread and reviewed the references in every chapter and offered her usual all-encompassing support. I hope that my niece will forgive me for missing her recital this year so I could finish this manuscript and promise to pay my family back for their support during yet another project.

# Introduction: Blurring Rhetorical Borders

*Heather Urbanski*

With the recent explosion of participatory digital media, rhetorical reality is quickly catching up with rhetorical theory. The idea of audience participation in texts is at least as old as Aristotle; now that theory is made manifest by digital media. Within the Humanities, we have long accepted a rhetorical view of reading as a transaction in which we re-create, or even re-write, a text each time we read it, but today's "Digital Generation" seems to take that theory to an entirely new level, often literally creating the narratives as they experience them.

Under the participatory entertainment umbrella, we see such active digital engagement with popular culture as fan fiction, Massively Multiplayer Online Role-Playing Games (MMORPGs), and even Fantasy Football. My interest in this topic was piqued when I heard Jane Espenson, formerly a writer on *Buffy, the Vampire Slayer*, remark at the 2006 World Science Fiction Convention that "there is a thin line between fan and pro" when it comes to Internet fandom, reflecting a rhetorical blurring between receiver and sender. In so many ways, today's digital technology allows an unprecedented variety of participatory entertainment to flourish, calling into question the traditional Rhetorical Triangle that separates sender, receiver, and message.

The Digital Generation seems to be no longer content to remain passive receivers of messages but instead demands to be part of their creation. For those of us who work with such students, this blurring of the boundaries raises significant questions, questions that need to be addressed from an interdisciplinary perspective. For example, from a pedagogical standpoint, how can we incorporate the experiences, literacies, skills, and interests of Digital Generation students into our classrooms? How will our rhetorical and media theories need to be re-worked to account for the interactivity inherent in participatory entertainment?

The writing and/or rhetorical component of participatory entertainment has the potential to be significantly different from the centuries of printed text that proceeded it. Similar, in many ways, to the shift from an oral to a print tradition famously maligned by Socrates, digital media seem to many to represent a revolution in communication. Even if that is a bit overstated, and many others would argue it is (or at least is premature), the impact of digital media on the way in which contemporary American students learn to communicate (and to write) cannot be denied. We cannot know for sure if today's digital media will truly revolutionize rhetoric or have more of an evolutionary impact, as we have seen with computer-mediated composition, but now is the time to begin considering its impact. While I realize that this collection of essays and profiles cannot provide all the answers, my goal for the project is to contribute to the current dialogue regarding how the experiences of Digital Generation students can and will impact our discourse, and thus our culture, in the upcoming years.

A key assumption of this collection is that, contrary to fashionable crisis rhetoric that "no one reads anymore," the Digital Generation actually engages in more rhetorical activity — creating, writing, analyzing, etc. — than perhaps any before. As Director of Composition, I often hear these twin complaints: "Students don't read anymore" and "Good writers must be good readers." Yet, as a fan, I know that many of the most rhetorically active and best critical thinkers I've encountered rarely "read," at least not texts traditionalists would claim. With "new" media — film, television, gaming — there are so many ways to engage the mind that the conventional construction "reading is fundamental" starts to look rather provincial and nostalgic. And that comes from a reader who moved, literally, more than one thousand pounds of books within the past year across several states. I love books, but not exclusively, and am often puzzled by contradictions in the current research: for example, one study decries that because of increased exposure to technology such as computers and videogames, "our skills in critical thinking and analysis have declined" (UCLA) while another, from the Digital Youth Project, praises those very same activities for providing today's teens with "basic social and technical skills they need to fully participate in contemporary society," skills built around social, autonomous, and self-directed systems (Ito, et al.). I designed this collection to capture those activities that don't fit into traditional print-based definitions of literacy and rhetoric and the chapters that follow describe and document the participatory activities and the ways they are changing how we see writing.

There is, of course, a valid question as to whether the "Digital Generation" of this collection's title even really exists, a claim Siva Vaidhyanathan directly challenges when he declares, "There is no such thing as a 'digital generation.'" Vaidhyanathan is rightly concerned with issues of access, describing the reality that "college students in America are not as 'digital' as we might wish to pretend. And even at elite universities, many are not rich enough" and warning that "talk of a 'digital generation' or people who are 'born digital' willfully ignores the vast range of skills, knowledge, and experience of many segments of society." The power of Vaidhyanathan's critique comes in his observation that the "generation" tag washes over the diversity of human beings and "excludes anyone on the margins," an exclusion that has real consequences because "we forge policies and design systems and devices that match those [generation-based] presumptions." As I have put this collection together, and as you review the chapters to come, I hope you will keep in mind the complexities of the issues under review and Vaidhyanathan's reminder that "technologies do not emerge in a vacuum."

## Fans and Digital Media: Cultural Factors of the Digital Generation

Even given that caveat, there are still identifiable cultural factors that contribute to the unique rhetorical situation of digital media, beginning with the subculture that is fandom: Fans and fandom do not fair very well in scholarship, as Joli Jenson observes: "The literature on fandom is haunted by images of deviance. The fan is consistently characterized (referencing the term's origin) as a potential fanatic. This means that fandom is seen as excessive, bordering on deranged behavior" (9). Jenson's analysis of the literature on fandom, furthermore, finds a passive role assigned to the fan, who is constructed as merely responding to a media or celebrity system. Yet the reality is the opposite, which Henry Jenkins describes as the "ability to transform personal reaction into social interaction, spectator culture into participatory culture" ("*Star Trek*" 266). This essential nature of fandom is at the heart of the ideas in this collection.

Fandom is in a state of transition, however, because of digital technology. As Jenkins has recently described, "New technologies are enabling average consumers to archive, annotate, appropriate, and recirculate media content" (Introduction 1). In addition, Jenkins observes, "Over the past decade, fandom has both been reshaped by and helped to reshape cyberculture" (5). Similarly, as Jonathan Gray, Cornel Sandvoss, and C. Lee Harrington argue, economic and marketplace forces have changed the view of fans to a more culturally acceptable "specialized yet dedicated consumer [who] has become a centerpiece of media industries' marketing strategies" (4). Yet, not

all fandoms are created equal, as some of the contributors later in this collection note, and as Gray, Sandvoss, and Harrington also observe, "As cultural
judgment has become increasingly detached from the state of being a fan, our
attention shifts to the choice of fan object and its surrounding practices, and
what they tell us about the fan him- or herself" (5).

If Stephanie B. Gibson is correct and "we are a culture inextricably bound
up with our electronic technology" (2), that technology brings "nonlinearity,
nonsequentiality, and interactivity" into everyday life (7). This digital media
is accessible, easy to use, interactive, and increasingly powerful and sophisticated, as Gray, Sandvoss, and Harrington also note (8). It is, for many intents
and purposes, global, and, as Charles Bazerman points out in *Shaping Written Knowledges*, technology plays a key role in enabling social activity which
in turn transforms the social situation: "social situations structure communication events" and "forms of communication restructure society" (128–29).

At the convergence of television and the web, specifically, according to
June Deery, the opportunity to use Internet technology "as a secondary
medium to supplement the primary medium" allows both producers and fans
to use "the Web's practically infinite ... ability to store and retrieve a greater
amount of efficiently organized information than other media" (166). This
inter-media communication, combining television and Internet, has allowed
fans "to be more active and participatory than audiences of the past" (162).

We find participatory entertainment at this intersection of fandom and
technology. As Gibson argues, "Gatekeepers, both literal and metaphorical,
are reconceptualized in the world of digital text" (9), thus allowing greater
numbers to storm the digital gates, as it were, because, Jenkins observes, "The
concept of the active audience, so controversial two decades ago, is now taken
for granted by everyone involved in and around the media industry" (Introduction 1). When it comes to television, in particular, contemporary viewers
demand more participation in their entertainment, and, Deery argues, television producers have had to respond (162). Even such mundane technology
as the remote control, according to William Uricchio, "established new patterns of interaction" (172) with our entertainment. In this growing cultural
insistence on participatory entertainment, fans of all kinds expect to be actively
involved, no longer content to passively receive messages. They demand to
be part of the creation of those messages.

## Describing the Digital Generation: The Goals of This Collection

While many mainstream news stories follow the model of "let's look at
the strange new world of (for example) Second Life," scholars tend to find in

the fast-developing digital media a ready outlet for pre-existing theoretical approaches to the world. The essays and profiles in this collection balance those perspectives, and several others, to examine what participatory entertainment looks like to those who engage in it, and how it works for them, from a variety of interdisciplinary perspectives. To do so, the chapters focus on how we use digital media for entertainment, for "play," as opposed to for work or for social/political activism with the goal of capturing the significant, complex rhetorical activities of participatory entertainment that may be outside the margins of more traditional academic scholarship in rhetoric or Cultural Studies.

As such, this project is primarily rooted in fandom of various kinds. From television fans, to sports devotees, to the dedicated gamers, and all others in between, the explosion of digital media has changed the way these constructed communities interact, as many scholars have begun to document. The pieces in this collection will contribute to that conversation, both culturally and academically and, as opposed to "early fan scholars who were outsiders to the fan communities they studied" (Gray, Sandvoss, and Harrington 3), the chapters that follow are written by those enmeshed in this digital culture, who are fans as well as academics, to provide the valuable perspective of those who maintain this hybrid identity as part of their everyday lives.

The essays and profiles in this collection represent the dynamism and variability in the rhetorical activity of everyday lives but this collection is not about defending digital media, or at least not primarily. As I tell my writing students, that approach assumes an inherently adversarial stance that seldom accomplishes much. While examples to the contrary abound, we are not engaged in a battle between print warriors and new media soldiers. When we use those metaphors, when we allow an aggressive, "take no prisoners," all or nothing mentality to dominate our *own* rhetoric, then what are our students learning? What are *we* learning, besides to harden our presuppositions into immovable objects?

Instead, I hope this collection will be seen as presenting many aspects of a *conversation*, where real knowledge is made through the process of immersion, understanding, analysis, and even critique. Binaries such as new media versus "old" or avatars versus "real" people more often than not impoverish the conversation and as a scholar who has jumped among more communities and disciplines than I care to count, that approach seems myopic to me. It has become almost a cliché by now but I can't help holding onto a concept so simple in its profundity: Instead of "either/or," I prefer "both/and." Ironically, that theoretical construction encapsulates a plaque I have hung in every apartment I have lived in: "I may not always be right. But I am never wrong." This multiplicity of perspectives and a resistance to simplistic binaries is admittedly something I developed as I "matured" but nonetheless, it was a guiding principle when I assembled this collection. As a writing teacher, I was anxious to capture these changes as they were occurring, to document and reflect the additional writing, thinking, and rhetoric that is occurring on computer screens all around us. And, true to my belief in "both/and," this rhetoric of digital media does not replace the tradition of textual and oral rhetoric that may be more familiar. Rather, it is another piece of the mosaic, another angle from which to approach communication and thought.

Not every instructor can, or even should, be leading raids in *World of Warcraft* late into the weekend nights, nor am I saying that every writing teacher should craft volumes of fan fiction in between grading student papers (though it probably couldn't hurt). While actually participating in these activities does provide valuable insight, as the chapters and profiles in this collection illustrate, awareness, understanding, and respect for the rhetoric involved in participatory entertainment is a key first step.

I am far from an expert, technical, pedagogical, or otherwise, but it seems to me from my own limited subject position, that we are on the verge of a significant cultural shift in the way we communicate. There is no shortage of scholars from whom we can quote to identify this shift but Gray, Sandvoss, and Harrington provide a particularly useful vantage point for this collection: "these changing communication technologies and media texts contribute to and reflect the increasing entrenchment of fan consumption in the structure of our everyday life" (8). The benefit of collections such as this, as Gray, Sandvoss, and Harrington observe, extends beyond their initial scope in popular culture "because they tell us something about the way in which we relate to those around us, as well as the way we read the mediated texts that constitute an ever larger part of our horizon of experience" (10). If we are to avoid becoming the cliché of the curmudgeon complaining about "kids today," then we must back away from the crisis rhetoric, be willing to demonstrate the flexibility and resistance to early closure that characterizes the best our discipline has to offer, and make room in our classrooms not only for the rhetorical activities described in this volume but also for those we cannot predict.

## *Overview of the Volume*

As Gray, Sandvoss, and Harrington describe, digital media is an integral part of our experience and experience is the operative term for the chapters that follow. Both traditional academic essays and less-conventional participant profiles from more than twenty-six different authors capture the rhetorical activities of the Digital Generation from a variety of perspectives, though a few notes of caution are needed. First, these are the work of fans and as such, are full of fan opinions and speculations. The goal of the collection was to be polyvocal and my contributors delivered. So, be warned if you are faint of heart or are particularly attached to one of the texts under analysis. Second, while this is for the most part a "family friendly" collection, several chapters do contain expletives in their quotes from online fan behavior. I don't expect readers to be easily shocked, but do want all to be forewarned. Finally, as is always the case with any print collection, the world has continued since these chapters were written and so changes in both the digital world and the fortunes of particular sports or movie franchises may make some of the details seem a bit out of place. Updates were made where possible but while details may change, the overall points are nevertheless still quite valid.

## Part I. React: Maintaining a Fan Community

We begin with what many would consider the "typical" fan behaviors of following, supporting, and critiquing their favorite shows and activities, ranging from the most socially acceptable of fandoms (the multi-billion dollar arena of professional sports) to one of the "lowliest" (the humble, and unfortunately disappearing, soap opera).

Melissa Ames's essay, "The Inter(Active) Soap Opera Viewer: *Fan*tastic Practices and Mediated Communities," begins the section with a firm grounding in the connection between television and its fan communities, paying particular attention to the ways in which the specific nature of a televised narrative (in this case soap opera's year-round, daily airings) influences fan activities. Ames then delves into more empirical work, examining the diverse Internet communities available to fans of one particular serial, *General Hospital*, and speculating on the implications of that variety for soap opera fandom.

The next essay, Michael R. Trice's "Going Deep: What Online Sports Culture Teaches Us About the Rhetorical Future of Social Networks," seems a study in contrast, in part because of the intentional juxtaposition of soap operas with sports fandom. There are more similarities, though, than might initially be apparent, as Trice's analysis of sports on the Internet and interviews with online sports journalists reveals. In this chapter, the nature of sports fandom as a community, and digital media as a new vehicle for communication within that community, becomes clear, which is perhaps unexpectedly not all that different from Ames's conclusions regarding soap opera fans.

Another traditional fan base, science fiction fans, is the focus of Marina Hassapopoulou's "Spoiling *Heroes*, Enhancing Our Viewing Pleasure: NBC's *Heroes* and the Re-Shaping of the Televisual Landscape." In this review of the "official" options made available to *Heroes* fans by the show's producers, Hassapopoulou both documents the evolving nature of television serials via "transmedia storytelling" and raises questions regarding the actual levels of participation allowed by what is billed as "interactive" features of the show's website and network promotions.

The nature of truth, history, and evidence in online fan communities are called into question by the mere presence of the "Delete" button, as Karen Hellekson's analysis goes in "History, the Trace, and *Fandom Wank*." Taking one particular fan blowup (documented by the community blog known as *Fandom Wank*) as an illustrative example, this chapter examines the ways in which fan communities are negotiating new standards of history in the digital age.

Leaving the "official" realms for the entirely fan-generated is Kimberly DeVries's "Writing Wonder Women: How Playful Resistance Leads to Sustained Authorial Participation at *Sequential Tart*." In this chapter, DeVries examines how one group of female comic book fans took the familiar fan 'zine into the digital realm, claiming a space for their own voices to be heard among what they found to be too often a sexist discourse within comic fandom. Her analysis of *Sequential Tart* is informed by her participation in the webzine as well as grounded in feminist and new media scholarship and reveals a fan community actively engaged in responding to and appropriating the texts they enjoy on their own terms.

In the first participant profile, "What the Frell Happened? Rhetorical Strategies of the *Farscape* Community" Sean Morey describes the role of digital media in another traditional fan activity: the save our show campaign. In this case, the show in danger was *Farscape* and while Morey and his fellow Scapers were not ultimately successful, this profile provides an interesting peek into the role of rhetoric in such fan activities in the digital age. And on an entirely different note is Thomas B. Cavanagh's profile "The Realtime Forum Fan," which provides an unexpectedly rhetorical spin on "watching the game." The forums Cavanagh describes take place while the applicable sporting event is occurring, and contrary to conventional iconography, fans are not sprawled on the couch or lounge chair with a beer (or several) but rather are in front of computers, *writing*. Starting on television, but not ending there, is Georgiana O. Miller's profile, "'As Seen on *The Colbert Report*': Or, Why I Love Reality TV," about the intersection of reality television and digital media. In this amusing and honest confessional, Miller reflects on her obsession and on how it seeps out of the television realm into other media aspects of her life.

## Part II. Re-Mix: Participating in Established Narratives

The second grouping of chapters moves into more specialized fan activities (fan fiction and fantasy sports) that may be less familiar to conventional portrayals of fans but that are also standard, core aspects of fan participation within these communities.

In "Making Our Voices Heard: Young Adult Females Writing Participatory Fan Fiction," Susanna Coleman's concentrated focus on one story, and one young-adult fan fiction writer, provides an intriguing glimpse into just how intensive and participatory this fan activity can become. Using the idea of "interruption" to capture the agency she observes in the impulse to write fan fiction, Coleman traces the research, community engagement, and finally rhetorical skills involved in bringing one story to fruition as a means to examine the implications for our broader understandings of fan participation.

Participation of a different sort is the subject of Julie L. Rowse's "*Dungeons and Dragons* for Jocks: Trash Talking and Viewing Habits of Fantasy Football League Participants." Taking on the hugely popular, and profitable, fan pastime of Fantasy Football, Rowse combines (auto)ethnography and interview techniques to examine two seeming inter-related aspects of the activity: the role of "trash talking" and the influence on televised game viewing habits. While her sample is small, and so her conclusions very difficult to generalize, the perspective from "inside" such fantasy leagues provides her with several intriguing conclusions from both a fandom and a rhetorical perspective.

The technical and rhetorical skill required for the fan activities under analysis jumps by leaps and bounds in the final essay for this section, Kim Middleton's "Alternate Universes on Video: Ficvid and the Future of Narrative." One part fan fiction, one part fan video, Middleton examines what she calls "ficvids" for the new digital literacies their producers display, including an understanding of narrative cinema's formal conventions combined with the incredible technical prowess required to pull individual shots out of existing scenes and then reassemble them into a new narrative plot. The rhetorical skills of ficvidders certainly call into question the crisis rhetoric so often in vogue, as Middleton deftly observes in this chapter.

The two profiles that round out this section take on fan fiction from perhaps unexpected contexts. Julie Flynn's description of the crossover, a particular type of fan fiction, places such fan participation within the realm of literary studies and narrative exegesis in "Dean, Mal and Snape Walk into a Bar: Lessons in Crossing Over." And from a completely different perspective, Kristine Larsen, a professor of physics and astronomy, describes in "Stars of a Different Variety: Stealth Teaching Through Fanfic" the fan fiction impulse as "an application of the scientific method" by sharing her own experiences following her fandoms into new and interesting topics for research and rhetoric.

## Part III. Re-Create: Creating Narratives within Established Frames

The fan participation in the third section takes the concept of writing and composition most fully into the digital realm, covering some of the "flashiest" examples of digital media: YouTube, Second Life, and MMORPGs.

The essays in this section begin with Diane Penrod's take on the cultural phenomenon that is YouTube, "Writing and Rhetoric for a Ludic Democracy: YouTube, Fandom, and Participatory Pleasure." With both a fannish and scholarly eye, Penrod examines the ways that fan videos posted on that site demonstrate a range of participatory responses to popular narratives. As opposed to the text-specific ficvids that Middleton examines in Part II, the focus in this chapter is on the broader questions that the sweeping, inter-generational narratives of *Star Trek*, *Battlestar Galactica*, and *Star Wars*, with so much text and meta-text available, raise within a popular culture that now has the technology to compose mash-ups, homages, parodies, etc. of its own and distribute them nearly instantaneously.

In Christopher Paul's essay "World of Rhetcraft: Rhetorical Production and Raiding in *World of Warcraft*," we find the first appearance of *World of Warcraft*, a key and significant MMORPG. In addition to providing a useful primer to such gaming environments and the concept of raiding that can be central to that experience, Paul also begins the work of breaking the conventional wisdom of gamers as couch potatoes, camped out in basements with controllers in their hands, mindlessly killing monsters in isolation. By contrast, Paul's analysis finds, succeeding in such games requires social and rhetorical skills of unexpected sophistication.

Continuing what might be described as the "explaining gamers" section is Matthew S.S. Johnson's analysis of the marketplace in the MMORPG *Guild Wars*, "Rekindling Rhetoric: Oratory and Marketplace Culture in *Guild Wars*." Using the concept of the ancient Greek marketplace (*agora*) as his jumping off point, Johnson examines the activity and experience of game play in what I think may be an unexpected way, arguing that such games recreate a "space" that has been lost in contemporary culture, a space for public critique and social action that may reappear and bring forth change in the "real" world.

Switching gears to another, oft-maligned virtual world, Second Life, Mark Pepper introduces readers to the concept of Machinima, the "filming" of a virtual space such as Second Life or a game environment such as *World of Warcraft*, in "Virtual Guerrillas and a World of Extras: Shooting Machinima in Second Life." In his narrative and analysis of his own experiences directing and editing such a production, Pepper highlights the way avatars are constructions within complex intersections of the real and the virtual world while also reflecting on the pragmatic meanings underlying the tensions between process and product when it comes to composition.

Finally, the essays in this section end with a collaboration among four authors: Andréa Davis, Suzanne Webb, Dundee Lackey, and Dànielle Nicole DeVoss. The resulting chapter, "Remix, Play, and Remediation: Undertheorized Composing Practices," presents a complex take on the concepts of remixing, play, and composition by weaving together the authors' own experiences with digital projects as a foundation to raise key questions regarding the nature of the writing process, and the genres and forms with which the process will be engaged in years to come. In some ways, this chapter inspired the structure for the collection and also stands outside that structure. It doesn't fit neatly into any of the three sections and yet that's why it seems a good way to end the Re-Create analysis section. Our composing processes will need to be recreated in the ensuing years, maybe in the ways these authors identify, maybe in ways we can't predict, even now.

In the first "gamer" profile, "Conf(us)(ess)ions of a Videogame Role-Player," Zach Waggoner starts us off, appropriately enough, within a single-player role-playing game, *Morrowind*. As he "confesses," the lure of creating an avatar/character and performing as that character in a rich virtual world is sometimes too tempting to ignore.

These identity and character elements are also important to Harald Warmelink's description of his experiences with *EVE Online*, an MMORPG, in "Born Again in a Fictional Universe: A Participant Portrait of *EVE Online*." The multi-player aspect of *EVE*, Warmelink describes, provides invaluable resources for learning such a complex game environment.

Taking those social aspects of MMORPGs in a different direction is Wendi Jewell's "A Place to Call Home: The Experience of One Guild Chat in *World of Warcraft*," which offers a profile of the Vorpal Bunnies, a guild within *World of Warcraft* that has the seemingly counterintuitive goal of being "family-oriented" within a game that has "Warcraft" right in its title. But, as Jewell's description of a guild chat session reveals, the Bunnies allows *World of Warcraft* players to bring as much, or as little, of their real-life roles into the virtual environment as they desire.

Finally, Catherine McDonald's profile is a little different: she is not sharing her story but that of her partner, who supplements his professional career with online strategy games, blogging, and digital music creation. From the perspective of a close, interested observer, "Magic Canvas: Digital Building Blocks" reveals the intellectual, social, and even rhetorical benefits that such digital pursuits provide because of the creative outlets they embody.

## Part IV. Teaching the Digital Generation

The final section shifts the focus onto the Digital Generation as students or, rather, as learners, because increasingly issues of teaching and learning do not have to occur in the traditional classroom. In fact, as Jenkins has identified, "Many have argued that these new participatory cultures represent ideal learning environments" that remain "distinct from formal educational systems in several ways" ("Confronting") and one of those environments and cultures Jenkins cites as an example is the fan fiction community that opens this section.

In "Encouraging Feedback: Responding to Fan Fiction at *Different Colored Pens*," Juli Parrish takes on the informal learning community of fan fiction by examining the nature and role of feedback on one site dedicated to two characters (Willow and Tara) from *Buffy the Vampire Slayer*. Grounding her analysis in one particular fan fiction story, Parrish argues that such communities function as peer writing groups and that the copious volumes of writing occurring at such sites not only needs to be recognized and studied, but also celebrated for the supportive, collaborative writing environments being created.

Taking a different subject, but with a similar goal, Elizabeth Kleinfeld is also concerned with an under-valued aspect of digital media in her essay, "MetaSpace: Meatspace and Blogging Intersect." Noting the contradiction between conventional wisdom regarding the decline of literacy and the explosion of self-sponsored writing, Kleinfeld uses her own experiences with blogs to examine the impact this increase in rhetorical activity can have on those who participate — students, professors, citizens, and fans alike.

Finally, in "Meeting the Digital Generation in the Classroom: A Reflection on the Obstacles," I share my (mis)adventures trying to incorporate some of the activities described elsewhere in this collection into my own life to examine one of the obstacles that may prevent instructors from integrating digital media into their pedagogy: individual technical know-how. Then, focusing on a broader level, I raise concerns that the nostalgia underlying so much of the critique of digital media might present an even bigger obstacle to those who teach the Digital Generation.

The final two profiles take us into the more traditional college classroom. In "Making Dorothy Parker My MySpace Friend: A Classroom Application for Social Networks," Ashley Andrews describes the opportunities in social networking sites for helping students encounter traditional texts, like *The Glass Menagerie* or *Huckleberry Finn*, in digital media terms. Her profile reviews the results of two classroom projects that provide a pragmatic grounding to the "virtual," ephemeral nature of the technology. Jentery Sayers, in

"Novel Cartographies, New Correspondences," also describes the application of digital technology in the writing classroom in pragmatic, pedagogical terms, but with a very different manifestation. Instead of engaging with literature, Sayers's students "map" the physical campus, collaboratively authoring, and then writing about, a "geoblog," utilizing technology and vocabulary that truly takes writing instruction into the Digital Generation.

As I noted earlier, the goal of assembling such a variety of perspectives from those directly engaged in digital participatory entertainment was to capture these rhetorical activities and contribute to a broader understanding of the Digital Generation. I believe that the mix of these experiences provides powerful evidence for the rich complexity of fan participation in digital media, a complexity that instructors and media watchers alike have opportunities to take advantage of in all manner of activities, both now and in the near future.

*Portions of this chapter have previously been presented at the April 2007 Popular Culture/American Culture Association's National Conference and at the 20th Penn State Conference on Rhetoric and Composition in July 2007.*

## WORKS CITED

Bazerman, Charles. *Shaping Written Knowledge: The Genre and Activity of the Experimental Article in Science.* Madison: University of Wisconsin Press, 1988.

Deery, June. "TV.com: Participatory Viewing on the Web." *Journal of Popular Culture* 37.2 (2003): 161–83.

Gibson, Stephanie B. "Literacy, Paradigm, and Paradox: An Introduction." *Emerging Cyberculture: Literacy, Paradigm, and Paradox.* Ed. Gibson and Ollie O. Ovideo. Cresskill, NJ: Hampton Press, 2000. 1–21.

Gray, Jonathan, Cornel Sandvoss, and C. Lee Harrington. Introduction: "Why Study Fans?" *Fandom: Identities in a Mediated World.* New York: New York University Press, 2007. 1–16.

Ito, Mizuko, et al. *Living and Learning with New Media: Summary of Findings from the Digital Youth Project.* Nov. 2008. MacArthur Foundation. 21 Nov. 2008 <www.digitalyouth.ischool.berkeley.edu/report>.

Jenkins, Henry. "Confronting the Challenges of Participatory Culture: Media Education for the 21st Century (Part One)." *Confessions of an Aca/Fan* Web log. 20 Oct. 2006. 7 June 2009 <http://henryjenkins.org/2006/10/confronting_the_challenges_of.html>.

_____. Introduction: "Confessions of an Aca/Fan." *Fans, Bloggers, and Gamers: Exploring Participatory Culture.* New York: New York University Press, 2006. 1–6.

_____. "*Star Trek* Rerun, Reread, Rewritten: Fan Writing as Textual Poaching." *Critical Studies in Mass Communication* 5.2 (1988): 85–107. Rpt. in *Liquid Metal: The Science Fiction Film Reader.* Ed. Sean Redmond. London: Wallflower Press, 2004. 264–80.

Jenson, Joli. "Fandom as Pathology: The Consequences of Characterization." *The Adoring Audience: Fan Culture and Popular Media.* Ed. Lisa A. Lewis. London: Routledge, 1992. 9–29.

University of California–Los Angeles. "Is Technology Producing a Decline in Critical Thinking and Analysis?." *ScienceDaily* 29 Jan. 2009. 3 Feb. 2009 <http://www.sci encedaily.com_/releases/2009/01/090128092341.htm>.

Uricchio, William. "Television's Next Generation: Technology/Interface Culture/Flow." *Television After TV: Essays on a Medium in Transition.* Ed. Lynn Spigel and Jan Olson. Durham: Duke University Press, 2004. 163–82.

Vaidhyanathan, Siva. "Generational Myth: Not All Young People Are Tech-Savvy." *The Chronicle Review.* 19 Sept. 2008: B7. *ChronicleReview.com.* 15 Sept. 2008 <http://chronicle.com/weekly/v55/i04/04b00701.htm>.

# I

*React:
Maintaining
a Fan Community*

# 1

# The Inter(Active) Soap Opera Viewer: *Fan*tastic Practices and Mediated Communities

## *Melissa Ames*

In today's cultural realm, everything exists within a hierarchy of sorts — fandom has not escaped this process of judgmental ranking and social stratification. Admitting to be a "fan" of something often earns people mixed responses depending on the subject of their devoted following. The more one's object of choice strays from the mainstream, the lower one exists on the fan hierarchy. If the masses find the fan subject matter to exist on the cultural periphery, fans are often quite ridiculed. As a pop culture scholar studying a "low-brow" entertainment form, I encounter the latter in regard to the genre of the soap opera.

What is often overlooked, however, is the utility of even the most "trivial" cultural artifact. While some do not see the point in analyzing mass-produced entertainment forms, others understand that much can be read beneath the surface of these products. The regular consumers of these items are doing a plethora of things with them and, as a result, they are affected not only by their interactions with these cultural products, but by the cultural status acquired in being associated with them. In analyzing this cyclical relationship among the soap opera, its diverse fan base, and the social-cultural setting it evolves within, I am attempting what Mary Ellen Brown calls "feminist culturalist television criticism," which Brown argues "addresses the issue of how ordinary people and subcultural groups resist hegemonic pressures and obtain pleasure from what the political, social and/or cultural system offers" (12). My analysis of soap opera fandom does this but also notes the situations when fans cannot, or simultaneously do not, always resist the hegemonic pressures filtering in from outside ideological system(s).

In order to study how soap opera fans both simultaneously reject and assimilate those hegemonic pressures on a daily basis, this chapter reviews existing fan research and studies the ways in which fans intermix with their chosen shows, social networks, program paraphernalia, and other outside depictions of what they cherish and who they are. The second part of this chapter deals with secondary products tangentially linked to the soap, products targeted at the traditional soap viewer: various fan websites and program paraphernalia. The overall argument throughout is that consumption is production and that although fans are not creating the actual texts themselves, they are "producing" in various ways through their active viewing.

## Fan*tastic Research Results: The Soap Fan — A Breed of Its Own*

Although popular culture now has a firm footing in academia, researchers often insist upon maintaining proper academic distance when analyzing their objects of study. However, when studying fandom, this sort of critical distance has proven to be unproductive because one often needs to have an investment in the community, or the entertainment outlet grounding it, in order to fully understand the texts being studied and to navigate successfully through its mass of followers. Both Henry Jenkins and Laura Mumford advocate approaching popular culture as a fan — the latter even admitting she wrote her doctoral dissertation on soaps while they played in the background (4). Having one foot in the foyer of the ivory tower and one foot in the cellar of fan circles is not an impossibility. In fact, it would be unrealistic to assume that any fan does not play a dual role of sorts in her individual pursuits. Jenkins explains this phenomenon by examining the *non*-autonomy of fan culture and argues that no one exists entirely in the realm of fandom alone, nor is that realm static in nature since it is responsive to the historical conditions surrounding it (3).

A glimpse into these forever changing cultural communities can be seen in Jenkins's ethnographic study of television audiences, *Textual Poachers: Television Fans and Participatory Culture*, where he analyzes fan culture by studying the various ways that television viewers actively interact with and rework the cultural materials they follow. Although he only mentions soap operas in passing, his analysis of *Star Trek* fans easily applies to those of my chosen cultural artifact.

Early on Jenkins discusses the etymology of the word "fan," a term which often carries a derogatory connotation. Considering the topic of this study, the most interesting part of the term's history is the fact that the word "fan" was gendered from the start: Jenkins reports that the word was first used "in reference to women theatre-goers, 'Matinee Girls,' who male critics claimed had come to admire the actors rather than the plays" (12). Moving beyond the birth of the term, Jenkins discusses the history of fandom and the development of fan practices up to the present televisual moment, focusing in particular on the communicative nature of the fan. This crucial criterion is interesting being that women are more often associated with oral culture and are (arguably) socialized to talk. Inadvertently, cultural forces have therefore primed women for easier entry into fan communities. Although fans can (and do) talk about anything, Jenkins found that most often television "fans offer moral judgment about characters' actions, they make predictions about likely plot developments or provide background about the program history to new fans" (81). The spoken dialogue fans embark on result in the text becoming endless in nature, a characteristic important in postmodern literary and feminine artistic practice.[1] Although the soap opera itself exists as an endless genre, one that has continuity, in terms of its run time, that surpasses all others, part of its textual extension comes from the conversations (oral or print) that surround it. The storylines do not stop on the screen; they are expanded through the informal discussions fans share with one another in person, through the online speculations found in Internet chatrooms, and even, on an individual level, through the lone experiences a viewer might have talking back at the screen in her own home.

So, sure, talk can be equated with activity, with secondary creation even, but more important, talk also breeds relationships. This idea of a shared viewing community can be seen with the soap opera viewer as well. In their research on soap opera fandom, Lee Harrington and Denise Bielby note the particulars of the community, claiming that it is not built around a traditional social structure but instead rests on a foundation of "common experience and feeling in the pursuit of affective ties to a soap narrative" (45). Part of the emotional ties fans have to one another stem from the fact that they value products that others in mainstream culture devalue.

Jenkins claims that almost all fans make "meaning from materials that others have characterized as trivial and worthless" (3). His studies have shown that, whether they do or do not actually exist on the cultural periphery, "fans resist cultural hierarchy with their own tastes and preferences" and are able to "raid mass culture, claiming its materials for their own use, reworking them as the basis of their own cultural creations and social interactions" (Jenkins 18). For Jenkins, fans are "active producers and manipulators of meaning," a conceptualization that reworks Michel de Certeau's view of "active reading as 'poaching'" (23, 24). Following this analogy, Jenkins parallels the producer-fan relationship with that of the landowner-poacher (32). In his conclusion, Jenkins makes two important statements that prove useful in this argument. The first is as follows: "I am not claiming that there is anything particularly empowering about the texts fans embrace. I am, however, claiming that there is something empowering about what fans do with these texts in the process of assimilating them to the particulars of their lives" (284). This line of thought easily clears up the problem some scholars might have in using soap operas for serious theoretical study or suggesting that they can be political tools for reformation. The soap opera by itself is not, as Jenkins clearly states, empowering, but the reading, the consumption, the appropriation of it by the female viewer can be. Utility is key.

Jenkins's second noteworthy conclusion comes with his last line: "Fandom does not prove that all audiences are active; it does, however, prove that not all audiences are passive" (287). This alone is the greatest retort for critics who claim that viewers are simply passive receptors gobbling up mainstream ideology in neatly formed cultural packages. Jenkins's study of fan culture proves that, while some viewers may passively take in television programming, that is not the case for every single viewer. So it can be argued that the viewer of a soap opera can actively consume the programming and, hence, refunction it in various ways. This concept of an active audience is perhaps the greatest hope of all scholars who wish to utilize popular cultural products for revolutionary means.

Since the term fan is gendered from the start, it should not be surprising that much of the research on fandom is likewise gendered. Many of the fan phenomena found by Jenkins in his study of fandom in general can be found in more narrow studies focusing on cultural products fashioned primarily for female consumers, the most important of which is that of activity. One such example of a gendered fan study that dealt with this fan trait would be Camille Bacon-Smith's *Enterprising Women: Television Fandom and the Creation of Popular Myth,* which deals almost entirely with the female science fiction fan community. She focuses heavily on the female followers of *Star Trek,* their practices, fanzines, communication patterns, narrative adaptation, conversations, reworkings of scripts, conferences, costuming, etc. Bacon-Smith's text is written in a semi-ethnographic/semi-autobiographical manner as both researcher and participant. Her major points are that women enjoy creation, a space for dialogue and belonging, and they are active in nature. Her key phrase to describe fan behavior is IDIC, "Infinite Diversity in Infinite Combination," and she echoes the previous conclusion concerning the impossibility of coming up with a one-size-fits all description of fans and their practices (6).

Bacon-Smith's notion of IDIC applies to followers of any genre. Whatever the cultural artifacts may be, fans are systematically drawn to them because they fulfill some need through the regular interactions with these products. Janice Radway's infamous work with the Smithson romance readers found that female fans approach texts that express "women's dissatisfaction with the current asymmetry in male-female relationships" (129). Radway found that by interacting with these texts regularly, female fans were able to get a daily fix of sexual empowerment by entering into a fictional world quite different from their own (50). However, Radway admitted that, even if they were reading to buck the system, they often were not aware of this purpose and most certainly were not vocalizing it. Despite the possible utility of a text like the romance novel, Radway notes that "women never get together to share together the experience of imaginative opposition, or perhaps the important discontent that gave rise to their need for the romance in the first place" (212). Moreover, she worried that such regular consumption was too passive a response to gender inequality and that it "might disarm the oppositional impulse" that sparked it (213). Nonetheless, despite this concern Radway does see value in the interactions fans have with these popular texts and advocates a conscious re-functioning of the fan behavior and fan communication so that it reaches another level of oppositional use. I would advocate the same move in terms of the soap opera. Just as Radway sees potential in the oppositional use of the romance novel and the conversations they spark, I see untapped opportunities within the genre itself, and the plethora of fan sites it inspires, to do feminist work — to stimulate conversations about why these fantasies are needed and how they contrast with society at large. It is an unlikely place for social work to occur, but not an impossible one.

Although the majority of fan research, and not just specific studies like Radway's, can be applied to the specific genre of the soap opera, there are some noteworthy differences between the media form of the soap opera and other pop cultural products. As Harrington and Bielby point out,

> Most media fans engage a closed text that makes limited installments of the official story available: a finite number of episodes, the occasional feature film or reruns in syndication.... [But] because serials' structure differs from that of other narrative forms, the fanship and fandom that surrounds serials also differs. The open-ended nature allows for an endless genre [21].

The questions then surface: Are fans' relationships and practices different when based on an endless genre? Do the regular interactions fans have with this endless medium offer up a different sort of utility, a different space for subversive cultural work?

I would argue that the genre's longevity, coupled with its seriality, changes the structure of the fan community to some extent. First, the longevity of the soap operatic form makes it more likely that fans will filter in and out of the group during the course of multiple years. While fans of television series that run for a finite time period do not often drop out of the fan group, soap circles do see member drop out. Because soap operas run for decades on end, they witness viewing depletion as shifting lifestyles and entertainment preferences cause fandom to dwindle and cease in individual cases. Longevity thus affects the nature of soap fandom. Second, because of the serial nature of soaps, the rapid delivery of installments means most fans cannot organize to watch communally like fans of other programming. The regularity of the soap also affects the type of fan communication and networking possible. Whereas other media products inspire meeting together "en masse" at conferences, co-producing fanzines, or exchanging derivative artistic work, soap fandom tends to lend itself more to participant isolation.

Largely due to the seriality and longevity associated with the soap, the Internet has risen as the ideal forum for soap opera fan communication as it offers an open-ended dialoguing space free of time restrictions. Of course, it could easily be claimed that the Internet functions in this way for all types of fandom, as it is used across the board as a communication forum for various groups and caters to the consumption of various cultural artifacts. However, the specific characteristics of the soap opera make this genre much more limited as far as fan communication options go. With the ceaseless distribution of soap opera episodes at extremely high intervals, the Internet is one of the few viable communication routes for the average soap opera fan.[2]

## The Soap Opera (Internet) "Connection"

In *Tune In, Log On: Soaps, Fandom, and Online Community*, Nancy Baym analyzes the Usenet newsgroup Rec.arts.tv.soaps (r.a.t.s) to study soap fan behavior (1),[3] conceptualizing r.a.t.s as a community and the computers they communicate through as social tools (1–2). Baym comes to the conclusion that r.a.t.s is an example of a virtual community, one joined by common interest, practice, and interpersonal communication. Using the term community forced her to justify "how people who rarely (if ever) met face-to-face, whose participants came and left, and who seemed to have such a limited communication medium managed to create not just a social world but a social world that felt like a community" (2). Limited or otherwise, the fact that r.a.t.s opened up a space for a constant string of communication is important as, once again, the oral nature of soap fandom flaunts itself even through this technology-based communication forum. Baym quotes one participant who claimed that she simply enjoyed "having some people to *talk* about the show with" (13, emphasis added). Baym notes the use of the verb "talk" to exemplify "the naturalness with which people apply a talk metaphor to online language use" (13). Her final determination is that interaction within the Usenet message system "is a novel hybrid between written, oral, interpersonal, and mass communication" (13).

Although the Internet does provide ample opportunity for this sort of program "talk," it would be amiss not to note that there are many other options on the Internet for soap opera fans. In order to see what a newcomer to Internet soap fandom would encounter, I analyzed a basic Internet search for fan sites devoted to one specific soap opera, *General Hospital*.[4] In an attempt to land myself on a few good sites I did what any advanced Internet searcher does — I "Googled" it. After a few misguided search prompts that directed me to a plethora of county hospitals, I searched using the phrase "General Hospital ABC Fan" and was overwhelmed by the number of hits I received — just over 145,000. After reviewing pages and pages of the listings, I realized the great variety of sites that housed information on *General Hospital* and that a lot more people were benefiting from these sites than happy-go-lucky communicating fans. In order to make sense of this mass of Internet options, I decided to group the various sites into categories by systematically analyzing just the first 100 hits.

I grouped the websites into six distinct categories, with some cross-listed under two different categories. The first three groupings were commercial sites and those with the potential to profit from site visitors. Category A sites were "official" corporate websites created by the actual network, its cable subsidiary, or various affiliated soap opera news networks. Approximately one-third, twenty-nine websites, could be cross-listed under this banner, including various pages from ABC, *TV Guide*, Soap Central, *Soaps In Depth*, *Soap Opera Digest*, and the Daytime Emmy Awards. Category B sites, of which I found fifty-five, were also well-established corporate websites, often functioning as information databases, entertainment information centers, or television specific sites. Some of these included informational blurbs, historical overviews, episode recaps, or critical evaluations posted on America Online, Wikipedia, BuddyTV, Amazon, Media Village, TV Fan Forums, IMDB, About, Soap Zone, Soap Opinions, and Soapdom — to name just a few. Category C sites were slightly different. These too were well-established sites devoted specifically to *General Hospital* but were not officially affiliated with the mother companies of ABC or Disney. Compared to Category A and B sites, these were more fan-directed than commercial and included MSN's *General Hospital* Fan Site, the *GH* Fan Club, the *General Hospital* Haven, and — the most cleverly titled — the Port Charles Herald. Approximately eight sites fell into this third category.

After analyzing the overlap in the categorizations, the commercial, or "official," sites (Categories A, B, and C) represented just under half of the first hundred websites available to novice fan searchers. Although quite a few of these offered links to fan forums, a surprising number were quite unlike what one would expect when searching soap opera fan sites. Under this collection of sites, searchers could easily click on a link and get transported to ABC's home page where they could fill out surveys, register for various contests, shop at the "ABC TV Store"; they could be connected to the megastore of Amazon.com and buy videotapes of noteworthy *General Hospital* Weddings and must have trivia books; or they could surf various sites and jot down the official mailing address to write to the studio, listen to exclusive *General Hospital* songs, etc.

The other three classifications of websites were all more fan-centered (often fan-created), less commercial, and more in line with what one would normally expect of a "fan site." I divided these into three categories based on the site's specific purpose. Category D sites are the closest to what one would consider a standard fan site, housing chatrooms, communication forums, fan event information, personal blogs, and so forth and ranging from informal to formal and established to non-established. Some of these sites were run through larger recognizable sources, such as Geocities, Angelfire, Soap Town USA, Fan Mail, or Myspace. Approximately two-thirds, sixty-four, of the sites produced by my search could be classified as Category D. More narrow in their focus, Category E sites were devoted solely to fan fiction. Only three of the one hundred sites advertised themselves in this way — one listed itself as a fan fiction site for the teens of *GH* and other ABC soaps, while another, titled "Carlie's Fan Fiction Page," advertised one specific fictional derivative of *GH—General Hospital Hungry Eyes*— and the third simply touted fan fiction alongside of spoilers and a critique of *General Hospital's* temporary spin off primetime weekly series on the Soap Opera Network — *GH Night Shift*. While writing fan fiction is not as common with soap opera viewers as with fans of other genres (like science fiction), this number is mostly likely under-representative. Upon closer analysis, quite a few Category D sites are likely to have links to fan fiction alongside of their communication forums, episode recaps, and social event listings; the fan publications are simply not often the major draw. The last group of sites, Category F, contained web pages devoted to specific characters and/or actors. On this given search, there were ten of these covering the following actors and actresses: Rick Springfield, Natalia Livingston, Maurice Benard, Jason Thompson, Finola Huges, Kelly Monaco, and Leslie Charleson. And, most amusingly, there was a Myspace under the name of "Carly," created to be a fan site for the character Carly Corinthos.

In short, television networks, entertainment journalists, and devoted program followers have crafted a variety of Internet sites for soap fans to use. By just attending to the first one hundred sites offered up out of a list of 145,000 plus, I was solicited to buy soap opera paraphernalia; I was asked to join fan groups; I was invited to message boards; I was offered pictures of both soap actors and their fans; I was tempted by plot spoilers; I was subjected to detailed episode summaries; I was informed about upcoming fan events; I was given historical overviews of the show, its writers, and producers; I was reminded of who won the daytime Emmys in years past; I was invited to a casting call for *GH* auditions; I was given the opportunity to read various interviews with soap actors and fans; I was instructed to write to *General Hospital* about my anger directed at the show for killing off longtime character Dr. Alan Quartermaine (Stuart Damon); I was invited to a purchase fan guides from a woman's Ebay account; and I was invited to click on one disheartened fan's website to read more about how *General Hospital,* with its heavy mob focus, has become just a "Lightweight *Sopranos* in Disguise." Quite obviously the breadth and depth of material available on the worldwide web for soap opera fans is incredible, inconsistent, and incalculable.

In some ways the use of the Internet by soap fans (and corporate profit by said use) is no different from that of other fan groups. However, due to the regularity of the episodes and the amount of "text" possible for viewers to comment on, it is safe to say that there exist many more opportunities for soap fans to comment and post about their shows in comparison to other programming. This unending range of material to view/read most definitely motivates a plethora of sites devoted to favored soaps. The large number of soap sites can also be explained by analyzing other characteristics of this media format. Soap operas house more characters than normal television shows, hence the multitude of soap actor websites. Soap operas have a duration that surpasses other narrative forms, so it only makes sense that there exist more archived episode recaps, spoilers, and news storylines devoted to them. The intricacies of the soap opera format itself shape the soap opera fan. So while soap fan practices align with those of other cultural artifacts, they also differ in part due to the unique characteristics of the daytime serial itself. Although academic research acknowledges this and many scholars have proved the complexity of soap opera fandom, outside depictions rarely acknowledge the depth and variety of soap fan groups and both the indirect power they yield over the production of their shows and the ways they are manipulated by those very same powers-that-be in the industry.

## Existing on the (Capitalistic) Cultural Periphery: A Look at Soap Products and Program Paraphernalia

Historically, and even more today in the age of the television-Internet coalition, the daytime fan has the ability to control some of this entertainment form's idiosyncrasies. Although many types of television programming are beginning to attend to the practices and preferences of fan groups, soap operas have decades of experience over the newer shows attempting to master this strategy. John Fiske discusses the three levels of any given televisual text: the primary, secondary, and tertiary levels with the program itself (physically created by outside sources, not directly altered by fans themselves) being the primary text (85). Items such as soap opera magazines or network websites (often systematically crafted by the producers with some direct contribution from fans) would fall into the category of secondary texts (85). The more unstructured communications, such as unscripted dialogue of fans to each other (be it informal, in person, and untraceable or written, electronic, and trackable) would fit into the third level of the text (85). Soap opera producers and writers have strategically utilized these secondary texts for years and, in recent decades of increased Internet activity, have turned to studying the tertiary texts when making important decisions concerning storylines, renewals of actor contracts, and so forth. Because of the swift pace at which these shows are written, produced, and aired, the creators have the ability (more so than any other type of programming) to quickly cast aside what is not working and make alterations as needed — a disliked romantic interlude will quickly fizzle, a popular recently deceased character will suddenly have a look-alike cousin breeze into town, an actor unsuccessfully playing a long term character role will find himself replaced with new blood, a well-received minor character slated to depart will suddenly find herself with a major plot line and contract renewal, etc.[5]

All of the above influences of fans are noticeable but not directly advertised. Although many fans understand the power they have (en masse at least) to control their favored entertainment form, their silent-party say in the show's creation is subtle in the way it unfolds. However, some soap operas have been more direct in allowing fans to wield their power and put in their proverbial two cents concerning various show developments. For example, the telephone-television tag team, especially useful in voting type situations, has been used by soaps in recent years. Louise Spence discusses how soaps across the networks have utilized 900 numbers to have fans vote on things such as which backup band should remain on the show, a name for a newborn baby, or the wedding dress a main character should choose (16). Soap websites also run similar polls and even contests that allow fans various opportunities such as attending the daytime Emmy awards, visiting the set, shadowing an actor for the day, or even starring in an episode of their favorite soap (the latter eventually turned into the reality show *I Wanna Be a Soap Star*) (Spence 16). Also these sites, definitely commercial creations in and of themselves, allow fans to let their love for their favored programs spill over into their outside lives through fan purchases (ones that, of course, simultaneously advertise their program affiliation to the network's profit).[6]

However, one of the most successful maneuvers that the networks use to fuel soap opera fandom comes not in the form of anything physical but instead comes in the form of experience. The networks strategically offer fans proximity to their fictional worlds and favored characters and help to minimize the distance between the fan and the show. Special events have become a huge deal in the soap industry and all three of the major networks have capitalized on this hyped-up media practice. Studies of these forums show how real life fans both do and do not match up to outside depictions of fandom (be they spawned from pop cultural parody, network pigeon holes, or academic analyses).[7]

## Consumption as Second-Order Production

In conclusion, soap operas and their viewers are often unjustifiably devalued by the cultural powers that be and much is overlooked concerning the genre itself and the behavior of its regular consumers. Because of the soap opera's "continued accountability to consumers, inscribing responsiveness to audiences within the production process, serials may offer cultural models for material transformation, models that come not from the directives of academic critics, not from marginal pockets of cultural resistance, but from within mass culture itself as a result of the influence of fans' voices over time" (Hayward 196). Hence, the daytime soap opera may provide one of the most ideal televisual sites for social work to covertly occur. Much can be done with television beyond its original, official "produced" state.

Again it all comes down to how "production" itself is conceptualized. In *The Practice of Everyday Life*, de Certeau argues that we must analyze how an object and/or representation is manipulated by its users, claiming that "only then can we gauge the difference or similarity between the production of the image and the secondary production hidden in the process of its utilization" (xiii). He speaks directly of television: "Television (representation) and time spent watching television (behavior) should be combined with analysis of what a consumer does/makes with time and images just like products purchased in a supermarket" (xii). He claims that consumption itself is a form of production, a form "characterized by its ruses, its fragmentation, poaching, clandestine nature, its tireless but quiet activity, in short by its quasi-invisibility, since it shows itself not in its own products but in an art of using those imposed on it" (131). Once we accept and internalize this argument that consumption is really just a different type of production (second-order production, I suggest), we will be one step further in proving that fans exist on the active side of the active/passive binary. Perhaps then those non-passive fans (and the academics who love to study them) can work on disrupting other binaries, for example the high-culture/low-culture binary that keeps the products important to so many hovering at the bottom of the cultural hierarchy where their utility is often overlooked.

## NOTES

1. In *Feminism, Postmodernism, and Affect: An Unlikely Love Triangle in Women's Media*, I compare the endlessness of the soap opera narrative to that of écriture féminine. Both exist as a form of female-directed storytelling and share similar characteristics, such as repetition and non-closure. Concerning the repetitive endless nature of écriture féminine, Helene Cixous, the creator of the term, writes that a "feminine textual body is recognized by the fact that it is always endless, without ending: there's no closure, it doesn't stop" ("Castration" 53). But this is not true of just écriture féminine. Mary Ellen Brown, also focusing on daytime soap operas, picks up on this tendency for women's stories to stick close to the narrative stylistic of the oral tradition which is "often circular, lacking a clear beginning, middle, or end" (1).

2. This difference is glaring when compared to traditional primetime programming. The fact that soap operas run all year round without break and air five days a week contrasts greatly with the practice of most evening serials which air only once a week for twenty-four — often non-sequential — weeks. Even compared to other daytime programming that runs all year round on a daily basis (talk shows like *Oprah* for example), the soap opera still remains an anomaly since, unlike its daytime neighbors, one will almost never find the soap airing a re-run episode at a later date. (There are a few exceptions to this rule now with Soap Network's new practice of retrieving soap operas from decades past and re-airing them on primetime cable. Still, this is not a "re-run" in the standard sense.)

3. A similar study was conducted by Christine Scodari in *Serial Monogamy: Soap Opera, Lifespan, and the Gendered Politics of Fantasy*. As an Internet lurker on soap fan sites, she studied the messages, transcripts, bulletin boards, and online chat room activity without participating in the dialogue, coming to many of the same conclusions that Baym does (1).

4. To be perfectly honest I too could be considered a newcomer in regards to most fan practices. Although a faithful viewer of *General Hospital* for nearly twenty years, I have only on occasion read soap magazines and almost completely avoided soap websites due to fear of spoilers since I am almost always a week or two behind the broadcast schedule, watching back episodes at my own pace.

5. Robert Allen actually attributes the soap opera "renaissance" of recent years to the secondary or tertiary texts, which he calls the "soap opera intertext" (88). Allen draws attention to all of the sources now "available that give fans information about soap opera actors and the 'behind the scenes' world of soap opera production in newspaper columns, specialized magazines, and television shows," arguing that "since the mid-1970s, an entire industry hyping the soap opera has emerged, one which rivals in scope, if not in size, the promotional infrastructure of Hollywood in its heyday" (88). Included in his conceptualization of this "soap opera intertext" would be newspaper columnists covering the beat, actors making public appearances, fan magazines, and journalism-type television shows about soaps.

6. This practice stems rather far back and even has carried into the primetime soap realm. For example, Ien Ang discusses the plethora of "I Love JR" or "I Hate JR" para-

phernalia available during *Dallas'* heyday in the eighties (15). Daytime soaps have offered viewers a variety of memorabilia connected to their shows. To list just a few touted by ABC: in the 80s, *All My Children* created a board game where players were able to be a character and travel around the board (the city of Pine Valley) fulfilling semi-storyline related tasks; in 2005, *One Life to Live* published the novel *The Killing Club*, a novel supposedly written by a character on the show that spawned a copy-cat murdering spree on the show itself; throughout the decades *General Hospital* has published a variety of show-related paraphernalia including *A Complete Scrapbook* full of character information and photographs, various trivia books testing the knowledge of loyal viewers, "Nurse's Ball T-Shirts" that were worn by characters on the show and aligned with its fictional annual AIDs charity event (although notably with the actual profits gained from the T-shirts sold actually going to support the cause), and in 2006 when the infamous Luke and Laura pairing was reunited for (none other than) sweeps month, the show's website allowed viewers to purchase a look-alike engagement ring that matched the one Luke gave his beloved bride. From time to time, the network at large will combine promotions, such as their line of clothes where viewers can browse through racks of clothes and accessories and buy things worn (or imitated from those worn) on the three serials or the holiday CD launched in 2006 that had songs covered by actors from each of the daytime soaps on ABC.

7. For further information see *Feminism, Postmodernism, and Affect*. In this I compare the results of self-reported fan behavior (collected through surveys at ABC's Super Soap Weekend) to the fan behavior depicted in soap opera parody films, such as *Nurse Betty, Delirious*, and *Soap Dish*, and theorized by many of the academics celebrated in the field and mentioned in this very chapter.

## WORKS CITED

Allen, Robert C. *Speaking of Soap Operas.* Chapel Hill: University of North Carolina Press, 1985.

Ames, Melissa. *Feminism, Postmodernism, and Affect: An Unlikely Love Triangle in Women's Media.* Saarbrücken, Germany: VDM Verlag Dr. Müller Aktiengesellschaft & Co., 2008.

Ang, Ien. *Watching* Dallas, *Soap Opera and the Melodramatic Imagination:* New York: Methuen, 1985.

Bacon-Smith, Camille. *Enterprising Women: Television Fandom and the Creation of Popular Myth.* Philadelphia: University of Pennsylvania Press, 1992.

Baym, Nancy K. *Tune In, Log On: Soaps, Fandom, and Online Community.* London: Sage, 2000.

Brown, Mary Ellen, ed. *Television and Women's Culture: The Politics of the Popular.* London: Sage, 1990.

Cixous, Hélène. "Castration or Decapitation?" *Signs: Journal of Women in Culture and Society* 7.1 (1981): 41–55

de Certeau, Michel. *The Practice of Everyday Life.* 1974. Trans. S. Rendell. Berkley: University of California Press, 1984.

Fiske, John. *Television Culture.* New York: Routledge, 1983.

Harrington, Lee C., and Denise D. Bielby. *Soap Fans: Pursuing Pleasure and Making Meaning in Everyday Life.* Philadelphia: Temple University Press, 1995.

Hayward, Jennifer. *Consuming Pleasures: Active Audiences and Serial Fictions from Dickens to Soap Opera.* Lexington: University Press of Kentucky, 1997.

Jenkins, Henry. *Textual Poachers: Television Fans and Participatory Culture.* New York: Routledge, 1992.

Mumford, Laura Stempel. *Love and Ideology in the Afternoon: Soap Opera, Women, and Television Genre.* Indianapolis: Indiana University Press, 1995.

Radway, Janice. *Reading the Romance: Women, Patriarchy, and Popular Literature.* Chapel Hill: University of North Carolina Press, 1984.

Scodari, Christine. *Serial Monogamy: Soap Opera, Lifespan, and the Gendered Politics of Fantasy.* Cresskill, NJ: Hampton Press, 2004.

Seiter, Ellen, Hans Borchers, Gabrielle Kreutzner, and Eva-Maria Warth, eds. *Remote Control: Television, Audience, and Cultural Power.* New York: Routledge, 1994.

Spence, Louise. *Watching Daytime Soap Operas: The Power of Pleasure.* Middletown, CT: Wesleyan University Press, 2005.

# 2

# Going Deep: What Online Sports Culture Teaches Us About the Rhetorical Future of Social Networks

*Michael R. Trice*

Facebook, Twitter, Flickr, Wikipedia — they all create a litany of what Web 2.0 means: social networking, interaction, crowd sourcing, bringing people together. We often speak as if they were the first to unite us, to create the anticipation of interactive exchange, or to encourage us to share our passion with the world. This passion is key, because, at its heart, Web 2.0 truly works to elicit the sense of community shared by a World Series, an Olympics, or a Man U match. What any social networking site wants is to excite the passion within its base of a Saturday afternoon at the stadium.

## Journalism, Sports, and Sex Online

*USA Today*'s website leads the pack when it comes to that place where social networking meets journalism. Assisting them is a little company in Austin, Texas named Pluck, which designed the system *USA Today* online uses to allow readers to rate articles, leave comments, and share recommendations by sending emails or links via Facebook. Pluck has conquered the journalism market for social networking with disturbing ease by designing social network platforms for media power houses like Hearst Communication, Reuters Media, Cox Newspapers, CBC, and *The Guardian*.

So a quick look at the *USA Today* website's front page should allow a reliable, if still slightly anecdotal, look at how often people comment on news articles. The most recent front page at the time of this writing is June 28,

2008; it features articles with the following number of comments: 79, 39, 36, 11, and 17. By comparison, the first five stories on ESPN.com from the exact same time have the following comment totals: 108, 1,477, 10, 60, and 3. These numbers incite two immediate thoughts regarding the online spaces. First — besides the one clear anomaly, a story on the 6–5 victory of the White Sox over the Cubs — the two sites appear to generate similar volumes of conversation regarding their articles. However, the anomaly suggests that a White Sox–Cubs game can generate four times the number of comments in this space as all other front page articles from both sites combined. Rhetorically speaking, this would seem to indicate an overwhelming sign that the White Sox–Cubs game fits the online space in a way the other news articles — whether sports related or not — have failed to do. This is additionally supported as the comments for the White Sox–Cubs article spanned not only the entire baseball game, but even days leading up to the game. The level of activity does not rest in a simple distinction between the two sites, as we can see through additional comparisons.

For a more direct comparison, the same story about Tyson Gay's record breaking performance in the 100-meter dash appeared on both sites, generating twelve comments on ESPN and seventeen on *USA Today*. That's a pretty comparable volume of commenting given the numbers observed earlier. It suggests that the key is not sports versus news or *USA Today*'s website versus ESPN.com, but rather the fact that the White Sox–Cubs article taps into an existing community, simply providing it a new space to exist — there is no attempt to create an instant community about a one-time story like the Tyson Gay story. Journalistic social media, in this case, worked better when it provided a new space to an existing community with a long history of social interaction.

|  | *USA Today* | *ESPN* |
|---|---|---|
| First Article | 79 | 108 |
| Second Article | 39 | 1,477 |
| Third Article | 36 | 10 |
| Fourth Article | 11 | 60 |
| Fifth Article | 17 | 3 |

Figure 1: Total Comments on First Five Articles on ESPN.com and USAToday.com for June 28, 2008.

The long participatory tradition of sports culture fits social networking in a powerful and perhaps unique way that extends well beyond other forms of online social networking: sports interaction itself is an immensely active form of social capital. The 2008 Summer Olympics helped define national identity and pride. Championship parades help unite cities. Pep rallies help unify colleges and high schools across the nation. Social media allow these one-time localized expressions of community to expand outside of their traditional geography.

Thus, it should come as little surprise that some of the most vital and vibrant social communities on the Internet involve sports, especially when a search for the word "politics" on Google turns up an overwhelming 437,000,000 hits — but a search for "sports" more than triples those hits at 1,390,000,000. More astounding, a Google search for "sex" turns up only 858,000,000 hits — only ⅗ the number of hits as sports. I should also note that all searches were conducted without any filters for safe content.

| Key Word | Politics | Sex | Sports |
|---|---|---|---|
| Total Hits | 437,000,000 | 858,000,000 | 1,390,000,000 |

**Figure 2: Google Hits for Politics, Sex and Sports (2008).**

Even if we add sex and politics together, they get about 95 *million* fewer hits than sports. While passion for sports may be part of this, what it should highlight is the power of the Internet to tap into and amplify existing social interaction.

## *Stadiums, Forums, and the Canons*

"Invention, arrangement, style, memory and delivery" has long been the victory chant for rhetorical scholars, a chorus that dates back to the first century AD work *Rhetorica ad Herennium*. This may be an old hat reference for those in the field, but one worth recalling for others to see just how old the canons are, even if we renegotiate them every fifty years or so. It is also worth noting that the Olympic Games pre-dated *Rhetorica* by over 800 years, running from 776 BCE through 393 CE (Perseus Project). So this little bridge we call the Internet pales next to the institutions of rhetoric and sports, yet it helps illuminates both.

When considering the rhetorical canons, the Internet appears to appeal largely to delivery. Never has space between locations mattered so little — and maybe this diminution of space has actually made location more important than ever by increasing the juxtaposition of local customs as the defining form of municipal identity rather than the relative spatial distance from other cities. In other words, the distance between Dallas and New York may matter less than the choices of those communities in fashion, speech, and the combined records of Cowboys versus Giants and Rangers versus Yankees. More so, fans of each team that have no connection to either municipality reflect upon its culture by joining in the online discourse of that community's team and fan base.

Sports teams have long assisted in defining the polis, Athens versus Sparta or the Coliseum of Rome. Even today the Rose Bowl, Fenway, Wimbledon, Augusta, Madison Square Garden, Yokohama International Stadium, and De Kuip all carry on this tradition of cultivating municipal and national identity through sports monuments. The thriving Internet sports community suggests a desire to connect across space and time via passionate competition. When fans can interact without travel, they may compete culturally in a more vital and thriving manner. No longer must they go to an event to compete for their city by supporting the local team, because now they can chant the praises of a municipality and its athletic embodiment across time and space via the Internet. In fact, they no longer need any connection to that locale beyond a passion for the team and a willingness to participate socially on behalf of that team.

Thus delivery is the canon with the most obvious benefit from the Internet. Yet, the same can be said for radio and television to a lesser degree (since these media lack the same reciprocity that exists on the Internet). However, what separates the community created within the Internet may well be more a matter of collaborative *arrangement* than one of reciprocal *delivery* because it is the fluid nature of arrangement that allows truly communal interaction. Just as an audience chants in a live stadium, on the Internet they can shout back and forth in a forum complete with interjections, the emotional release of instant response, and an informal textual style that allows an arrangement on the Internet previously unique to speech, particularly social speech.

More so than a wiki or even a political blog, sports sites offer the raw negotiation of meaning via speech championed by Mikhail Bakhtin (Mason). What more personifies the *We-experience* of Bakhtin than a crowded sports arena or the Olympic Games (Voloshinov 86)? Here groups engage in a vocal competition of which team will negotiate victory and pride via direct interaction. Sports fandom offers a powerful communal foundation that, while identifying with a local sense of self, thrives on communication with others across time and space. The Internet offers a powerful ability not to create this interaction, but to further amplify and expand it.

## Looking at the Experts

To help develop a picture of the current state of online sports communities, I sought the input of two leading journalists: one from ESPN.com and one from SI.com (*Sports Illustrated*'s website). Both cover college sports (primarily college football) and each has at least one book on the subject. But, most important, both have a reputation of responding to emails, writing interactive columns, and even participating in live chats with their readers.

Stewart Mandel of SI.com responded by email, while Ivan Maisel of ESPN.com responded via Gmail Chat. I've transcribed the interactions with only a few edits for spelling and accuracy. However, by juxtaposing both sets of interviews under various headings, the differences in context and rhetorical space between email and chat become evident. Thus, it is worth noting which space is which.

Much of what follows lacks the formality of style found in traditional scholarship. However, the Internet suggests such reduction may be required for a broader sense of community.

## Introductions

*Could you provide us a summary of your experiences as a journalist? Where have you worked, how long, and in what media?*

STEWART MANDEL: I have been with my current employer SI.com (formerly known as CNNSI.com) since 1999. I started as a producer who wrote on the side and switched over to being a full-time columnist in 2002. Previous to that, I worked briefly for ABC Sports Online (now defunct), did internships at the *Cincinnati Enquirer* and *ESPN the Magazine* and wrote for school papers in both high school and college.

*Could you start with a little background on your work in sports journalism? How long and what forms of media?*

IVAN MAISEL: I spent 11 years at Sports Illustrated (in two equal shifts). I spent 10–11 years at four different newspapers, all in sports. My fifth anniversary at ESPN.com is in a couple of weeks.

## Going Online

*You seem to have made quite the impact online by utilizing SI.com columns, blogs, mailbags, and even a MySpace page. So what pushed that? What are the ups and downs of all this interactivity?*

STEWART MANDEL: It started with the Mailbag, which is itself a more interactive form of journalism. I've been doing that since 2003. As I started to realize that I'd built a loyal following and the Mailbag readers themselves could theoretically constitute a "community" of their own, I started the MySpace page. I had no idea what the response would be. I was blown away last year by not only how many people signed up as "friends" but how they formed their own community amongst each other via my comments board or MySpace group. For me, the main benefit is primarily promotional, with the "friends" serving as sort of a built-in mailing list, but there have also been

plenty of times when the "networking" part paid off. When I heard Brent Mus-
burger mentioned my book on the air during the USC–Nebraska game, I sent
out a bulletin on MySpace asking if anyone had recorded the game and could
post a digital clip for me. Within 24 hours, the clip was up.

*You also climb into the trenches within your own comment sections (to your Mail-
bag column). Is there more emotion in your interaction than with typical print
columnists? Do you think being more interactive in your response levels the ground
between reader and writer?*

STEWART MANDEL: One of the main benefits of writing online is that
the feedback from what you write is immediate. Within minutes of a column
or blog post going up, I can see what exactly the reaction is, whether it's
through e-mails or blog comments. And if something happens to spark a
debate, then yes, there are times when I go in there and add my own two
cents. To me, this type of writing is far more rewarding than traditional print,
where you are basically writing to a vacuum. The last two years, I had a weekly
column in the magazine. Even though *SI* has such a wide reach, with millions of readers, I could count on one hand the numbers of e-mails I received
the entire two years about something I wrote in there. I much prefer the give-
and-take of the web.

*At ESPN, you integrate a large number of media types in your approach (TV,
web and so forth). How does that affect your job?*

IVAN MAISEL: It makes me think I haven't become one of those old gray-
headed, dead-eyed guys I used to see playing out the string in a press box. I
have always dreaded the notion of becoming one of them. But this job evolves
so rapidly it's all you can do to keep up. It has been a blast.

*The mailbag environment in which you have sometimes written might be one of
the most interactive forms of journalism today. How does writing on the web differ from traditional print?*

IVAN MAISEL: Everyone is different. But I'll tell you how I see it. The
tone is more informal. It's chattier, less formulaic in structure. What we're
trying to do, at least what I think ESPN.com is trying to do, is marry the
shoe leather of journalism with the informality of the web. There is plenty
of material on the web of people spouting off what they think. We tell you
what we think but we have done some reporting, too. I like the chattiness of
it. I like the personality of it. I don't like how a small percentage of readers
interact by spouting in rude, vulgar terms. But if you can say something and
not suffer the consequences of getting punched in the nose, I guess you're
more liable to say it.

## Responding to the Fans

*Fans can be brutal at times and supportive at others. How does the visibility of their views affect your journalism? For example, if we hold the Jeni Carlson[1] incident in mind, would the sports journalism community have known the extent of fan support for Gundy without the web comments? I know in following the story that I was shocked at the brutal conviction of some comments.*

STEWART MANDEL: To me, the fans are a part of my beat. In other words, to truly cover what's going on in college football on a weekly basis, you can't just follow solely the exploits of the coaches and the players. Oftentimes, the collective mood or reaction of a fan base is in itself a story — whether it's calls for a certain coach's head, or, like this week, the strong feelings of many LSU fans about Nick Saban. So that end, message boards, blog comments, etc., are extremely helpful for gauging these things. However, one must also always keep in mind that the people who post on message boards aren't necessarily representative of the "average" fan. These people tend to be in the 99th percentile when it comes to their passion, the strength of their convictions, their obsession with the sport or team, etc., thus causing such brutal diatribes at times.

*You talk of preferring the rewarding nature of the web. Could you elaborate on what makes that rewarding? You speak of vacuum versus give and take in comparing the two media. What is it about the sense of community that you find most rewarding?*

STEWART MANDEL: I'm speaking specifically about the instant feedback — knowing whether the article touched a nerve, what the response was, whether people loved it or hated it. And I should also add that these readers provide many of my story ideas to begin with. It's through them that I'm able to get a sense of the pulse of college football, what it is people are talking about. It's like having your very own market research group. I think in the pre–Internet age, writers decided for themselves what they thought the audience wanted to read, without having any idea whether that was actually the case.

*So do you read comments posted about your columns? If so, how does ESPN's social networking options affect how you write or reflect on columns for the website?*

IVAN MAISEL: I read most of the email I get. My goal when I took the job was to respond to all of it. Sometimes the volume overwhelmed me. But I am not as quick to answer anymore. I tried to answer it based on a respect for the reader. But the more I read email that didn't respect me, I thought, what do I need this for? Sometimes I respond, "I didn't realize that if we disagreed, that meant I was (fill in whatever vituperative term used). I thought that meant we disagreed." Sometimes I respond, "Hey, some eighth-grader is using your email account and sending me some real immature, uninformed, vulgar email. Thought you'd want to know." Lately, I just [hit] delete.

*Do you worry that interactive journalism might threaten objectivity? Is it too easy now to become involved with the fan community and move from journalism to entertainment?*

IVAN MAISEL: I have a powerful motivator that prevents me from doing that: employment.

*We actually did exchange emails once in 2005 over the merits of Texas and USC earlier in the season.*

IVAN MAISEL: Hope I was polite.[2]

## Sports Online: Now and the Future

*What's the value in this interactivity? Do you see it as something that can be expanded to other forms of journalism beyond sports? Do you think the world is ready for Wolf Blitzer's mailbag?*

Stewart Mandel: I think sports is inherently more suited for interactivity than other types of news because so much of what we love about sports is the debates and the opinions and the arguments. In that way, it's not altogether different from politics and I don't think it's any coincidence that the two most popular types of blogs are sports and politics. I'm sure there are ways that mainstream news could also incorporate interactivity, but it's a fine line. People look to Wolf Blitzer to report the news first and foremost, they aren't necessarily seeking his opinion about said news.

*In a similar vein, does even this little bit of controlled interaction constitute a form of accountability that some people feel the fourth estate has lacked? Or even just the appearance of accountability?*

STEWART MANDEL: Sure — if you make a mistake these days, people are going to know about it. There are several "watchdog" type blogs devoted entirely to sports journalism. Much of it swings toward the "bitter" side (i.e., the most successful writers in our business are the ones bloggers seem to attack most relentlessly), but in general, increased accountability shouldn't be viewed as a bad thing.

*Okay, in your dream world, where do you want to go from here with your journalism, online and otherwise? What other outreaches and interactions? Any concerns?*

STEWART MANDEL: I honestly don't know. Things are changing so quickly. I work for a publication that did not even exist when I started college. I didn't set out to be an online writer because I did not even know that opportunity would exist. So I kind of like to think that ten years from now, I might be writing for an entity that doesn't yet exist today.

*What do you see as the strengths of a standard online column versus an interactive column? Or vice versa?*

IVAN MAISEL: The standard [online] column has going for it everything that journalism has always brought: news, storytelling, communication, bringing the community together. It's just delivered in a manner that doesn't depend on an alarm clock going off at 3 A.M. The strength of an interactive column depends upon the writer selecting the questions that best set him up to give informative, entertaining answers. In that sense, it's about as fair as an Egyptian election. I control both sides of the debate. I have had a few readers chastise me for unnecessary sarcasm in my answers. But that's how I communicate with just about everyone. It's a hard habit to break.

*Like a radio call-in with a great screener?*

IVAN MAISEL: But I'm my own screener. When I do web chats, I pick the questions. Sometimes, I have to do them on the phone, with someone in the office reading me questions. They always pick questions that I would never pick. I don't want to answer, "Who do you like in the Tech-State game?" Blah-blah-blah. I'd rather talk about an issue, or a specific team.

## Writing Spaces

*Where are you answering these questions and what device(s) are you using?*

STEWART MANDEL: In my apartment, on a Dell laptop.

*Oh and do you have any fan forums that you frequent? As a one-time Texas undergrad, I almost hate to admit that one of the best amateur sports forums I've seen is www.soonerfans.com. ;) Do you have any forums that you've come to admire from near or far?*

STEWART MANDEL: There are a lot of very good (if slightly partisan) team sites — WeAreSC.com, Warchant.com, GatorBait.net, etc., etc. Lately I've come to enjoy several college football blogs that don't necessarily cater to one team: EveryDayShouldBeSaturday.com and TheWizardofOdds.blogspot.com.

*If you would, please share where you're doing this chat and on what piece of equipment?*

IVAN MAISEL: I am sitting in my attic, which is my office, in my home in Fairfield, CT. Most of the time my yellow lab is up here snoring, but since the kids got home from school she has ditched me. I have green leaves out one window and yellow out another. Behind me is a wall of bookshelves with 4–500 sports books, which I use for reference and to procrastinate. Got a TV up here, too. It's pretty nice.

## The Rhetoric of Sports

*Could you elaborate on the similarities you see between online sports communities and political blog communities? Is there a potential for harm if the opinions outweigh the reporting, much like some of the backlash over pundit-heavy news networks? Can we predict the coming of a Colbert of sports?*

STEWART MANDEL: I can't say I've spent too much time on political blogs, but yes, what you say is already occurring. You can see it in particular with the popularity of Rivals.com or Scout.com team sites. These are fan-driven sites with actual, reported articles; however, most often, the writers are not trained journalists. In almost every case they are a fan of the team they're covering and they're gearing their content toward that audience. Many fans have come to prefer this sort of blatantly biased, sometimes opinionated writing over traditional, mainstream journalism and in fact have such a skewed sense of objectivity (kind of an inherent part of being a fan) that they view someone like me as having a "bias" against their team if I write anything remotely negative. In reality, I'm the objective one, but they've become conditioned to reading something that's overly pro–Ducks or pro–Huskies, etc. In that sense, it reminds me very much of the CNN/Fox News debates. I would gladly take on the role of Colbert of sports if offered.

*Web chats are so spontaneous, how does that feel?*

IVAN MAISEL: It feels like the American economy must be going down the tubes. I have gotten as many as 1,200 questions in a 45-minute chat. That's not 1,200 people. There's always one guy who thinks that if he keeps hitting the send button that I'll answer his question, when in fact that's a guarantee that I won't. To paraphrase Justice Potter Stewart's line about porn, I may not be able to define obnoxious behavior but I know it when I see it. But it is a lot of people. It's quite strange.

Regarding the first line of the last answer: why aren't these people working?

*Some of them are. I know I sent in a few chat questions while sitting behind the desk at Apple Computers on the occasional Saturday.*

IVAN MAISEL: If they're participating in a chat, they're not working. That's my point!

## Conclusions

With the insight of our intrepid reporters added to this chapter's initial observations, the overwhelming strength of online interaction emerges from established community — or, at the very least, a sense of belonging to an existing culture. While we should never dismiss the productive and conjoining power of the Internet, such productivity emerges in direct connection with the communal and cultural support for that productivity that originates from connecting existing passions. This support works best when it pre-dates the Internet so that the online spaces improve the arrangement and delivery of an existing community and discussion, whether sports or journalism or cooking recipes.

What sports sites excel at is transferring this existing sense of community into an online community. Certainly the Internet's ability to reduce spatial concerns and emphasize the power of chosen cultural identities aids this sense of community. Understanding what makes sports sites so successful can help us to further examine how to use community as a foundation for productivity. By tapping the right community institutions, the current productivity of sites such as Wikipedia and Facebook could be just a drop in the bucket. The trick arises in our need to acknowledge and understand the rhetorical value of not just entertainment and fandom, but other elements of traditional culture that can translate into the new arrangement of social networking.

In short, rather than attempting to reinvent the wheel online, social networks need to adapt to existing community needs to tap the passion of competition, the pride of fandom, and the sense of community that already exists. The power of the Internet lies not predominantly in creating new communities but in creating specialized arrangements for existing communities to enhance their rhetorical power and reach.

Whether the existing community is ten people or ten million, the Internet works better at amplifying the connective needs of a community through existing passion rather than attempting to generate that passion from scratch.

## NOTES

1. Jeni Carlson was a writer for *The Oklahoman* singled out for personal attack by the head coach of Oklahoma State, Mike Gundy, due to an article she wrote concerning a quarterback switch. The fallout became a YouTube and Internet sensation in late 2007, even spawning a few local TV ads.
2. He was.

## WORKS CITED

Bolter, Jay David. *Writing Space*. Mahwah, NJ: Lawrence Erlbaum, 2001.
Cicero. *Rhetorica ad Herennium*. Trans. Harry Caplan. Loeb Classical Library, 1954.
*ESPN.com*. 28 June 2008. 28 June 2008 <www.espn.com>.

Mason, Bruce. "A Million Penguins (analysis)." 2007. De Montfort University. 23 May 2008 <http://www.creativewritingandnewmedia.com/>.

Sports Illustrated. *SI.com*. 28 June 2008. 28 June 2008 <www.si.com>.

The Perseus Project. "Ancient Olympics FAQ 11." 13 Aug. 2004. *The Perseus Digital Library Project*. 16 May 2008 <http://www.perseus.tufts.edu/Olympics/faq11.html>.

*USAToday.com* 28 June 2008. 28 June 2008 <www.usatoday.com>.

Voloshinov, V. N. *Marxism and the Philosophy of Language*. Trans. Ladislav Matejka and I. R. Titunik. Cambridge: Harvard University Press, 1973.

# 3

# Spoiling *Heroes*, Enhancing Our Viewing Pleasure: NBC's *Heroes* and the Re-Shaping of the Televisual Landscape

*Marina Hassapopoulou*

"Chat with other fans online!"

"Mash-up your own music video!"

"Create your own comic book!"

"Voice your opinion in the online poll!"

"Vote for your favorite character!"

These calls (pulled from NBC's *Heroes* website in 2006-07 during the first season of the show) are just a sample of the exhortations mainstream television networks continually make to their viewers through show websites. Viewers are challenged to become something more than viewers: they are encouraged to become active contributors in the production process. The emphasis on viewer participation suggests that, in the digital age, we can't just watch a TV show; we have to be immersed in the show's digital periphery in order to have the full viewing experience. In fact, these days we do not even have to own a television to watch a TV show, since the "old" medium — television — has been remediated into newer media. We can now watch our favorite TV series whenever and wherever: online, on our iPods, and even on our cell phones.

While watching television is not yet in danger of becoming a nostalgically outdated pastime, the increasingly digital means of promoting television shows indicate that this "old" medium might not be able to sustain itself without support from new media.

45

The changing landscape of television has inevitably influenced — and has, in turn, been influenced by — a generation of digitally-savvy (or at least digitally aware) viewers. In order to cater to these viewers, television executives have adopted a cross-media approach to the creation and development of TV shows, with transmedia storytelling a prime example of how digital media are reshaping the realm of television. According to digital media critic Henry Jenkins, transmedia storytelling refers to the unfolding of a narrative through various media sources that aid the concurrent development of various facets of that narrative.[1] In other words, transmedia storytelling relies on contributions to the main story from several media outlets, such as television, magazines, videogames, and websites, all of which help develop and enhance the main storyline(s).

Moreover, many television shows now have an interactive dimension that gives viewers the chance to become actively involved in the storyline. ABC's *Lost* was one of the first shows to actively encourage its viewers to look beyond the televised narrative by creating websites for fictional elements of the show such as the Dharma Initiative research project. New media offer numerous opportunities for promotional tie-ins, allowing consumers to feel as though they have discovered new facets of their favorite storylines on their own. In the case of NBC's *Heroes*— a TV show that offers plenty of opportunities for the development of "theories" (although not as many as ABC's *Lost*) and thus fosters viewer speculation — the network has taken the concept of viewer interactivity to a new level, offering such options on the official *Heroes* website as hyperlinked graphic novels that fill in the gaps of the televised narrative while also allowing viewers to participate in the show's narrative development, of ordinary people with extraordinary abilities who try to cope with the responsibilities that come with their supernatural powers.

In 2007, NBC executives and *Heroes* creator Tim Kring tried to initiate a reverse version of the voting procedure of reality competition shows like *Big Brother* and *American Idol* by asking viewers to choose a new character to be introduced to (rather than eliminated from) the show. The process was supposed to work like this: *Heroes: Origins* would launch with six stand-alone episodes that introduced six new heroes and viewers would then vote online for their favorite. The most popular new character would then be incorporated into the actual series, giving viewers a say in how the narrative developed and allowing them to be indirectly involved in the show's creative process. If NBC's fan forums are any indication, the promotion of *Origins* created much excitement among viewers looking forward to the prospect of contributing to an executive decision about the show. All potential new characters were to be introduced via the *Heroes: Origins* series, but the 2007-08 strike by the Writers Guild of America put a damper on those plans. Instead, fans were asked to create their own hero on NBC's *Heroes* website, with the best one then starring in a new online live-action series. Even though the promotion did not go as planned, the *Heroes: Origins* concept remains a powerful example of the ways the digital world can create opportunities for engaging viewers in their favorite shows and generating new ways of consuming and interacting with televised material.

## Heroes: *Breaking Boundaries through Transmedia Storytelling*

Transmedia narratives are an indication that the entertainment market has realized that, to paraphrase Jenkins, successful products will flow across media until they become prevalent within the culture at large (Thorburn and Jenkins). Transmedia storytelling relies on what game designer Neil Young calls "additive comprehension," where consumers look to various media platforms for a complete understanding of specific narratives (Jenkins, "Transmedia"). By offering supplementary narratives such as character backstories while mimicking the aesthetics of the graphic novel paintings featured in the actual show, the *Heroes* online *manga* (Japanese-style comics) provides just such additive comprehension, particularly because these online comics contain hidden "Easter Eggs" (in the form of digital images of eggs) that provide hyperlinks to bonus pictures from the show as a reward for diligent readers. Taking transmedia storytelling in another direction, the NBC *Heroes* website also offers a link to the official *Heroes* Wikipedia entry that accumulates information on the show's development under sections such as Events, Episodes, Locations, and a surprisingly addictive *Heroes* 360 feature that takes viewers inside fictional characters' websites and cell phones, while also providing interactive maps. Many fans post comments on character blogs, addressing the characters as if they were real people.

Unlike more open-ended shows like *Lost*, the creators of *Heroes* do their best to fill in the ellipses in the televised narrative through new media avenues, instead of allowing viewers to engage in unguided inquiry about the show.[2] In general, *Heroes* viewers are more interactive in the sense that they have to search beyond the televised narrative for answers, but they are not independently *active* because answers have been planted for them and all they have to do is *find* (not contemplate or imagine) them. In essence, they are just consumers sent on an Easter Egg hunt with too many clues.

*Heroes'* creators have provided many other ways to sustain viewer interest while the show is on hiatus, including the aforementioned online graphic novels and webisodes exclusive to NBC's official *Heroes* website.[3] In the digital age, transmedia storytelling has reshaped the concept of viewership to something more interactive and multifaceted. Viewers are not "just viewers": they have the option of expanding their role to that of active contributors in a show's development. However, as will be discussed later on, viewers are never granted full creative privileges, and thus can only make contributions within parameters established by producers and network executives.

Arguably, the more a commercial product (such as a TV show) stretches out across a variety of media, the less control its producers maintain over it. Mainstream producers are not always successful in regulating consumer-driven production, but in the case of *Heroes*, producers have managed to somewhat control the extent to which consumers have a say in the show's televised content. They do so by allowing devoted viewers to have more creative freedom in the show's digital components such as the official forums and online activities that include making customized music videos using clips from the show. In this way, *Heroes* producers have limited fan activity to mostly the digital realm of the show rather than the televised narrative.

In transmedia franchises that originate from, or become most known through, film or television, consumer participation usually takes place in the digital extensions of that film or show. In the case of *Heroes*, viewers are offered the chance to "interact with *Heroes*" (according to NBC's official *Heroes* website) through new media avenues (such as mobile phone text messages offering "clues" regarding what to look for during the on-air broadcast), but this interaction seldom qualifies as consumer-driven production. Text messaged clues about *Heroes* and webisode spin-offs, for instance, make the TV show appear more three-dimensional to its consumers because it is not confined to a single medium, but this does not necessarily mean that consumers actively contribute to the show's narrative database; most of the time, they just consume the multifaceted product in its various forms. In other words, *Heroes* fans are more interactive with the producers' existing storyline material, but their productivity operates within a pre-existing, producer-generated narrative database.[4] NBC's online interactive graphic novels are an example of how the *illusion* of independent production is given to consumers (users choose the direction of the story in *Heroes* digital comic books from several possible narrative twists), whereas, in fact, the extent of consumer production has already been predetermined by traditional producers (i.e., the narrative database has been established by the producers, so consumers are mostly remixing existing material). But, since the modes of consumption have significantly expanded in the digital era, many consumers are under the impression that they have become more autonomous in their consumption of the franchised material.

## *If You Can't Beat Them, Join Them: The Making of Prosumer Culture*

The marker of success for a TV show is when viewers turn into something more passionate: fans. Television shows — and, more specifically, their fictional characters — can be considered some of the most influential driving forces of fandom. Building a solid fanbase is what TV executives are counting on when it comes to securing a stable demographic. Early academic fandom studies have claimed that "fans [and consumers in general] operate from a position of cultural marginality and social weakness" (Jenkins, *Textual* 26), but this position has dramatically shifted in recent years as fans have been allowed a more active role in the creative development of their favorite shows and movies. Before fandom became a creative force operating from *within* the mainstream, fans were independently producing DIY (do it yourself) videos of their favorite shows and films from a culturally marginalized position. *Buffy the Vampire Slayer* (created by Joss Whedon and airing from 1997 to 2003) video tributes are a noteworthy example of underground fan experimentation with the show's narrative potential.

Many contemporary television shows, however, now incorporate more opportunities for audience participation, not just through voting on television (*American Idol*–style) but also, and more so, through new media avenues. The emphasis on viewer participation indicates that TV executives acknowledge their viewers' active role in both interpreting their shows' narratives and appropriating them. Arguably, this has always been the case, but now media producers also accept the fact that consumers want to not only produce but to also infiltrate mainstream modes of production. To keep up with the changing role of the media consumer, media producers are beginning to encourage consumers to become "prosumers,"[5] thus encouraging their participation in the production of media content. Nevertheless, media producers still wish to maintain their traditional primacy over media content, and so they try to keep user-generated content in check.[6] In other words, producers still wish to regulate the realm of consumer production (e.g., UGC: user-generated content) and thus exert control over independently-produced media content. Essentially, media conglomerates try to attract more consumers by offering them — *us* — new ways to interact with media content, while also trying to keep consumer input at bay by confining it within specific boundaries. At times, those limitations are too subtle for consumers to notice or care, but their existence is, nonetheless, undeniable.

Even though *Heroes* has undoubtedly left its mark on popular culture — with the most notable proof being the "Save the cheerleader, save the world" quote from the show which turned into a popular catchphrase — there are factors that prevent it from being classified as a cult phenomenon of the same status as, say, David Lynch's short-lived television series *Twin Peaks* (ABC, 1990-91). One reason for this is the regulation of *Heroes* fan activity by mainstream producers. In the past, fan activity would accumulate in more "underground" (or independent) avenues such as fan fiction and fan websites. The official NBC website for *Heroes*, by contrast, fosters a significant amount of fan activity, which means that there aren't as many independently-operating fan communities as there were when shows like *Twin Peaks* and *Buffy the Vampire Slayer* were beginning to gain a cult following and status.

The gradual incorporation, or, acceptance, if you will, of fan-produced work (such as online fan fiction) into the mainstream has (somewhat ironically) given producers more control over fan-produced material. This is not an entirely negative thing, though, because producers demonstrate to fans that their ideas matter. In the case of *Heroes*, producers have attempted to create a two-way communication system between the show's creators and its fanbase by launching the *9th Wonders* website, which is, according to its creators, "the official/unofficial fan site for *Heroes*" where fans, cast, and producers can all ask and answer questions about the show. The website's welcome message states that the cast, the creators, and the fans are "all in this together" as the site tries to establish a communal middle-ground between consumers and producers, reflecting the impact new media have on the promotion of TV shows and the concept of fandom. To an extent, collaborative websites like *9th Wonders* support the assertion that we live in a participatory culture in which its "members believe their contributions matter, and feel some degree of social connection with one another [or] at least they care what other people think about what they have created" (Jenkins, "Building").

## Spoilers Welcome: When Fan Practices Become Appropriated

NBC's attempt to incorporate prosumers into the televised content of *Heroes* is perhaps best represented by the launch of the *Heroes* Theories contest, where viewers were encouraged to submit videos of their theories about the show's enigmas to the NBC website in hopes their work would be aired on the network. NBC's Theories has, in a sense, recontextualized the meaning of spoiling. The "spoiling" of television shows used to be an unsanctioned community-building activity, where fans would share their predictions and knowledge about the shows through independent forums such as fan websites. Jenkins' case study of the CBS reality show *Survivor* demonstrates the lengths fans go to in order to uncover secrets about the show and, conversely, the lengths producers go to so as to prevent the leaking of information (*Fans*). Spoiling could be considered a communal practice: discussion forums act as sites of inquiry where viewers collectively share and negotiate spoiler information. It is believed that TV producers casually "eavesdrop" on such websites (or even offer misleading spoilers) to see if show secrets are in danger of being demystified, but this information had never been officially confirmed until networks began hosting their own fan forums on official show websites to monitor such discussions more easily.

In an interesting twist, though, NBC's *Heroes* Theories contest has, in a way, legitimized the act of spoiling by *encouraging* consumers to solve the show's enigmas during the first season (2007). The contest asked viewers to submit videos of their predictions of what will happen in the show via the *Heroes* website. The prize for the winning entries was that they would be broadcast on NBC. In this way, NBC managed to incorporate spoiling practices into the show, rather than run counter to them. At the same time, *Heroes* Theories eradicated a significant part of the community element in spoiling practices by pitting fans against each other. Although some fans offered constructive feedback on other fans' Theories videos and posts, the competitive nature of this kind of spoiling, combined with the allure of seeing one's work on television, took away the community-building element integral in "traditional" spoiling practices.[7]

Fan communities revolve around the principles of reciprocity and interdependence and thus provide a contrast to the self-interest of formal economy (Jenkins, *Convergence* 280). However, with the convergence of grassroots and formal sectors, Jenkins argues, the "loyalty and [...] sense of 'identity' or 'belonging'" characteristic of grassroots communities (e.g., fan communities) is no longer contradictory to the corporate principle of "forming ties on the basis of calculation, monetary or otherwise" (*Convergence* 280). In the case of *Heroes*, a loosely-knit fan community has been created around the various promotional activities initiated by NBC. Fans form precarious communities when they post, for example, their individual *Heroes* Theories and vote for their favorite submissions. Ultimately, though, it was NBC that determined the duration and longevity of such communities. The establishment of a Theories deadline by NBC, for instance, implied that once the deadline had been reached, this specific video-sharing community would either dissolve or migrate to other sites like YouTube or independent fan websites.

My own *Heroes* theory is that the show's producers were running out of ideas by the end of the first season. The creative sterility was evident in the anticlimactic first season finale of the show. In my opinion, the rationale behind NBC's Theories contest is as follows. Fan video submissions become property of NBC and are not returned to their creators (according to the submissions agreement), which means that the content of the videos is owned by the network. NBC explicitly warned participants that they would not be given any credit if their submission was used (although *where* it might be used was not made clear). Viewers were asked to respond to only specific questions about the show surrounding their speculations about the show's mysteries. It seems to me that NBC would not go to such lengths to encourage viewer input if they did not have a higher purpose in mind. Perhaps video submissions were (or will be) used by *Heroes* producers to generate more creative ideas and determine what direction the show will follow. If my speculations are correct, then fans are indeed contributing to the creative development of the show ... they are just not officially getting credit for it.

The Theories contest led prosumer videos to concentrate on the NBC website, instead of other sites like YouTube. Arguably, websites such as YouTube can be viewed as democratized sites of production, and thrive under collaboration and shared content.[8] In the case of other TV shows like *Lost*, the majority of fan and hater videos are posted and shared on YouTube. In the case of *Heroes*, however, YouTube is usually populated with the fan videos that were *rejected* from the NBC website (with the exception of the popular *Zeroes* parody series, which is too long and off-topic to compete in the Theories contest anyway). Unlike YouTube, NBC offers prizes to *Heroes* prosumers for various contests, the most coveted reward being television airtime. This means that prosumers tailor their media according to NBC regulations in order to win, regulations that can seriously stifle creative initiative. For instance, Theories submissions could only be a maximum of 60 seconds long, and prosumers were asked to "speak directly to the camera and frame [themselves] from the chest up ... quality counts, no mumbling!" What NBC defines as "quality," I interpret as an attempt to stifle individual creativity. The regulations do not leave much room for stylistic experimentation and are more heavily focused on content (i.e., the theories conveyed) than form. Regulations forbid "idea misappropriation," which further restricts the content of the videos because applicants are not allowed to parody (and, subsequently, critique) the existing material. Despite all these restrictions, prosumers were still eager to submit their work to NBC.com instead of more democratic sites like YouTube.

YouTube has become an alternative outlet for user videos rejected by NBC. Even though those videos bear the stigma of mainstream rejection, some of them are far more innovative than the "talking heads" videos populating the NBC website. TheyCallMeSloppyPat's *Heroes* photo essay, for example, was not accepted by NBC because it was not in the video format specified by NBC. TheyCallMeSloppyPat states, almost apologetically, "I don't have a camera, but I made do. Turns [out] this video doesn't meet any of their criteria but whatever I want to share my theory." His "whatever" attitude seems to be a defensive response to the rejection he has received from NBC, and in his case YouTube is merely a secondary avenue for sharing his work. This once again suggests that most prosumers strive for mainstream media recognition, and feel jaded when they do not receive it. For users like TheyCallMeSloppy Pat, their work does not seem to matter unless it becomes accessible to as many viewers as possible.[9]

It should be emphasized, however, that the *Heroes* fan-related activities do not completely restrict consumer creativity and interpretation. Even if we look at *Heroes* as a database of "closed texts" regulated by network executives and NBC publicists, critics like Umberto Eco and John Fiske would argue that the inherent heterogeneity in audiences produces a negotiation between the production-controlled signifiers and their decoded meanings. Unfortunately, though, at the time this chapter was being written, I could not find sufficient evidence to support this point in the user-generated content pertaining to *Heroes*. This indicates that even though negotiated readings of the show did exist during its first season, resistant *products* (such as videos) were scarce. On the contrary, more open-ended shows like *Lost* have allowed fans more freedom to produce alternative interpretations, which are evident in prosumer content such as YouTube videos that challenge the heteronormative aspects of the show.[10]

A prosumer video posted on NBC.com was one of the few examples where user creativity shined through, even within the strict parameters set by NBC. User Yen-Feng's top-rated video entry for the Theories contest manages to stick to the NBC regulations by answering a specific question, but does so in a relatively unique manner. Yen-Feng uses special effects such as smoke and digital image manipulation to make his theory more engaging. This video does bend some of NBC's rules, however. The prosumer does not always speak directly to the camera (as per contest rules) since he incorporates stills from the show into his video. I believe that the reason why NBC has not disqualified this video is because it would have made a popular "reject" entry on YouTube. Yen-Feng's video indicates that, even though consumer participation in mainstream media content sometimes acts as a promotional gimmick, user-generated content can still find ways of being creative within established frames.

However, in the case of *Heroes* and many other shows, fan creativity needs to be stimulated by an enthusiasm for the show itself. A recent look at the *Heroes* peritexts indicates that the interactive dimensions to the show have not been able to sustain high viewership ratings, at least up to this point. The official *Heroes* website keeps expanding its interactive features, but so far there has not been another attempt for viewer involvement as participatory as the

Theories contest. To an extent, this suggests that even if viewers wish to become more than just viewers, the television show has to be good enough to inspire them to consume its other, digital facets. If the "dominant" product starts to deteriorate, as is the fate of most TV shows, then the amount of prosumption begins to decrease because, in certain areas, prosumption is driven by fandom.

## Uncertain Direction: What Is the Future [Name] of Prosumption?

The digital universe's state of perpetual evolution makes it impossible to draw definite conclusions about its impact on contemporary modes of media consumption and production. The need to come up with new terms like "prosumers" to identify our functions as members of an ever-expanding digital landscape not only suggests that the traditional role of the media consumer has changed, but that it has not yet stabilized (and probably never will). What is evident is that "prosumption" changes the way we interpret and remix existing media content such as televised narratives.

As media production tools become more accessible to amateurs, DIY aesthetics characteristic of, for instance, fan-made videos are gradually infiltrating commercial media and creating a more diversified content. A relevant example from *Heroes* is a televised promo for both the show and the Theories contest.[11] This *Heroes* promotional video fused Theories entries with footage from the show and was broadcast on NBC in 2007. The video amalgamated (and reformatted) the DIY amateur aesthetics of fan videos with the stylized format of the television series to produce a new kind of aesthetic hybrid. The analysis of the *Heroes* Theories contest shows that media consumers are still only allowed to produce their own material within established parameters in broadcast media, but it also suggests that prosumers are gaining more influence within mainstream media production. Moreover, the remixing of existing new media material by the digital generation introduces more ideas and diversity into media content as a whole. Even the less participatory act of remixing existing material, such as "found footage" from TV shows, encourages media consumers to look beyond dominant narratives (e.g. those established through television) and also beyond dominant modes of consumption to construct their own meanings — not just mentally, but also in more concrete ways, such as through fan videos. Of course, not every media consumer wishes to be a prosumer: some consumers just want to watch TV!

In any case though, media prosumption helps consumers interact with media content in a more hands-on manner by encouraging them to experiment with various forms, formats, software, and narratives; whether they choose to do so is up to them. When it comes to film and television, the act of "prosuming" means that viewers become more reflective about the very format of new and old media, and more conscious of the ways in which producers and consumers are in a dialectic with each other through media contents and forms.

## NOTES

1. For more information on transmedia storytelling, see Henry Jenkins's blog, *Confessions of an Aca-Fan: The Official Blog of Henry Jenkins* <http://www.henryjenkins.org/>.

2. Moreover, NBC engages in common fan practices before allowing fans to do so too. NBC's cross-media promotion of *Heroes* has so far done the majority of activities Jenkins identified as "poaching" (appropriational) practices in his book *Textual Poachers* (1992). Accordingly, NBC has recontextualized content, it has expanded the series timeline and dimensions (e.g. in terms of character depth and back-stories) through new media tie-ins, and it has enticed viewers through media cross-overs (e.g., *Star Trek* references, Japanese manga). All these are identified by Jenkins as fan practices that still take place years after the publication of *Textual Poachers*. The only difference is that now such poaching is not restricted to marginalized fan communities, but is also used as a marketing strategy by media conglomerates. In a more recent study, Jenkins rightfully claims that even "if creators do not ultimately control what we take from their transmedia stories, this does not prevent them from trying to shape our interpretations" (*Convergence*, 123).

3. It is hard to keep track of all the Web-based components of the show, since new things are constantly being added to NBC's *Heroes* website. This comes as no surprise because the show's creators have stated from the very beginning of the show that *Heroes* was meant to be a transmedia franchise.

4. New media critics like Lev Manovich see the database and the narrative as separate and often opposing concepts. However, the term "database narrative" is a more adequate category because it conveys the convergent nature of database and narrative that is facilitated by new media. Marsha Kinder suggests that this database structure "exposes or thematises the dual processes of selection and combination that lie at the heart of all stories and that are crucial to language: the selection of particular data (characters, images, sounds, events) from a series of databases or paradigms, which are then combined to generate specific tales" (Willis 40). In light of this observation, the interactive viewer is not a "true" contributor to the work but simply a participant who remixes existing material. In this way, participatory works can actually retreat in the opposite direction to that of a truly participatory objective.

5. The portmanteau "prosumer," a fusion of the words "producer" and "consumer," refers here to active media consumption and was first coined in the late 1970s and early 1980s by futurologist Alvin Toffler. This term has been criticized for its ambivalent connotations but, for the purposes of this chapter, I use the term as a shorthand for active (i.e. *pro*ductive), non-corporate consumers/viewers, in order to distinguish from corporate modes of production. However, I feel it is important to mention at least a couple of reasons why the term is problematic, so as not to seem as though I am simplistically applying it to my own analysis. One of the reasons why this term is problematic lies in the uncertainty of where to situate prosumers: do they operate within the logic of consumer culture, or do they retain a certain independence from the mainstream economy? In general, the answer to this question depends on the kind of prosumption taking place and

the circumstances under which it is taking place. Another issue with the term is that "prosumer" misleadingly suggests that a prosumer is *equally* a producer and a consumer, whereas in fact this is rarely the case. A prosumer is either more of a producer or more of a consumer; in this particular case study, the latter holds true.

6. Admittedly, the term "producer" does not adequately reflect the complexities in distinguishing between large corporations and more independent producers. However, for lack of a more suitable term, I use "producer" to refer to those in charge of mainstream media avenues such as network television channels.

7. Moreover, the large number of video submissions NBC received indicates that many prosumers would like to see their work shown on television, not "just" online. The fact that very few *Heroes* theories were aired on NBC indicates that network producers still maintain control over televised content — something that undermines the foundations of participatory culture.

8. While the democratic principles of such websites can easily be challenged (especially since both sites are subject to regulation and selective filtering by a minority of users), the vast increase in prosumer media content online is undeniable.

9. Another important restriction in NBC's Theories contest is the fact that all prosumer submissions must come from U.S. and D.C. residents. This excludes a huge international demographic that constitutes a significant part of the show's fanbase. The apparent justification for this exclusivity seems to be that non–U.S. and D.C. residents do not get access to U.S. network television.

10. Interestingly, the creators of Heroes have even tried to control how *Heroes* fans interpreted a character's (Zach) sexuality on the show. Zach was initially intended by the creators to be gay, and this was suggested through his character's MySpace profile, though not on the actual show. However, network executives and NBC publicists later denied that Zach is gay, which sparked fan speculation and debate on the Web. For a more detailed analysis see Brian Juergens' "*Heroes* Straightens Up Its Gay Character."

11. The video is available on YouTube: <http://www.youtube.com/watch?v=VupiA DrchmA>.

## Works Cited

Digestor 2365. "Zeroes." *YouTube*. 8 Feb. 2007. <http://www.youtube.com/watch?v=IW JJBwKhvp4>.

"Heroes Theories Promo." *YouTube*. 3 April 2007. 20 Oct. 2008. <http://www.youtube. com/watch?v=VupiADrchmA>.

Jenkins, Henry. "Building the Field of Digital Media and Learning. Confronting the Challenges of Participatory Culture: Media Education for the 21st Century." *Digitallearning.org*. 10 June 2007 <http://www.digitallearning.macfound.org/atf/cf/%7B7E45C 7E0-A3E0-4B89-AC9C-E807E1B0AE4E%7D/JENKINS_WHITE_PAPER.PDF>.

_____. *Convergence Culture: Where Old and New Media Collide*. New York: New York University Press, 2006.

_____. *Fans, Bloggers, and Gamers: Exploring Participatory Culture*. New York: New York University Press, 2006.

_____. *Textual Poachers: Television Fans and Participatory Culture*. New York: Routledge, 1992.

_____. "Transmedia Storytelling 101." *Confessions of an Aca-Fan: The Official Blog of Henry Jenkins*. 2007. 30 June 2008. <http://www.henryjenkins.org/2007/03/transmedia_ storytelling_101.html>.

Juergens, Brian. "*Heroes* Straightens Up Its Gay Character." *AfterElton.com*. 11 Dec. 2006. 30 May 2007. <http://www.afterelton.com/TV/2006/12/heroes.html?page=0%2C2>.

*NBC.com: Heroes.* 2006. 12 Feb. 2009. <http://www.nbc.com/Heroes/>.
*9th Wonders: The Official/Unofficial Fan Site for* Heroes *Fans.* 2007. 12 Feb. 2009. <http://www.9thwonders.com/>.
TheyCallMeSloppyPat. "My Heroes Theory." *YouTube.* 3 March 2007. 30 May 2007. <http://www.youtube.com/watch?v=I9w5VVB0CZQ>.
Thorburn, David, and Henry Jenkins, eds. *Rethinking Media Change: The Aesthetics of Transition.* Cambridge: MIT Press, 2003.
"Welcome to Heroes Wiki!" *Wikipedia.com.* 2007. 30 June 2008. <http://heroeswiki.com/Main_Page>.
Willis, Holly. *New Digital Cinema: Reinventing the Moving Image.* New York: Wallflower Press, 2005.
"Yen-Feng's Theory." *NBC.com: Heroes.* 2007. 1 June 2007. <http://www.nbc.com/Heroes/theories/galleries.shtml#mea=88217>.

# 4

# History, the Trace, and *Fandom Wank*

*Karen Hellekson*

"I can't respect you as an author when you go around telling your readers that you're dating HIM," read the handwritten words on a caricature drawing of actor Zachary Quinto, best known for his role as Sylar on television's *Heroes*. The image appeared on *Fandom Secrets* (http://community.livejournal.com/fandomsecrets/), a Web site for the fan community modeled on well-known site *Post Secret*, which publishes postcards sent in by people sharing a secret. The anonymous fan artist's secret: "I wish you had some way of validating your story so I can read your fics without wondering whether you're delusional, doing it for attention or telling the truth."

Turns out she wasn't the only one wondering whether this unnamed fan fiction writer is actually dating Quinto. "I'm dying to know what's going on, but nobody is speaking up. Is it a real situation? Is it a joke? Anyone have some juicy details?" one fan wonders.[1] Why yes, in fact they do. "This is where the fun stuff begins," another fan writes a couple days later in a densely hyperlinked blog post:

> It comes to light that [the fanfic writer] is using her psychic mother to figure out who's been posting secrets about her and sending her 800+ f-list [friends list] after them. And her point of contact with Zachary Quinto is her 12-year-old medium sister. That's right folks, apparently she's dating him on the astral plane! And he sends her letters and family heirloom earrings through spirits, through her medium sister ... or something.[2]

It didn't take long for the ruckus about this fabulously zany tidbit of information (dating Quinto? on the astral plane? through her medium sister?) to escalate to stunning proportions. As the situation became public, the deletions began: *Fandom Secrets* took down the image and its related discussion. The fan fiction writer in question defended herself, then began deleting her blog posts. Her friends stuck with her, then, feeling betrayed, fled en masse. Three broke silence to reveal all, and one stayed behind to defend. Everyone, it seems, had an opinion.

*Fandom Wank,* an online community-authored blog, exists to publicize events like this, and it's the reason I watch the site. It can be cuttingly mean, but — dating Quinto? on the astral plane? through her medium sister? It's pure gold. The site's purpose revolves around the creation of multiauthored, multivocal documents, like the one I just described. The site welcomes wank — a fan-appropriated term used to describe these fan upsets, from British slang meaning "masturbate"— from fandoms of all flavors. Anything is fair game for the site, as long as it results in things like peevish posts, angry exchanges, destroyed online friendships, people announcing they are leaving fandom forever (the so-called fandom flounce), and people anonymously revealing what they probably shouldn't. *Fandom Wank*'s topics range widely. A quick glance at the site as I write this reveals wanks about fan misappropriation of money meant to pay for a Web site; several wanks about Stephenie Meyer's latest novel, which was leaked on the Internet; and the cancellation of *Stargate: Atlantis* and the ensuing fan reaction. Each of these topics results in escalating exchanges, and each originary post, which summarizes the problem at hand and the fan reaction that makes it wanky, hotlinks to all manner of evidence, allowing interested readers to click through and find support for the original poster's assertions. But the mere generation of these documents is not the point of the activity. The fan community uses the creation of wank documents to explore community standards regarding the quality and veracity of evidence.

These wanks are, I argue, historical writings imbued with community-specific meaning. These documents comprise a collaboratively authored text that brings together relevant traces, documentation, and testimony. The goal is to construct a persuasive document that revolves around coming to a consensus about the events' believability. A piece of evidence, like a *Fandom Secrets* image that results in extensive commentary, is presented, examined, discussed, and judged. The work posted at *Fandom Wank* illustrates contemporary activities of historiography and documentation on the Web within a specific community, foregrounding notions of authority and meaning making. Hotlinks, downloaded Web pages, and saved images, in conjunction with assessments of the veracity of interlocutors, are all used to support and provide authority for assertions. Such documentation makes up the trace, to use Paul Ricoeur's term for documents or artifacts that prove an event occurred (13–14). *Fandom Wank* illustrates that the trace has moved beyond the realm of physical reality. Handwritten artifacts that prove an event occurred have given way to an electronic, hyperreal equivalent.

## Blogs and History

Before I address *Fandom Wank* in more detail, I want to discuss why blogs are the best medium for the creation of this kind of text. Web 2.0 has been driven forward by the utilization of powerful, easy-to-use tools (Tapscott and Williams 19). As I've argued elsewhere (Busse and Hellekson 13), and as others have noted (Lovink 214), fans and other users have a long history of repurposing tools to their own ends, while at the same time the capabilities of the tool affect the social experience. A blog can be a fan fiction archive, for example, which permits categorization and commenting, thus guiding the interaction. Free blogs at popular fan sites, like LiveJournal.com, can be set up and customized in minutes, and simple coding makes entries easy to create. Most important, blogs have media-rich features, which permit "the use of images, audio files, hypertext links, and the audience commenting system" (Thomas 201). Commenting is a key component of this mode of making history, as I'll discuss later; comments, or discussions appended to a post, are often used to present further evidence. Although blogs are often thought of as representing the voice of an individual, they can be customized to permit many people to post. At the LiveJournal.com and Journalfen.Net fan-friendly blog domains, this kind of blog is called a *community*. Although access to a community may be restricted, posters usually just have to sign up and obtain a user name to be able to read, post, and comment.

As Jean Burgess notes, blogs were formerly thought of in generic terms based on their formal features: entries are dated with the most recent post first, calling to mind the historical genre of the chronicle; blogs are updated frequently; links are posted as well as commentary. But this is insufficient, she argues: "We need to understand the ways in which the formal and technological features of blogs combine dialogically with remediated 'speech genres' ... and existing social contexts and conventions to form hybrid sub-genres." Burgess proposes that "existing speech genres (conversation, debate, personal storytelling) need to be articulated with ossified academic writing genres (the essay, the research report, the literature review, the critique)" in a *hybrid sub-genre* (108). Sites like *Fandom Wank* are an example of such a hybrid sub-genre: they combine conversation, debate, and personal storytelling with historical documentation. The multivocal nature of a text so created is of particular interest because within history, such texts are rare given that the single author's viewpoint is firmly embedded in historical discourse (Berkhofer 190).

The very features that permit such ease of posting also permit activities that, within the realm of historical documentation, are deeply troubling. Posters can alter the date and time of a blog post. Many blogs permit comments to be edited, and all of them permit comments to be deleted, either by the commenter or by the blog's owner. Posters can delete their entire blog with the push of a button, or they can move the blog wholesale to another domain, thereby breaking all the links made to the original blog's posts. It's also possible to lock entries, even after the fact, so only a specific subset of designated readers can see them. Trace and documentation can be altered: when entries can be manipulated, edited, deleted, or locked, they seem impermanent and transient. Historian Bernadine Dodge notes of online documents, "The basic tenets of our profession are now unspeakable, for how does one talk of authenticity, authority, provenance, original order or evidential value in a world where time and space have dissolved?" (350–51). Let me reframe her question: how can the hyperreal substitute for the real?

The answer may lie not in the document or its representation, but in those analyzing it. Ricoeur notes, "Under the condition of a broad agreement among specialists, one can say that a factual interpretation has been verified in the sense that it has not been refuted at the present stage of accessible documentation" (338). Something is true, in short, because a community of people agree that it's true. This is the basis of truth by consensus so important to the judging of Web content (Tapscott and Williams 274–75), and mocked by political commentator Stephen Colbert when he coined the term *wikiality* on July 31, 2006: "We can all create a reality that we all can agree on; the reality that we just agreed on."[3]

Ricoeur and Dodge both have in mind the historian, who has been trained in the applicable standards of the discipline. But in the case of blog-based, trace-conserving, history-constructing sites like *Fandom Wank*, the specialist historian gives way to the specialist fan skilled in reading and writing in a very particular *lingua franca*. These members of the community present evidence and then decide on its appropriateness and interpretation.

## Fandom Wank

*Fandom Wank* is just one of several dedicated wank sites, all of which have the same basic structure and rules. The language used in the posts is dense and inaccessible to the nonfan, thereby delineating the community. On its "about" page, FW provides rules related to quality of evidence. Posters may not link to locked material, or material in some forum type that isn't freely accessible to all: "The general rule is don't cut-n-paste from anything that requires the approval of someone else (private journal owner, moderator, et cetera) to join." In related advice, "if it gets locked after being wanked, it's okay. Post text, screencaps, whatever. But if it starts out locked and inaccessible and *stays* locked, that's a big fucking no." A similar wank site, *Bad*

*Penny*,[4] neatly summarizes fannish consensus: "Documentation, people. If you want to do a tell-all about a fan's or group of fans' ethical wrongdoing, make sure you can back it up. Links, screenshots, sources. 'Show me the evidence!'" The documentary evidence falls into the following categories, many of which are cut-and-paste elements: hyperlinks to Web pages; saved Web page code, in case the page is taken down; screen captures (caps) of Web pages or other online sources; quotations from e-mails or posts (usually permission is obtained before an e-mail is posted publicly, but public posts may be reproduced with attribution); records of IP addresses, which track the identity and location of a particular computer when a post is made, although these may be made anonymous via Web proxies and thus are not wholly reliable; and first-person testimonial accounts.

Most of these forms of documentation lack permanence and can be removed from the Web at any time. When something hits FW, it's big, and as soon as the involved parties realize what's happened, the lockdown and deletion frenzy begins. To illustrate the nature of evidence in this kind of wank document, I refer back to the wank I described to open this essay. "How NOT to Date a Celebrity" was posted at FW on February 17, 2008, and the purpose of the wank was to learn whether a *Heroes* fanfic writer was actually dating Zachary Quinto (figure 1). I've chosen this wank not only because of its sensational elements, which resulted in a lot of reader interest, but also because it provides examples of the sorts of documentation I want to discuss. All the posts I quote from are openly browsable. I have redacted user names to protect fans' privacy, but this wank also has an unusually high proportion of anonymous posts. The document comprises many threaded comments that must be clicked on to unfold, so I provide the comment page number and some keywords from the first comment, which remains unhidden, so interested parties can find the discussion. This wank ranges beyond FW: wank-style documentation exists at a number of other community sites and personal blogs.

Important to the discussion below is the relevance of testimony, which is fraught because of the divide between the desired objectivity and the inevitable subjectivity (Torstendahl 306; Breisach, *Future* chap. 13; Berkhofer). The people on Quinto's astral-plane girlfriend's blog who are permitted to read her locked posts provide an example of testimony, of which Ricoeur notes,

> And I do not see that we can go beyond the witness's triple declaration: (1) I was there; (2) believe me; (3) if you don't believe me, ask someone else.... I have said that we have nothing better than our memory to assure ourselves of the reality of our memories — we have nothing better than testimony and criticism of testimony to accredit the historian's representation of the past [278].

**Edited again:** Annoying sock is ~~annoying~~ revealed to be a freetheelves supporter. What a surprise.

**A Note to the Mice (and anyone else asking)**
We actually have rules here on Fandom Wank. Rule number 6 states **Do not link to locked material.** So no matter how much you want proof or lulz or whatever from FTE's super sekrit filter posts, you can't have them. Please stop being morons and asking for them. Certainly don't post them! The mods will take your mouse power away.

**Hey look!** A mouse wrote this wank a Theme Song!

**Yet Another Edit:** Some of the former super secret filter friends are doing a little Q&A Thread.

**A Note to the Mice (and anyone else asking) Part 2**
Snacky says "summarizing the flocked posts is pretty much a no-go here too. This is a JF-wide thing, not just a FW thing, and we'd really like not to piss off the JF admins and respect their wishes."

Let's review.
Don't link to locked posts.
Don't ask to be linked to locked posts.
Don't c&p locked posts.
Don't encourage the posting of locked posts.
Don't summarize locked posts.
Don't [verb of your choice] locked posts!

---

**Page 1 of 6**
<< **[1]** [2] [3] [4] [5] [6] >>

**(Post a new comment)**

**flightstothesea**
2008-02-17 10:55 pm UTC (link)

MY GOD, IT'S FULL OF WANK! o.o

(Reply to this)

**negativecosine**
2008-02-17 10:57 pm UTC (link)

I keep thinking that her "medium sister" refers to the sister that's neither small nor large.

(Reply to this)(Thread)

(no subject) - **mistressrenet**, *2008-02-17 11:02 pm UTC*
  (no subject) - **negativecosine**, *2008-02-17 11:06 pm UTC*
  (no subject) - **angstymcgoth**, *2008-02-17 11:42 pm UTC*

**Screenshot of the *Fandom Wank* post entitled "How NOT to Date a Celebrity," posted on February 17, 2008, illustrating hotlinks and threaded comments.**

Screen caps and first-person accounts are both ways to assert "I was there." Screen caps, however, have higher evidentiary value because they are factual and disinterested in a way that a person can't be. Collections of neatly sorted links provide a kind of authority and accreditation as well: posters line up hotlinked facts that are left to speak for themselves.

The originary FW post contains many examples of community-appropriate documentation. As is custom, the poster hotlinks items in her description of the wank, but she also immediately provides specially saved evidence: "The next day, the entire thread of [the original] wank [on LiveJournal.com] disappears. Too bad the internet never forgets." Hotlinked to the last few words is a .zip file containing saved Web pages with the original exchange — her support. Literally hundreds of comments are appended to the originary post, kicked off with an all-caps exclamation: "MY GOD, IT'S FULL OF WANK!" This wank also generated artworks: one poster wrote a theme song ("You may disagree but I'm not insane! / I date Sylar on the astral plane!"), and an off-site discussion of this topic, hotlinked from the FW post, resulted in several Sylar/Mohindar wedding images, dedicated in one way or another to the person whose astral-dating assertions started it all. The original FW post was updated several times with late-breaking information; such edits are prefaced, as is customary, by a boldface indication that the information was added: "Edited," "Edited again," "Hey look!," and "Yet Another Edit" all provide updated news and fresh links, including off-site links to detailed summaries of information.

But in addition to the recorded traces, it's necessary to take into account the veracity of the source. Sometimes those involved in the wank will attempt to steer discussion by disguising themselves with a different user name and posting their own support. Such partisans are called *sock puppets* or simply *socks,* and unmasking them is a worthy endeavor. And with this wank, it didn't take long for socks to join the fray. On the first page of comments, one commenter writes, "One of [her] friends revealed themselves as the sockpuppet!" A link to a now-locked LiveJournal.com post is provided, along with a quotation from the post: "*Sorry to anyone who found the sock annoying. He was my best attempt at diplomacy during a really shitty time.*" The anonymous post immediately below the wank comment notes, "IT GETS BETTER!!... Also she has just admitted being [user name] in the wank post. We have sockpuppets!" Although the links in this wank point to posts where people admit to being sock puppets, the subtext here is that whatever evidence a sock provides must be discounted as partisan; they are merely muddying the waters.

On the fifth page of comments, a side discussion about Quinto begins with "look what this mouse [poster] found" and includes a hotlink to damning commentary by Quinto's alleged astral-plane girlfriend on a celebrity-gossip site that implies that the two of them have met in real life. In response, an anonymous poster writes, "Should any of this be capped (it's public now)? she's been on a delete rampage before and she can find it by looking here now. i can't cap it right now though." Luckily, it's covered: the next comment says that "a mouse has capped the thread." Here, community members exhibit a concern with capturing unlocked evidence while the getting's good because they anticipate deletion, thereby preserving it and retaining its status as a trace. Yet the link to the gossip site provides support for astral-plane girlfriend's assertion: have they actually met? could they really be dating? This text is read critically by FW posters. Maybe they've met, maybe she's lying, or maybe she's nuts, but in any case, the assertions here are in line with assertions she makes elsewhere, in forums with different audiences.

On the second page of comments, a long thread directly explores the quality of the evidence presented at FW. One commenter writes,

> I'm still waiting for some actual proof that she said anything about dating ZQ on the astral plane. There are too many anonymice making wild allegations without screenshots and too many named people saying they're on her flist [friends list] and haven't seen any crazy at all.... The only evidence that's shown up so far is something she said that could easily be read as proof, BUT is also ambiguous enough to be a mistake or brain fart on her part.
>
> So. Proof plz, or the whole thing starts smelling like the "OMG Usagi Kou orgy with a soda bottle!" rumors.

This commenter is troubled by the poor quality of the evidence. Alas, it initially seems that the shocking assertions may not hold up: the original posts detailing the astral-plane dating were locked and thus according to community rules may not be duplicated. "Looks like there are some caps, but it's unclear whether they're locked posts or not" is immediately followed by, "Aaaaaand, at least one of the capped posts is locked. ::sigh::" One poster writes, "3 of her inner circle ... have come forward and confirmed EVERYTHING. Not to mention her supporters who believe her or think it is O.K. for her to lie or believe that she is-dating-ZQ-through-her-medium-sister. That is all the proof you need." The response to this is, quite reasonably, "It's not." However, a flurry of posting in various other forums finally provides the support the original poster required: "Oooookay, I found the 'declaration of war' screencaps where the anons [anonymous posters] seem to be getting their information. I'm convinced." The proof that satisfied this reader was not "he said/she said" and secondhand reports describing locked posts, but a screenshot with the information she required, provided by someone she considered reliable.

On the first page of comments, under the comment thread with the first line of "Could someone please shoot the sockpuppet?," one person writes, "Does this mean we can look forward to the wanker(s) coming here and defending themselves?" In response, another commenter writes, "Why do I have a sudden desire to know everyone's IP address?" Another writes, "...so. What are the odds of getting an IP from the OP [original poster] of that post?" Here, the importance of knowing IP addresses is foregrounded: IP addresses will be logged, which will permit them to be analyzed. These addresses are useful because they can unmask sock puppets: if several posts written under different user names come from the same IP address, then they came from the same computer, and therefore they probably came from the same person. The desire to separate posters from socks illustrates the desire to understand the quality of the assertions posted: if they are from a sock, the information is skewed, perhaps even invalid. Yet what socks say is still integrated into the larger text and must be considered, if only to be dismissed.

In addition to figuring out whose testimony to accept and whose to reject, and in addition to hotlinks, saved Web pages, and screen caps, commenters provide their own memories and their own take on the events, thus giving valuable first-person accounts. Several people who commented anonymously (most likely because they didn't want to pay for an account with named posting privileges) signed their screen names, clearly identifying themselves as people in the know, including one of the "3 of her inner circle" alluded to above. On the second page of comments, one poster asserts her authority by noting, "And I'm one of the 137,356 people on her flist (but not on the hallowed filter of doom and fail and mental) and she's conveniently deleted her post where she waged war on poor [user name] because her mother saw a picture of her and 'confirmed' that she was the one sending [Quinto's astral-plane girlfriend] 'hate mail.' She's also deleted posts of her flouncing and threatening suicide." Although she cites her authority ("I'm one of the 137,356 people on her flist"), she honestly admits she's not part of the inner circle and so is limited in what she knows. But she also adds her voice to the chorus of people trying to learn more so they can assess the veracity of the wanky assertions. Her post characterizes Quinto's astral-plane girlfriend as someone unreliable, although by the time the wank has burned itself out, the consensus seems to be that she honestly believes what she's saying, so she is possibly insane and thus to be pitied, not mocked.

The goal of FW as a community is to use the tools available to record events in the fandom, whether important or just plain amusing, by using strategies that further cement the social group's rules (Hodkinson 192). A quick round of locks and deletions, as well as the locked nature of some of the original material, meant that in this particular wank, hard traces were hard to come by and thus screen caps were particularly important. Many other topics were considered relevant and discussed at length, including Quinto's sexual orientation, the astral-plane girlfriend's public declarations of sanity, and the necessity of death before one can be contacted by a medium. The assertions of authority and the posting of particular kinds of permissible content, all described in densely fannish language in a fan-run forum in order to create a novel truth-telling historical document, fulfill the group's rules of submissible evidence while keeping outsiders at bay (as should be evident from the excerpts I provide here, which are examples of typical posts), which dually purposes the text as exclusionary and documentary. To adequately analyze a new media text, researchers need to learn to negotiate this zone of exclusion: jargon, standards of appropriateness, and so on all conspire to keep the group together while providing stumbling blocks to easy entry into new forums.

## Conclusion: Textual Production as Social Practice

"Pulled by the archive out of the world of action," Ricoeur writes, "the historian reenters that world by inscribing his work in the world of his readers. In turn, the history book becomes a document, open to the sequence of reinscriptions that submit historical knowledge to an unending process of revisions" (234). Wank documents comprise a series of exchanges that attempt to attain consensus through this process of revision — in this example, the truth of the original assertion is queried. Blogs permit the realm of the social to be placed on an equal footing with the realm of the documentary trace. The entirety of "How NOT to Date a Celebrity" seeks to ascertain whether a *Heroes* fanfic writer actually thought she was dating Zachary Quinto on the astral plane. This exemplar wank illustrates how FW and similar sites continually revise an event and seek to document it by providing a forum for communal sharing of information, which occurs until the wank burns itself out. The documents so generated may be revisited later by a historian, who will use the hyperlinks (if they remain intact), screenshots, and other evidence to reconstruct events and the sort through the often overwhelming amount of evidence to pull together a story with the benefit of hindsight. One particularly well-known example of this sort of activity in the fan world is "The Ms.Scribe Story," by charlottelennox (available at *Bad Penny* in several parts beginning June 15, 2006). This document — which, interestingly, was treated as fan fiction and not a historical document when it was posted — revisits posts and wanks to construct a compelling argument that Ms.Scribe, a fanfic writer, used a variety of shady techniques, including socks, to gain prominence in Harry Potter fandom.

Traditional historical writing valorizes the disinterested, objective observer, although postmodern concerns with the lack of objectivity and history's links to fiction writing have shaken the discipline's foundations (Iggers; White) and reopened debate on the nature of history making. Matt Hills addresses the point of objectivity in terms of fandom by noting, "Fan cultures ... are neither rooted in an 'objective' interpretive community or an 'objective' set of texts, but nor are they atomised collections of individuals whose 'subjective' passions and interests happen to overlap" (113). In other words, fandom is not monumental but fragmented, linked by commonalities of practice that still may vary from fandom to fandom. In wanks, this is literalized as fragments of comments appended to an originary post resulting in a fraught subjective/objective text that needs to be decoded according to the community's consensus of what is appropriate: "I was never once under the impression that I had to believe any particular way at all, just provide whatever support was appropriate," one fan writes of the "How NOT to Date a

Celebrity" wank.[5] A poster may be revealed as an insider, in which case her words carry more weight, or as a partisan sock, in which case her words may need to be dismissed altogether.

Calls for better documentation sit next to posts gleefully reveling in the sheer absurdity of it all. The intent of the wank is to entertain as it explains. But all posts will be weighed and judged according to community standards, which include standards of assessing the veracity of records of traces as well as the credibility of the poster. The document so constructed in turn becomes part of a larger, densely hyperlinked, collaboratively authored metadocument. In the world of Web 2.0, wank documents provide a valuable example of how the trace may be retained in a world of easily deleted ephemera.

*A version of this paper was presented in March 2008 at the International Convention for the Fantastic in the Arts, in Orlando, Florida. All URLs cited were active and freely available on September 7, 2008. Thanks to Sarah Bewley, Craig Jacobsen, Shelley Rodrigo, and Mafalda Stasi for their comments.*

## NOTES

1. http://www.journalfen.net/community/fandom_lounge/, for February 15, 2008.
2. http://www.journalfen.net/community/fandom_wank/, for February 17, 2008.
3. http://en.wikipedia.org/wiki/Wikipedia_in_culture#Wikiality.
4. http://www.journalfen.net/community/bad_penny/.
5. http://stopthewank2.livejournal.com/, for February 26, 2008.

## WORKS CITED

Barnes, Harry Elmer. *A History of Historical Writing*. 2d rev. ed. New York: Dover, 1962.
Berkhofer, Robert F., Jr. "A Point of View on Viewpoints in Historical Practice." *A New Philosophy of History*. Ed. Frank Ankersmit and Hans Kellner. Chicago: University of Chicago Press, 1995. 174–91.
Breisach, Ernst. *Historiography: Ancient, Medieval, and Modern*. 3d ed. Chicago: University of Chicago Press, 2007.
_____. *On the Future of History: The Postmodernist Challenge and Its Aftermath*. Chicago: University of Chicago Press, 2003.
Bruns, Axel, and Joanne Jacobs, eds. *Uses of Blogs*. New York: Peter Lang, 2006.
Burgess, Jean. "Blogging to Learn, Learning to Blog." Bruns and Jacobs 105–14.
Busse, Kristina, and Karen Hellekson. "Introduction: Work in Progress." *Fan Fiction and Fan Communities in the Age of the Internet: New Essays*. Ed. Karen Hellekson and Kristina Busse. Jefferson, NC: McFarland, 2006. 5–32.
Dodge, Bernadine. "Re-imag(in)ing the Past." *Rethinking History* 10.3 (2006): 345–67.
Hills, Matt. *Fan Cultures*. London: Routledge, 2002.
Hodkinson, Paul. "Subcultural Blogging? Online Journals and Group Involvement among U.K. Goths." Bruns and Jacobs 187–97.

Howell, Martha, and Walter Prevenier. *From Reliable Sources: An Introduction to Historical Methods.* Ithaca: Cornell University Press, 2001.

Iggers, Georg G. *Historiography in the Twentieth Century: From Scientific Objectivity to the Postmodern Challenge.* 1997. Middletown, CT: Wesleyan University Press, 2005.

Lovink, Geert. *Zero Comments: Blogging and Critical Internet Culture.* New York: Routledge, 2008.

Ricoeur, Paul. *Memory, History, Forgetting.* 2000. Trans. Kathleen Blamey and David Pellauer. Chicago: University of Chicago Press, 2006.

Tapscott, Don, and Anthony D. Williams. *Wikinomics: How Mass Collaboration Changes Everything.* Expanded ed. New York: Portfolio, 2008.

Thomas, Angela. "Fictional Blogs." Bruns and Jacobs 199–210.

Torstendahl, Rolf. "Fact, Truth, and Text: The Quest for a Firm Basis for Historical Knowledge Around 1900." *History and Theory* 42 (2003): 305–31.

White, Hayden. *Metahistory: The Historical Imagination in Nineteenth-Century Europe.* 1973. Baltimore: Johns Hopkins University Press, 1990.

# 5

# Writing Wonder Women: How Playful Resistance Leads to Sustained Authorial Participation at *Sequential Tart*

*Kimberly DeVries*

> I believe that to envision gender (men and women) otherwise, and to (re)construct it in terms other than those dictated by the patriarchal contract, we must walk out of the male-centered frame of reference in which gender and sexuality are (re)produced by the discourse of male sexuality (de Lauretis 17).

Since its earliest days, the Internet has been not just a tool used for communication and research, but also a site for community building. Because it permits easy communication over great distances, the Internet has allowed many people who might never have met to connect in a safe (because virtual) and often anonymous environment, leading to the development of many communities that involve some level of role-play, if only in using a name other than that connected to one's physical identity. Some of these virtual communities have become sites of resistance in which members of a marginal group can (re)construct their identities without being constrained by the dominant culture. Teresa de Lauretis felt this identity work was necessary for women when in 1987 she wrote *Technologies of Gender: Essays on Theory, Film, and Fiction,* from which the opening quote is taken. Now in the early part of the twenty-first century, when many groups including women use online spaces for this purpose, their activities are shaped not just by the already existing structures they seek to escape or subvert, but also by the social and technical dynamics of the web.

Many scholars have posited the web as a combination of tool and locale that will allow disenfranchised groups to form stronger communities and speak with stronger voices. This utopian view was prevalent until the early 1990s, and then began giving way to a more complex understanding that is still developing today. Manuel Castells offers a comprehensive history of the Internet and web in *The Internet Galaxy* and notes that the social structure of the web has been shaped both by the communities that built it and by the design of the technology itself. In this chapter, I explore the longevity of the unusually successful monthly webzine known as *Sequential Tart* to determine how the community and its technological platform have interacted so successfully. I draw on a variety of theorists in considering this community, but also allow the Tarts speak for themselves by including several extended excerpts from the webzine.

*Sequential Tart*, a pun on the description of comic books as "sequential art" and on "tart" as a derogatory term for women who are too forward, has defined itself using the following epigraph at the top of every issue:

> **sequential tart (si-kwen'shel tart) n.**—1. a Web Zine about the comics industry published by an eclectic band of women; 2. a publication dedicated to providing exclusive interviews, in-depth articles and news, while working towards raising the awareness of women's influence in the comics industry and other realms [www.sequentialtart.com].

In fact, the topics covered now reach far beyond comic books to include film, television, music, books, events, and a variety of cultural phenomena ranging from alternative sexualities entering the mainstream, to a grandmother's feelings about her first computer, to the interplay of high and low culture. More than sixty women contribute, some once or twice a year and some offering several contributions per month, and many have participated since the late 90s. What inspires such sustained participation? Many factors may enable it, but the place to start is the actual origin of the webzine.

## Secret Origins

*Sequential Tart* began in 1997 after a group of women comic book fans who all belonged to another email list grew irritated with the sexism in *Wizard* magazine (a print and online magazine about comic books):

> [W]e didn't like their extremely limited coverage of the [comic book] medium ... [and how] we just couldn't find a magazine about comics that we liked to read, one that talked about the kinds of comics we were reading, in the way we wanted to see them discussed [Keller].

The women agreed that stereotypes about what kinds of comics women were or ought to be reading were at least partly responsible for the lack of discourse representing their views; the male dominated industry assumed women preferred cute and fluffy comics, while violence and sexual content were largely ascribed to male tastes. Because at the time these women felt that breaking into the established discourse in either fan communities or in the industry itself was impossible, they decided to create their own space. This allowed them to structure the 'zine and the organization of people using only the aspects of traditional publishing models that served their purposes, rather than trying to meet industry expectations. From the start, the women who formed *Sequential Tart* criticized not only the industry, but anyone, including women, who tried to pigeonhole the female comic-book readership. According to Katherine Keller, a founding member, they were

> sick and tired of being told (as it were) what kind of comics women liked or would/should like. We weren't reading a damn one of them. We were sick of hearing about *SIP* and *Bone*. Fuck that. We were reading *Preacher*, and *Hellblazer*, and *Invisibles,* and *Starman*, and we knew a lot of other women who were reading (and loving) the same comics. We liked violence, blood and gore. We didn't like "nice" books [Keller].

The original Tarts recognized that merely rejecting the existing discourse and comic books themselves was not the answer, as this would not change the discourse and would merely deprive women of the enjoyment many experienced through comic books as well as remove their voices even further from cultural commentary. Rey Chow has argued against a feminist strategy of simply withdrawing from the discussion of cultural production, arguing that because the concept of "image-as-feminized-space" (16), breaks down when we acknowledge that women enjoy some of these "stereotypical" and male-defined images as well, we must rather shift our focus from the "moment of production to the moment of reception" (19). Thus the issue becomes not what the creator intended, but what women viewers make of these comics. The Tarts clearly chose this route by focusing on their own interpretations rather than on the creators' purposes, claiming a position not only distinct from male stereotyping, but also far more complex than that described by some earlier women resisters. However, they were not only working against gender stereotypes. In another theoretical frame, we can also consider that the founders of *Sequential Tart* were resisting "overflow" from big comics publishers and the surrounding "media convergence" of magazines, TV shows, websites, and movie tie-ins while at the same time using these materials to create their new space (Jenkins, "Convergence" and *Convergence*; Brooker).

In his work on fan cultures, Henry Jenkins reminds us that media convergence is a type of cultural convergence and is about how media is both produced and consumed. It is both top-down and bottom-up, referring both to corporate producers trying to use every possible medium to attract and hold an audience as well as members of the audience appropriating material from all kinds of sources and media to create new content (*Convergence* 18). *Sequential Tart* represents a pioneering effort in the latter category that continues to this day in its work to reclaim popular media by reinterpreting it and re-inscribing meaning to suit the Tarts' own interests and ends, rather than those of corporate producers.

*Sequential Tart* began by resisting a male dominated discourse and because nearly the entire comic-book industry was male-dominated at the time of *Tart's* inception, they were simultaneously resisting media overflow, the deliberate effort by media companies to saturate a market through more than one channel (i.e., TV, comics, and the Internet). Rather than only react against the stereotypical images and messages being pushed through all of these channels, the Tarts instead focused on the responses of women readers; they opened a dialogue in which problematic representations of women could be discussed without denying or outlawing the enjoyment women experience reading comic books. Thus, rather than rejecting or eliminating comic books themselves, they reclaimed and redefined this art form. In addition to creating their own space apart from, yet intersecting with, the world of "fanboys," the Tarts also promoted women taking control of the way others respond to and interpret real women as icons or objects. Thus, the initial impetus behind the creation of this webzine was an impassioned rebellion against gender stereotypes and corporate overflow, but rather than focusing on reaction, instead a new space was created that attracted and continues to attract both writers and readers.

That original impulse, however, would not have been enough to ensure survival on its own. Use of the Internet has strengthened the community of both participants and readers around *Sequential Tart*. In addition, the survival and continued vitality of *Sequential Tart* may also be attributed to several identifiable factors: the structure of the offline fan community from which it developed; the tone of the webzine itself; technological innovations by the editorial staff; visible connections to the offline lives of the staff; and flexibility in allowing evolution in both the roles of staff members and the format of the webzine.

More than ten years after its creation, *Sequential Tart* has been notably resilient in the face of changing technologies and readerships as well as changes to lives of its core contributors. In *The Internet Galaxy*, Castells argues that individualism is becoming "the dominant trend in the evolution of social relationships," a trend that is supported by the Internet (128–29). He argues that unlike those examples in which online interaction occurs in tandem with offline physical encounters, most online communities are "ephemeral" and are being replaced by networked individualism, for example in the proliferation of blogs as a primary social space.

Several characteristics, cultural and technical, have made the Tart community sustainable even within the shift Castells describes. To begin with, the comic book fan community and the comic book industry have always shared a quite permeable border and unlike many other forms of entertainment or publishing, the industry has always been characterized by a do-it-yourself approach, and a complicated, ambivalent relationship with copyright laws. Since the golden age of American comics at least, fans of and participants in this industry have long been grappling with issues surrounding authorship and participation often assumed to have been made prominent by the expansion of the web. Familiarity with these issues and other characteristics of comic book fan/creator communities appear to have contributed to their remarkably smooth transition to and success on the web.

Comic book creators[1] have never needed institutional credentials to get started. Even the major American publishers, Marvel and DC, still find new talent by trawling conventions and now, websites, for talented writers, illustrators, inkers, etc. Because fans become creators with relative ease, they feel a far greater sense of ownership over the media and tend to be more active in related organizations or communities. At the same time, because publishers have a long history of abusing the rights of individual creators, and comic history has been peppered by many bitter and highly publicized lawsuits, both fans and creators are very well aware of intellectual property issues. In fact, legal disputes over rights are such a problem for individual writers and artists that many well known creators and publications, including those mentioned here, have commented publicly on the problem in an effort to educate others.

In these ways the production of comic books and the activities of fans sometimes share characteristics with both open source projects and hacker communities — two groups that Castells argues have strongly influenced the development of Internet culture. *Sequential Tart* includes both fans and creators, and all of the staff were comic book fans participating in offline fan communities long before joining *Tart*, so all shared the above experiences and knowledge which act as a common ground from which to negotiate other differences. This shared experience supports the maintenance of a very open and supportive tone in the webzine, even when it is critiquing the industry or individuals therein.

## A Tart Point of View

The friendly and open atmosphere may seem at odds with the original goal of raising awareness of women's roles in the comic book industry and critiquing stereotypical representations in the books themselves. However, a positive approach does not mean being uncritical. While reviews tend to be friendly and enthusiastic, articles written in *Sequential Tart* can be biting, ironic, or even regretful when considering comic books, creators, or publishers who persist in stereotyping women, gays/lesbians, people of color, or men in some way. For example, an entry in the "Bizarre Breasts" column pokes fun at the hyper-developed breasts women now sport in many mainstream comics. It is humorous, but also makes a real argument about the illusionary, or perhaps delusionary, proportions many artists assign to female characters. Lisa Jonté, author of the article and creator of the images that accompany it, frames her critique as the findings of a committee charged with studying the mutagenic effects of environmental disaster on superheroines. The dry humor of her report is capped by the stinging mockery of the following footnote:

> While some heroine's breasts are merely abnormally large, some are so distorted that they appear to have become separate entities from their host bodies, with an all-round cleavage that suggests that said breasts are in fact completely detachable. This researcher witnessed a pair of the aforementioned "balloon" breasts as they broke free of their minimal restraint and wafted gently heavenward. After several moments of frustrated calling, (in which the breasts did not return) the owner, one Vengeancia, was forced into pursuit of the truant ta-tas [Jonté].

Note that in the footnote mentioning "Vengeancia," Jonté, herself a professional illustrator, takes aim at Scott Clark, creator of "Avengelyne," for being so poor an artist. Rather than commenting directly on the inherent sexism of Clark's illustration, Jonté makes the argument that the proportions he represents are not only unreal, but can only be the product of an environmental disaster, which makes the world of his comic series dystopian in a way Clark probably didn't intend. Thus we see an example of how *Sequential Tart* revises the response to the representation of women in comic books, but in a way that avoids being strident or alienating to male fans.

However, sometimes a member of *Tart* takes quite a serious tone in criticizing representations of women in comics. But again the main focus is on offering a more positive alternative. In the excerpt below, Rebecca Salek makes this critical move when she comments on *Wizard Magazine*'s list of the ten greatest comic book heroines, arguing against their interpretation of what a great heroine is:

> But — why only mainstream characters? Why only spandex-or kevlar-clad super heroines? Why only current characters? And why are they all white (with the exception of Cassandra Cain)?
>
>    \*\*\*
>
> There are other kinds of heroines besides super heroines. Police officers, for instance. Comic books are filled with strong female police detectives —

not to mention private detectives. Space ship captains. Spies. Archaeologists. Witches. Elves. Goddesses. Angsty teenagers. And ordinary women who struggle through the pain and joy and uncertainty of everyday life.

In the above passages, Salek addresses the basic and obvious problem of racial exclusion, but, perhaps more important, she also points out a lack that may not be as obvious to casual comic book readers: the diversity of story-lines built around women has not been recognized. By focusing only on busty white superheroines, *Wizard* sends the message that no other women characters are at all interesting. In fact, by this measure, no real women are interesting or worth our admiration either. By this standard, nothing that real women might actually do deserves to be chronicled; strong admirable women exist only in fantasies. Salek goes on to consider how this contemporary Top 10 List does not even reflect the minimal progress made by the mainstream comic book publishers in representing women and people of color, finally asking:

> Are comics so white-biased (historically, even unconsciously) that there are no credible Native American, Hispanic, African-American or other contenders?
>
> ***
>
> Everyone who reads this article — draw up your own list. Send it in to Tart. Send it to Wizard. Send it to every comic or pop culture or art list to which you subscribe. Share it with all your friends. Get a conversation going.
>
> ***
>
> The louder the conversation, the more attention it will attract, and The Powers That Be will take notice. They'll notice just how important these characters are to us — and treat them with more respect and dignity. Give languishing characters a second chance. Maybe even invent a few new role models for our daughters.

This article was posted along with the rest of the April issue on April 1, 2002. By April 10, sixty-eight responses had been posted on the Tartsville bulletin board service (BBS) offering a wide array of admired heroines, and sharing what individual posters liked most about them. This public BBS serves to strengthen the community around *Sequential Tart* by helping readers connect with each other and with the Tarts themselves — and the line between these groups is often quite blurry.

## Real People Living Real Lives

The Tarts and their readers demonstrate and reinforce awareness of each other as real people rather than mere names in a by-line in many ways. Some of these are deliberate, such as the construction of the *Sequential Tart* masthead that allows each Tart on the staff to create a detailed persona that is then available for all readers to examine. Each member of the staff is asked to create a "bio" by filling out a simple online form that requests information on costume, superpowers, sidekick, secret origin, overused quote, etc., thus framing each Tart as a superhero. Interestingly, while all have some fun with these personae, they in fact also turn out to be quite accurate descriptions of each Tart's real self, in terms of appearance, occupations, and attitudes. In fact, this activity is one response to Salek's point that there are no mainstream comic book heroines who were angsty teenagers or ordinary women. The Tarts not only promote the independent comic books that contain this kind of character, but they also provide examples with their own lives, and do it in a way that is fun rather than didactic. The pleasure in this modeling seems to be not in reinventing yourself, but in reinterpreting and playing with the way readers understand your identity. These personae allow each Tart staff member to create a first impression that will enhance rather than contradict later live encounters.

While not all readers visit the staff biographies, in writing articles and reviews for *Tart*, staff members also tend to refer often to their own experiences and preferences, explaining how these influence their reactions to the topic under discussion. This way of writing keeps the Tarts solidly visible as real people and allows readers to evaluate whether they generally agree with that writer — and thus how useful the opinion is. Further, in this way the Tarts model a different response to comics and to culture generally: simply by demonstrating another view rather than always arguing explicitly against the mainstream.

## Commitment to a Community

Women at *Sequential Tart* seem to take a different path than that described by Sherry Turkle in which Internet users create alternate experimental personae, useful though that path may be (180). Rather than creating and presenting new identities in the online community, the Tarts rewrite the interpretations made of their real, original identities. The staff biographies allow the Tarts to literally transform their real selves into superheroines, lest readers have any doubt. A similar tone finds its way into the *Tart* public bulletin boards as well, where writers who in other circumstances might be on the cultural fringe, like men who favor handbags or Utilikilts,[2] are seen as cool and whose opinions are valued. Transforming interpretations rather than identities allows the members of *Sequential Tart* to change perceptions more directly, to give members a greater feeling of control, another factor in the webzine's continuing growth and health.

Finally, many people join and remain in the community around *Sequential Tart* for a very common reason: they are trying to find others who share their interests and the Tarts, by virtue of their existence, offer hope of this. Members of the comic book subculture often experience being marginalized and mocked in the American mainstream culture and thus are hungry for community. Once finding one, they tend to be intensely loyal. This loyalty among the Tarts can easily be observed at the San Diego ComicCon and other national conventions. The *Tart* staff and friends often turn out in force, have a special dinner, attend other events together, and may gather in the evening to swap whatever cool comics were acquired that day. These events have sometimes taken on the feeling of a family reunion.

Along with the shared goals of promoting comics and changing attitudes about women that unite the *Sequential Tart* staff, those writing for *Tart* empower each other in ways that inspire commitment and continued participation through continued writing. Regardless of individual differences, the Tarts support each other's identities as they are presented. Following this rule has allowed members to productively discuss quite difficult issues. For example, in January 2002, a poster who goes by the name Zackman started a thread at about 7:00 A.M. called "Blowing Women up in Movies," in which he begins:

> Looking back at movies like Bad Boys, Last Boy Scout, & Art of War, as well as some horror movies, I somehow began to ask myself this question: Wouldn't it be logical(?) if women victims in the above mentioned movies get, er, raped by the bad males, instead of being bludgeoned with a foot-long hammer, mowed down by an Uzi, or being blown out by a .45?

By noon, two other men and one woman who post regularly had asked if he was thinking about where he was posting this message, if he was seriously advocating more rape in movies, and whatever he was trying to ask, to please clarify. All three of these posters made it clear that they were prepared to take issue with the question and with Zackman, but all offered him the chance to explain, and one said that rather than go on, she'd let others do the "thumping." At this point posters are already showing better manners than is usual on many BBS systems, and that is recognized by the moderator who posts just after 12:00 P.M.

Pam Bliss, the moderator, responds in a way that shows awareness of her position both as moderator with certain responsibilities and as woman who has a personal reaction to the topic. She posts first as Moderator, "Pam B," and then as a regular member, "Pam Bliss." As Moderator, Pam simply lets everyone know that she is watching the thread closely, and that so far it looks ok, but she also asks, "Please be careful with this one, ladies and gentlemen." In choosing that particular phrase, Pam models a scrupulously polite tone, and reminds posters that they, as "ladies and gentlemen," should make courtesy a priority in this thread. In her next post as regular member, Pam announces the removal of her moderator hat and then enters the discussion with a refinement of Zackman's question that helps move talk in a more academic direction. In all of the subsequent messages, while most posters are still talking primarily about the issue of women being raped as a plot device, they all also comment briefly on how they reacted to the question, and on Zackman's manner of asking. The thread peters out after one more post from Pam, praising everyone's good and courageous behavior. Most striking here is the way numerous posters, all of who were upset to some degree by the original question, offered replies that not only were thoughtful, but quite candid in exposing views for which they might be attacked. While online communities sometimes do foster more openness, this tends to occur more in terms of personal revelations that cannot really be argued with, rather than through considered statements of opinion on controversial topics. The willingness of participants to speak openly reflects the trust these people have for the community as a safe place, and also the deliberate fostering by moderators of the belief that everyone there is well intentioned and reasonable.

Insistence on this foundational assumption allows community members and staff to present themselves in a more "real" way,[3] and may be responsible for what I would describe as a remarkably ego-less management of the Tart organization. Because no one seems to feel they have to defend their "territory," *Tart* has been able to reorganize itself several times with ease. Editrices have swapped assignments to avoid boredom, and members have taken on new responsibilities like creating and updating a Wikipedia entry, MySpace and Facebook pages, and experimenting with new ways of offering content. Most striking is that Tarts can both gain and shed authority comfortably. For example, last year an editrix who faced too many competing demands from work stepped down to the level of contributing Tart, which means that she doesn't have to contribute every month, but also doesn't share much in decision-making. This was a step she decided on and to my knowledge the transition didn't involve any arguments from anyone, either for or against.

However, the loyalty-inducing manner of *Tart's* birth and the warm community dynamics would not be enough to sustain it if participation was too time-consuming or technically difficult.

## *Design for Participation*

*Tart* has always been a work of love, depending on the volunteer efforts of women who can write, or code, or create graphics, or otherwise contribute needed labor. In its early days, each monthly edition was jointly authored via several mailing lists, one for discussion among all members, one for monthly staff, one for submissions, and one just for editrices. The editrices then coded the html pages by hand, which was enormously time-consuming, even after they taught even the least technically inclined Tarts to use the webzine's standard <span> tags. An even greater burden fell on Lee Atcheson, who has been webmistress from the start. She created the entire *Tart* website from scratch, hosted it on her server, which she also administered. This continued until 2002 when she created (again from scratch) a web-based system for submitting reviews that maintained a database of information entered in each text field. For example, once information has been entered for the DC/Vertigo comic book imprint, it need not be re-entered for subsequent reviews. Thus the system accumulates and builds on the labor of individual contributors for the benefit of all. In 2006, a similar system was created for the rest of the content as well, including monthly columns, convention reports, and other regular features of each issue. With this addition, not only is data available from previous inputs, but also after each writer adds her work and an editrix ok's it, the content is wrapped in standard pages automatically, rather than having to be hand-coded every time. So now the writers and editrices can focus entirely on the actual writing and are largely freed from repetitive coding or data entry.

These changes were necessitated by the increasing demands on the staff's time, and especially on Lee Atcheson's, from work, families, and other responsibilities — in other words, we were all growing up. So we see a technical solution to a typical problem in the division of labor. Most volunteer "community" projects are actually run and built by one or a few core people with heterogeneous participation from the rest (Schäfer), and this certainly has been true at *Sequential Tart*. But that model is difficult to sustain over years, so *Tart* has moved to make contributing and formatting content much easier in a technical sense. This year Lee is also working on setting up at least one other Tart to assist with web development as well, and training others is now something we are trying to actively pursue, rather than relying on the ad hoc approach.

*Sequential Tart* attracts writers because it presents an alternative to paper and webzines that are both corporate and sexist (not to mention racist and homophobic). But the most crucial factors behind *Tart*'s survival and success appear to depend on three very different aspects of the site, two social and one technical. First, everyone in the whole community, including the publication and the larger group that participates via the bulletin board, supports each other both online and off. Further, members move up and down through the hierarchy without any of the acrimony that often accompanies redistribution of authority in communities or groups that lack formal organizational structures (something I have never heard of happening in any other group).

Finally, through the innovation of members with the relevant technical skills and because we recognize the value of collaboration, women can join and contribute to the monthly publication with ease. Tarts keep writing because *Tart* is supportive, flexible, and uses a design that facilitates participation.

## NOTES

1. In the comic book industry, creator is used as a term to cover both writer and artist since many people do both.

2. A many-pocketed kilt for men (and women) who would like to wear skirts yet still work in a machine shop or lumberyard. Details at the website: http://www.utilikilt.com/.

3. By "real," I mean both closer to their physical appearances and to their legal identities as well.

## WORKS CITED

Atcheson, Lee. Email to the Author. 15 April 2002.

_____. "It Lives! In Which the ST Booth at MegaCon Takes on a Life of Its Own." *Sequential Tart* April 2002. 9 June 2009 <http://www.sequentialtart.com/archive/apr02/art_0402_10.shtml>.

Bliss, Pam, Stephen Geigen-Miller, Rose, Spook, and Zackman. "Blowing Up Women in Movies." Online Posting. 2002. *Tartsville*>Pop Culture forum. 9 June 2009 <http://www.sequentialtart.com/community/Forum4/HTML/000331.shtml>.

Brooker, Will. "Living on *Dawson's Creek*: Teen Viewers, Cultural Convergence, and Television Overflow." *International Journal of Cultural Studies* 4.4 (2001): 456–472.

Castells, Manuel. *The Internet Galaxy: Reflections on the Internet, Business, and Society.* New York: Oxford University Press, 2001.

Chow, Rey. *Women and Chinese Modernity: The Politics of Reading Between East and West.* Theory and History of Lit. 75. Minneapolis: University of Minnesota Press, 1991.

de Lauretis, Teresa. *Technologies of Gender: Essays on Theory, Film, and Fiction.* Bloomington: University of Indiana Press, 1987.

Jenkins, Henry. *Convergence Culture: Where Old and New Media Collide.* New York: New York University Press, 2006.

_____. "Convergence? I Diverge." *Technology Review.* June 2001. 9 June 2009 <http://www.technologyreview.com/BizTech/12434/>.

_____. *Textual Poachers: Television Fans and Participatory Culture.* New York: Routledge, 2001.

Jonté, Lisa. "Bizarre Breasts." *Sequential Tart* July 2001. 9 June 2009 <http://www.sequentialtart.com/archive/july01/bb_0701.shtml>.

Keller, Kathrine. Email to the author. 17 April 2002.

Norton, Mike. "What is the deal with you women!?!?!?" Online posting. 2002. *Tartsville*> Neighborhood forum. 9 June 2009 <http://www.sequentialtart.com/community/Forum6/HTML/000367.shtml>.

Salek, Rebecca. "The Ten Greatest Heroines in Comics Today According to *Wizard Magazine* or, The List O' Big-Busted, Super Powered White Women (with the Odd Exception)." *Sequential Tart* March 2002. 9 June 2009 <http://www.sequentialtart.com/archive/mar02/art_0302_3.shtml>.

Schäfer, Mirko Tobias. "Participation Inside? User Activities Between Design and Appropriation." *Digital Material: Tracing New Media in Everyday Life and Technology.* Ed. Marianne van den Boomen, et al. Amsterdam: Amsterdam University Press, 2009. 147–58.

Turkle, Sherry. *Life on the Screen: Identity in the Age of the Internet.* New York: Simon and Schuster, 1995.

Wilding, Faith. "Where Is Feminism in Cyberfeminism?" *Old Boys Network.* 9 June 2009 <http://www.obn.org/cfundef/faith_def.html>.

# 6

# What the Frell Happened? Rhetorical Strategies of the *Farscape* Community

*Sean Morey*

In the middle of *Farscape*'s fourth season, the Sci Fi Channel announced that it was canceling its critically-acclaimed and first original program. It cited decreased ratings as a reason for cancellation, even though *Farscape* had already been extended through a fifth season. This premature cancellation prompted an enormous response from fans who used many rhetorical strategies to get *Farscape* back on the air. While some of the tactics they used were not original, others were quite inventive and used various new media available to them, most important the internet.

In fact, the campaign was born in a new media environment when, on September 6, 2002, in an online chat room, David Kemper (Director/Producer), Ricky Manning (Executive Producer), and Ben Browder (Commander John Crichton) leaked the news that the fifth season of *Farscape* would be canceled, leaving the fans wondering, "What the FRELL happened?" (Theorist). In an instant, to this digitally-assembled audience, the electronic delivery of information mobilized fans to traverse different networks and nodes and take action against this injustice. As a devout *Farscape* follower, I learned of the news early the next day, and followed the threads of how to, as the campaign called itself, "Save Farscape."

In spirit, the Save Farscape campaign shared its roots with the letter-writing campaign to save *Star Trek* from cancellation in the 1960s. One of the first actions that the *Farscape* fandom community (calling themselves Scapers, an analog to Trekkies) took was writing to the Sci Fi channel; hardcopy letters might be taken more seriously than convenient email. However, this act became more symbolic in nature. While written texts were certainly important to furthering the cause (one of my acts of participation included writing scholarship about *Farscape*), it became clear that the Scapers worked in a digital environment. And since much of new media is image-driven, Scapers turned to the appeal of visual rhetoric as a way to spread their message.

Identifying as a Scaper, I participated in several of the projects to revive *Farscape*. The chief tool that I used was also the tool that kept the community working together as a whole: the SaveFarscape.com website.[1] The website was quickly launched after the Kemper, Manning, and Browder announcement, and provided updates about the cancellation, information about the Sci Fi channel (such as the names and addresses of where to mail letters), new rhetorical ideas, and what different Scapers were doing. From their use of new media tools, it became clear that the Scapers were digitally savvy, and put their media skills to good use.

I immediately ordered a fan-made t-shirt, bearing digitally-produced *Farscape* character portraits that bore the caption "Wanted: Farscape Season 5." These portraits were also put onto coffee mugs, posters, and other items to spread *Farscape* iconography. This kind of fan-produced artwork resurfaced consistently and the many rich images of the *Farscape* universe became central to the campaign, as though it were political. And in one sense, we all felt some sort of democratic call to arms, to protest that unilateral decisions about this show could not be made without the voice of the audience. Sci Fi delivered their message, and we Scapers were delivering back.

And key to getting a fifth season of *Farscape* was the fifth rhetorical canon, delivery,[2] which clearly became digital delivery; besides the website, fans found many means to accomplish this. In one instance, Scapers wearing Save Farscape t-shirts attended an airing of CNN's now canceled *Talkback Live* on September 17, 2002. On a few cutaway shots of the audience the fans could be seen several rows back. However, one of the individuals was able to stand up and ask a question, visually delivering the message on live, national television. In addition, Scapers pooled money to buy and air a 30-second television commercial to help save the show (Kahney). However, it was not necessarily the message that created the rhetorical effect, but the delivery itself. The use of these different media created the message that Scapers were unhappy about the cancellation, causing other media, such as CNN news reports, to cover the story and increase exposure. Not many people other than *Farscape* fans would identify with a Save Farscape t-shirt, but the act of delivery on cable television caused the networks in general to take notice, especially the Sci Fi channel. And while it is difficult to gauge just how useful any of these individual projects were, or if they produced their intended effects, the organizing power of the Save Farscape Web site helped to make their net effect greater than the sum of their parts.

We also worked with the show's creators, actors, directors, and producers in order to confront the Sci Fi channel. After a sustained effort, Scapers and *Farscape* personnel were unable to save the fifth season, but we were able to convince Sci Fi to agree to a four-hour miniseries to conclude the loose ends and cliffhangers at the end of season four. However, even though *Farscape* received a second, albeit brief, life, we continue to work together to get more *Farscape*. Recently, the Sci Fi channel announced that they would revive *Farscape* in a series of webisodes. Not cable TV, but perhaps a medium more appropriate to the rhetorical use of new media by the *Farscape* community.

## NOTES

1. The website SaveFarscape.com was eventually transformed into WatchFarscape. com, as the campaign decided that it needed to emphasize "watching" *Farscape* as the chief way to increase ratings and convince the Sci Fi channel that it was worth saving.

2. One method to increase viewing involved literally delivering DVD copies of *Farscape* to public libraries: see <http://library.watchfarscape.com/>.

## WORKS CITED

Kahney, Leander. "SciFi Show's Fans Pay for TV Plea." 23 Nov. 2002. http://www.wired. com/services/feedback/letterstoeditor. *Wired*. 27 June 2008 <http://www.wired.com/ culture/lifestyle/news/2002/11/56550>.

Theorist, Cosmic. "The Nitty Gritty on How Farscape Got Cancelled." 20 Sept. 2005. *Watch Farscape.com*. 27 June 2008 <http://www.watchfarscape.com/index.php? option=com_ content& task=view&id=93&Itemid=25>.

# 7

# The Realtime Forum Fan

## *Thomas B. Cavanagh*

One could argue that the experience of watching a sporting event on television is superior to that of seeing it live. Television viewers have the advantage of play-by-play announcers, expert commentary, relevant statistics, and instant replay, not to mention the conveniences of home (and not having to fight crowds and parking lots). Yet, sports fandom tends to be an inherently social pastime. Fans gather in giant stadiums and arenas to cheer their teams. In college football, single games at venues such as the University of Michigan can draw and seat more than 100,000 fans.

There is a reason that fans congregate like this. An undeniable energy is created by crowds, whether at the local cinema, at a live theater performance, or at a sporting event of any level. People enjoy the experience more when they can be around and interact with like-minded others. Of course, often only a minority of any team's fans has the means or time to attend live games. Yet fans still gather to experience the event. They can be found at Superbowl parties, sports bars, and other ad hoc locations.

However, as more and more societal interaction moves online, so too are sports fans congregating in online discussion forums. The combination of Internet discussion forums and sports is not new. For as long as there has been Internet discussion, it has been a medium for sports fans to interact. Typically, such discussion forums have fueled pre-game trash talk and hype, as well as post-game gloating (and misery). But now a new type of discussion has emerged, one that has evolved out of these pre-game fan forums: the realtime fan forum.

In realtime forum discussions, conversations that once took place only in smoky sports bars over pitchers of beer now also occur online. Like-minded fans gather virtually and independently to watch games on television and talk about it online. Realtime forums are characterized by several key features, each of which is addressed in more detail below:

- They occur online.
- They are text-based.
- They are contemporaneous with a sporting event.
- They are abstracted from their context.

## They Occur Online

It may seem obvious, but the single most defining characteristic of real-time fan forums is the fact that they occur online. The fans interacting with each other do not see each other and probably don't even know each other. Although a comparison could made between the realtime fan forum and the local sports bar, where fans who may not know each other gather to watch a game and have a friendly argument, the comparison breaks down quickly. The realtime fan forum is a unique medium. The analogy might be appropriate if the sports bar were configured so that fans were separated from each other by partitions and were only permitted to communicate via writing. No longer is communal fandom limited to geographic boundaries — a single neighborhood or even a single city. With internet-based interaction, fans from literally all over the world interact, comment, complain, and gloat; and not once do they ever see each other.

## They Are Text-Based

Realtime forum fans communicate exclusively via text. They do not interact via telephonic means or Voice Over Internet Protocol (VOIP). Doing so would make the interaction no different than two or more fans watching a game while talking on the phone, an entirely different and long-established practice. While mainstream sports web sites such as Sports Illustrated, Fox Sports, Yahoo Sports, and ESPN offer realtime fan forums, such interaction can also occur via instant messenger (IM) or other chat venues. Typically, real-time forum interactions include liberal amounts of IM-style text abbreviations (e.g., OMG, LOL). Not only do these abbreviations and emoticons provide a kind of emotional frame of reference for otherwise sparse text, they enable rapid communication between participants. Just as abbreviations facilitate rapid text-messaging, they perform the same function in fan forums, where speed is essential. If participants want to comment on a play, they must do so quickly, before the next play occurs.

## They Are Contemporaneous with a Sporting Event

With the exception of cultural touchstone experiences such as the Academy Awards, sporting events are somewhat unique in attracting fans to comment on the proceedings as they occur. This is the aspect of realtime forums that makes them different from forums used only for pre-game hype. Realtime forum fans participate in active dialog *while a game is still in progress.* Fans actively comment on individual plays, commiserate over bad field position, and speculate about their team's chances for a conference championship. This interaction all occurs during confined temporal boundaries and, unlike most traditional fan forums, realtime forum communities only exist for the duration of the event (although discussions can be archived for some time after the event).

## They Are Abstracted from Their Context

Absent in realtime forum discussions are detailed descriptions of game-related activities. There may be *reactions* to game-related activities (e.g. "Did you see that catch?!!" or "That ref is blind!"), but there are rarely descriptions of the events themselves. The rhetoric generated in these discussions relies entirely on the external game information to provide context. Realtime forum interactions require that the game-related context be provided by other electronic means, typically, although not always, via television. The actual discourse is separate — abstracted — from the events to which they refer.

## The New Rhetoric

While fans may be driven to these realtime game forums for social reasons, the result is that a whole group of people who, in the past, would simply be passive observers of a game are now *actively writing* about it while it takes place. It is an entirely new domain of writing and rhetoric that did not exist before the availability of the Internet. Fans are co-creating this new experience in a realtime collaborative writing process with its own rules and expectations. Drawing on established "netiquette," IM abbreviations, and other digital communication conventions, realtime forum fans are establishing what Michel Foucault called discursive formation. The form and function of the discourse community are emerging and being negotiated concurrently with the active life of the forum. What Foucault calls the "rules of formation" are still being determined and the game forums of today may not even resemble the forums and interaction norms of the game forums of the future. Through their new digital rhetoric, realtime forum fans are defining the rules and boundaries of live online fan discourse.

Of course, this online fan interaction inherently changes the home viewing experience, layering it with a digital/social dynamic that could previously only be realized by getting in a car and driving down to the local sports bar. Formerly isolated fans are now connected by a shared interest in sports and computers. These fans no longer simply watch a game. They watch a game while simultaneously discussing it on their computers. With one eye on the television screen and the other on the computer monitor, they create their own fan experience unique to the new digital culture.

## WORKS CITED

Foucault, Michel. *The Archaeology of Knowledge.* London: Tavistock Publications, 1972.

# 8

# "As Seen on *The Colbert Report*": Or, Why I Love Reality TV

*Georgianna O. Miller*

When I say I'm a reality TV fan, I mean it. Take Gordon Ramsay as an example. I don't just watch *Hell's Kitchen*. I also watch *Gordon Ramsay's Kitchen Nightmares* and *The F Word* on BBC America. This is amazing for a number of reasons, including the fact that I work full time for a university, so it's not as if I don't have enough to do. It's also kind of amazing because I've been a vegetarian for at least 8 years and can't eat 90 percent of what he cooks. However, when I discovered that my boyfriend wanted to go to London to celebrate after taking the bar exam, I strong-armed him into eating at one of Ramsay's restaurants.

This entailed poring over Ramsay's extensive website and using their online reservation feature to request a table a month and a half before we left. We went to Boxwood Café, where a two-person, three-course dinner costs about £150. When my boyfriend went to the bathroom I confessed to our server that I was a Gordon Ramsay fan, thereby scoring us a tour of the kitchen. I also bought an autographed cookbook — full of those same meaty recipes that I can't eat. Needless to say, I blogged about my meal on MySpace when I returned.

Perhaps I'm starting to sound like an obsessed fan — which, let's face it, I probably am. However, aside from all its other various appeals (such as the dark and ruthlessly strategic side of human nature that it reveals), the various "reality" genres have made TV approachable in a way that it has never been before. This approachability enables us to not only enjoy what we watch, but to weave the experience of watching into other facets of our lives — many times, digitally.

In his 1967 work *Society of the Spectacle*, Marx scholar Guy Debord claims, "In societies dominated by modern conditions of production, life is presented as an immense accumulation of spectacles. Everything that was directly lived has receded into a representation" (7). This has grown perhaps even more true in the decades since the work's publication, and perhaps particularly with the advent of reality television. "Reality television" consists of ordinary people in extraordinary situations; its close cousin, what VH1 calls "CelebReality," consists of already extraordinary (i.e., famous) people in ordinary situations.

In some ways television functions to make the world smaller — *Survivor* small talk at parties and *The Bachelor* water cooler gossip. However, in so many other ways it has made us spectators, distracting us from the business of our own lives. In this way it is easier to call and vote for your favorite *American Idol* contestant to secure the stardom of a complete stranger rather than work for your own career advancement, or visit a *Big Brother* speculation forum at work when you know your boss's computer tracks the URLs you visit, or read about Jackie Warner's tips on the *Work Out* website rather than, well, working out.

Stephen Colbert, of Comedy Central's *The Colbert Report,* takes perhaps the fullest advantage of the potential crossovers between traditional TV and its various digital manifestations. He sold his *White House Press Correspondents' Speech* on iTunes, and after he challenged his audience during his nightly broadcast to send his book to the top of the bestseller list, it indeed became iTune's bestselling audiobook of 2006. When Hungary held a contest to name a new bridge spanning the Danube, Colbert gave his viewers the URL for the contest and encouraged them to vote online. Within three weeks of making this call to action, "Stephen Colbert híd" was not only the first-place name for the new bridge, it had 7 million *more votes* than the entire population of Hungary. Similarly, after Colbert coined the term "wikiality" in July 2006, Wikipedia.org was forced to temporarily close its entry on African elephants when *Report* viewers virtually descended upon the site at Colbert's request, revising the entry to state that the population of African elephants had tripled in the previous six months.

True fans of the show can't even get tickets unless they're internet-savvy. The only way to get tickets (when they're available) is to apply using a link on the show's page on the Comedy Central website. When I was going to New York City for a conference, I used the link to request tickets over two months in advance. I was fortunate in that there was an audience interaction in the episode filmed the day I was there, and they showed me on national TV for a full 5 seconds before cutting to commercial. That episode led to my own digital participation in the *Report* phenomenon — that episode still lives on my DVR. And my computer. And my iPod. Heck, I linked the YouTube clip to my MySpace page and changed my name to "As Seen on The *Colbert Report*" until the show's website removed the link. I got phone calls from people who'd seen me on national TV, e-mails from ex-students — the 'net's ability to broadcast my participation gave me *my* fifteen minutes of fame.

Hey, did I mention that Jayla, a contestant from Cycle 5 of *America's Next Top Model,* is a waitress at a dive bar in my town? I kept ordering beers until I got up the courage to tell her that I was a fan. And then there's the time I dragged my San Diego friend to an area bar frequented by Sadie, runner-up from *The Bachelor: Rome.* Or that time when, after watching *Celebrity Fit Club,* I bought Dr. Ian's *Fat Smash Diet?* The *Top Chef* cookbook is on my gift list. I tried to get my boyfriend to buy tickets to the *So You Think You Can Dance?* tour for my birthday, but unfortunately we were in London eating at Gordon Ramsay's restaurant when tickets went on sale, and by the time we got back to the States they were out of our price range. Maybe next year....

## WORKS CITED

Debord, Guy. *Society of the Spectacle.* Trans. Ken Knabb. Oakland: AK Press, 2006. Trans. of *La Société du Spectacle.* Paris, 1967.

# II

*Re-Mix:*
*Participating in*
*Established Narratives*

# 9

# Making Our Voices Heard: Young Adult Females Writing Participatory Fan Fiction

*Susanna Coleman*

I was eight when I wrote my first fan fiction story. It consisted of a few hundred words scrawled in my diary, the beginnings of a convoluted tale about the Teenage Mutant Ninja Turtles meeting characters from Disney's 1990s cartoon series *DuckTales* and *Darkwing Duck*. Decades later, I am still writing fan fiction on a daily basis, having composed stories based on over fifty fandoms that range from cartoons to such "academic" texts as *Beowulf,* Plato's *Phaedrus*, and Thurber's "The Secret Life of Walter Mitty." However, both my fan fiction and the very nature of my life as a fan have evolved. As an eight-year-old, still years away from Internet access, I was a fan in isolation: I would watch a show and write or draw about it in my diary, but my participation ended there. Now, however, my fan fiction writing process goes beyond simply reading, watching, or playing a text[1] and then writing a story about it. Because of my involvement with fan communities on the Internet, I am instead a full participant within the text.

For instance, I spent seven months in 2007 and 2008 writing "The Lying Game," a 43,000-word fan fiction for *Darkwing Duck* (while my fan fiction has evolved, my tastes in television have not). As part of the composing process, I participated with other fans in a number of online activities: I watched episodes of the show posted on YouTube by other *Darkwing* fans, discussed characters' personalities and motivations with fellow fans via text messaging and chat, and viewed other fans' reactions to my work in the textual feedback they left on finished chapters of "The Lying Game" posted online. Consequently, I not only wrote a story that conforms to the characters, setting, and worldview present in the series, but I also engaged actively with *Dark-*

*wing Duck* by participating with other fans to both analyze the existing text of the show and create new texts about it.

Such extensive online participation raises the question of *why*: what do I and the other women who comprise ninety percent of fan fiction authors (Jenkins, *Fans* 43) achieve with the Internet that we could not accomplish without it? I argue that online participation in fan fiction enables female fan fiction authors to have a voice in the elements of popular culture with which we fill our free time. Our participation goes beyond merely consuming cultural products such as television shows, movies, and videogames. Instead, we invest considerable time and effort online both researching the original text that is the basis for our fan fiction and *interrupting* this text as we write, reshaping it into what we deem a more satisfactory narrative and exposing this new text to other fans. I take the term "interruption" from Nedra Reynolds, who describes it as an activity through which women gain agency — the ability to speak and be heard — by interposing into masculinist discourse with their own voices. While Reynolds focuses on interruptions in male-dominated conversations relating to composition studies (66), interruption is also an activity which comes naturally to female fan fiction authors as we improve upon and expand our fandoms. In this chapter, I examine this strategy of participation by interruption in a fan fiction story by "Madam Luna," another young adult female author who moves from passive consumer to active agent. In addition, I explain how we can apply these strategies to curricular writing, using participation to better understand and articulate our own voices within "academic" texts.

As is evident from the above description, fan fiction is simply a story written using someone else's characters. Those outside the fan fiction community may have had a brush with the genre through the publication of books in which authors write or rewrite stories using others' characters, plots, and settings. Such novels differ from the majority of amateur online fan fiction in that they are published in print, they are sanctioned by the producers of the texts from which they draw, and their authors receive payment for their work. However, books such as *Wicked,* inspired by *The Wizard of Oz,* are still fan fiction, still stories composed using the ideas of others. Some novels even retell the stories of classic, canonized literature; in these cases, fan fiction may be taught alongside the text on which it was based, as in an undergraduate literature class I took in which we read *Wide Sargasso Sea* immediately after *Jane Eyre.* However, even non-sanctioned fan fiction is easily available to a mass audience via the Internet. Although early fan fiction was originally published in fan magazines known as "zines" (Kustritz 371), the Internet is now the distribution medium of choice for most authors: online publication is quicker and cheaper, and with large fan fiction archive sites such as FanFic tion.net, FicWad.com, and AdultFanFiction.net, authors can reach a much larger audience. Fan fiction, both online and off, brings with it an array of terminology such as "fandom," which refers to an original text or franchise on which a fan fiction story is based, and "slash," which denotes a story featuring a romantic relationship between two characters of the same gender.[2]

Once considered the domain of crazed fans who should, as William Shatner famously put it in a *Saturday Night Live* skit, "get a life," fan fiction has begun to earn more serious attention as interest in the field of digital writing has increased. Much valuable research has already been accomplished on fan fiction (see, for instance, Hellekson and Busse), particularly on how both young (Jenkins, Thomas) and adult (Kustritz, Jenkins) fan authors participate in their fandoms by rewriting elements which they find incompletely or unsatisfactorily addressed by the original texts. In fact, in her study of slash fan fiction authors, Anne Kustritz concludes that the primary reason authors write fan fiction is to improve upon the original texts from which they draw, especially when "the concept and the characters are not being fully exploited by the source product" (374). Henry Jenkins even notes that fan fiction can affect how a fan views the original text itself, creating a "greatly expanded narrative and a more fully elaborated world" (*Textual* 177). This research has indicated what fan fiction authors already knew: we are not merely passive consumers of our fandoms. We *participate* in them, reshaping them and drawing in other members of the fan fiction community.

In keeping with this insiders' knowledge, there is a need for research from within the fan fiction community so that that theories of fan fiction better reflect the practices of actual authors. Jenkins, for instance, discusses his discomfort with "the imbalance of power between scholars and the audiences they wrote about," which leads to "increasingly inaccurate depictions of fan practices and perspectives" (*Fans* 61). I seek to correct that imbalance, for while I take an analytical approach to fan fiction, I do so from the perspective of a fan fiction author. In addition, unlike most researchers, I base my analysis on a particular fan fiction story by Madam Luna, using it to demonstrate the participatory efforts of its author through a first-hand account of her writing process.

At the time of my research, Luna was a seventeen-year-old high school senior with whom I had communicated online for three years; I first came in contact with her when I visited her now-defunct website containing fan fiction and art relating to the *MAD Magazine* comic strip *Spy vs. Spy,* of which we are both fans. Luna agreed to participate in my study by allowing me to read and analyze some of her fan fiction and to ask her specific questions about her writing. She indicates that like myself she has been involved with fan fiction from an early age and that she has composed it for school assignments. When asked why she writes fan fiction, Luna responds, "It's a hobby. It's something fun to do that doesn't require very much obligation on my part, and I can pick up and leave off my stories whenever I please." She also cites feedback as the primary benefit she gains from writing fan fiction: "Benefits from fan fiction, for me, are purely in the form of reviews and feedback. I love getting reviews and comments, it's a definite ego boost. It is a major role, but then again, I've never been very torn up over the distinct lack of feedback I get from stories I write about more obscure fandoms. I just shrug and keep on writing."

There is something of a contradiction in Luna's statements: she explains that the benefits she receives from writing fan fiction are "purely in the form of reviews and feedback," yet she also notes that she is not distressed when she does not receive any feedback on her work. Therefore, it seems that reader response is not the *only* reason fan fiction is enjoyable for Luna. I suspect that much of the satisfaction Luna receives from writing fan fiction comes from the fact that she is actively participating in the fandoms she enjoys. When she composes fan fiction stories and publishes them online for others to read, she not only rewrites the fandoms for herself but also influences *other* fans who read her reimagining of the fandoms. The key quality of Luna's participation is this *re*writing, *re*imagining: she participates in her fandoms by interrupting them in order to shape them into what she wants them to be. In her responses to my questions, Luna herself did not consciously identify any sense of empowerment as a benefit of fan fiction. However, when examined closely, Luna's fan fiction does exhibit ways in which her participation through interruption gives her agency over the fandoms for which she writes.

In order to investigate Luna's participation in and interruption of fandom through fan fiction, I analyzed a story she wrote based on a Japanese videogame series titled *Pop'n Music*, which consists of over a dozen individual games. Luna describes *Pop'n Music* as "'abstract' rhythm game[s]," pointing out that "[t]he characters themselves have no backstory in the game[s], [only] in descriptions given on the web sites and in the accompanying manuals and art books, which is where most of the information regarding character relations and backstories come [*sic*] from." Just as Reynolds sees feminists gaining agency by interrupting the masculinist discourse of composition studies, Luna participates in the *Pop'n Music* fandom by interrupting it throughout the fan fiction examined here, a story titled "Married to the Sea"; after careful online research into the fandom and its characters, she makes changes to the fandom which allow her to rewrite it in her own voice.

In composing her fan fiction, Luna first participates online in *Pop'n Music* through research: instead of simply writing about the characters as they appear in the games, she engages other online sources to flesh them out into three-dimensional figures. As she mentions, one such source is an official Japanese "art book" for *Pop'n Music* which provides illustrations and detailed descriptions of all of the games' characters. While the book was only printed in Japanese, bilingual *Pop'n Music* fans have translated it into English and made this translation available to other fans online. Luna uses the characters' descriptions in the art book to develop the personalities they exhibit in her fan fiction. Yet her participation in the fandom goes even farther than merely looking up the characters in a book. Because she cannot read Japanese, Luna depends on other fans to make the art book accessible to her through scanned images of its pages and accompanying English translations of its text. Thus to research the characters about whom she wishes to write, Luna moves through at least three layers of participation in *Pop'n Music*: playing the games, studying the art book, and communicating with the fans who make the art book accessible to her. The Internet is vital to at least two of these layers, for she likely would have access to neither the art book nor its translation without going online.

On the surface, Luna's reliance on the art book demonstrates no interruption of *Pop'n Music*; if anything, her use of an official reference seems to show a strict adherence to the fandom. However, her careful research ultimately becomes a vehicle for her interruption. As I will explain in more detail below, she deliberately changes a key trait of one character as he is described in the art book. Luna's use of the art book is a case of the oft-cited maxim of writing: she has to know the rules before she can break them. Her familiarity with the fandom gained from the art book is clearly demonstrated in "Married to the Sea"; this familiarity can be interpreted as Luna's proof to her readers that she is a knowledgeable fan of *Pop'n Music*. If an author makes the *faux pas* of writing a fan fiction that is "out of character" from the fandom, she will often receive negative reviews and criticism from other fans. However, Luna's knowledge of the character's background gives her credibility among fans and therefore agency; their acceptance of her as a knowledgeable author will keep them reading when she not only breaks the rules but rewrites them completely.

After her online research of *Pop'n Music* is complete, Luna continues her participation in and interruption of the fandom through the text of "Married to the Sea." This fan fiction is a slash story written in the third person but told from the point of view of the *Pop'n Music* character Warudoc, a technologically-adept pirate captain who makes and sells robots. The other main character is Captain Jolly, a pirate who is described in-game as the "king of the sea" and in the art book as liking "pretty flowers" and disliking "land." The story takes place during a windless night on which Warudoc's mechanized ship *Mariner Z* comes across Jolly's stranded, wind-powered vessel. Warudoc boards Jolly's ship with the intent to either loot it or make a trade with its desperate crew. Jolly offers half of his spoils in exchange for being towed back to shore; in addition, he buys dinner for Warudoc to show his gratitude. Afterwards, Warudoc offers to pay for a visit to a nearby hot spring, where he has difficulty bathing due to the hook which has replaced one of his hands. Jolly assists him and offers to let Warudoc sleep on his ship with the caveat that he, Jolly, will be setting sail early in the morning. Warudoc protests that Jolly will get "lost" if he sails off again; when Jolly is offended at the perceived attack on his navigational skills, Warudoc clarifies that he means lost "somewhere on the other side of the world where I can't find you." Warudoc declares that he'll follow Jolly in his own ship, and the story ends with them going to Jolly's cabin together.

"Married to the Sea" begins with an "author's note" in which Luna directly addresses her readers to explain some of the changes she made to the games' setting and characters. As in some novels, the author's note in fan fiction is a fairly common device which allows authors to address their readers directly in order to explain elements of their stories, to offer thanks for support or feedback, or to give credit to those who helped with the construction of the story. In this manner, Luna uses her author's note to explain the changes she made to the *Pop'n Music* fandom in "Married to the Sea":

> Author's Note: AU,[3] if pop'n music fanfiction can be said to be "AU" at all. Maybe in the fact that beautiful women aren't one of Warudoc's interests here? And I just made up the Mariner Z, and did away with the concept of Earth for consistency with the White Land/Hige Land/Fairytale Kingdom countries [*sic*].

In this note, Luna interrupts the narrative of the *Pop'n Music* games by changing several things: (1) as discussed in detail below, she alters a key characteristic Warudoc possesses in the *Pop'n Music* fandom, (2) she invents a ship for Warudoc to sail, and (3) she relocates the games' characters and setting to another planet. The creation of the *Mariner Z* and relocation of the games' setting are both moves designed to make "Married to the Sea" function as a narrative: Warudoc could not have come upon Jolly at sea without a ship, and such fictional countries as "the White Land" and "the Fairytale Kingdom" preclude the possibility that Luna could have easily set her story on Earth. With these changes, Luna participates in the *Pop'n Music* fandom by rewriting and thus interrupting it.

Luna's greatest interruption to *Pop'n Music* is the rescription of the character of Warudoc as evidenced in the author's note and later in the story itself. In the games and other official texts of the fandom, Warudoc is a somewhat flat, stereotypical pirate. Luna quoted this fan translation of Warudoc's profile in the art book when I asked her to describe him: "If you were to rank evil by looks, he's [*sic*] be the number one in the world. No, he's the most stylish pirate captain in the *universe*! His name is Warudoc. All the gold, silver, treasure and beautiful women in the world are his property.... Although if you try to talk to him, all you'll get out of it is bragging."

According to this profile, Warudoc not only exhibits the characteristics of greed and iniquity (stereo)typically assigned to pirate characters, but he also is distinctly masculinist with his "property" of "[a]ll [...] the beautiful women in the world." However, Luna envisions Warudoc as a much rounder character than the art book describes, and she gives him a motivation for his behavior: "I see Warudoc as being — not really a 'softie on the inside,' but he tries so hard to play the 'evil villain and nothing else' not that he really dislikes doing anything to the contrary, even when he wants to. It's a reputation thing." According to her, Warudoc's vices are deliberate actions performed not for their own sake but in order to portray the dark image he wishes to maintain. Kustritz discusses such rewriting of fandoms' masculinist characters as a key feature of fan fiction: "Fan writers 'repair the damage' done to these characters at the hand of the writers and producers of the source product by making them into real people with personalities, faults, needs, illogical desires, and weaknesses" (375).

Luna's first "repair" of Warudoc is evident in her author's note, where she indicates that "Married to the Sea" is AU because "beautiful women aren't one of Warudoc's interests here." Luna demonstrates her participation in the *Pop'n Music* fandom with this part of the author's note, for she acknowledges just what she has changed about Warudoc. By referencing the art book's description of the character, Luna shows her familiarity with him, proving to other dedicated fans that she has done her research. Again, this makes them more likely to accept and favorably receive her fan fiction. More important, this part of the author's note also works to remove a characteristic which clashes with Luna's desire to compose a slash story. As described in the art book, Warudoc corresponds to Kustritz' description of "[t]he men captured and rewritten by slashers" who are "suited to rescription because they embody many of the things that are wrong with the patriarchal system of traditional romance" (376): he represents the possession and control of women by men. Luna's "rescription" of Warudoc both begins to correct this troubling masculinist characteristic and allows her to write him as a character interested not in beautiful women but in other men.

Luna continues to undermine this aspect of Warudoc's character as "Married to the Sea" progresses. Although she begins the story with Warudoc as the party in control of the events of the story, by the end of the fan fiction, Luna has rewritten him into a subordinate position. In the rescue operation which occupies the first third of the story, Warudoc exhibits traditionally masculine characteristics. Early in the story, Luna gives a detailed description of him based on his physical appearance in *Pop'n Music*: "The captain was a leathery old seaman at the ripe age of fifty-three, though he never hesitated to knock it down a few notches, depending on the company he found himself in. Like any self-respecting pirate, he'd been in enough battles to lose an eye and a hand, which he'd replaced with a patch and a golden hook respectively." The depiction of Warudoc as "leathery," his mature age, and the implied bravado of the eye patch and hook possessed by "any self-respecting pirate" all work to establish him as a tough, strong, stereotypically masculine character. In addition, Luna again participates in the *Pop'n Music* fandom through this description, for she relies on Warudoc's physical appearance in the games to construct how he looks in "Married to the Sea."

The opening events of "Married to the Sea" also work to illustrate Warudoc's dominance. His mechanical ship does not rely on wind power as Jolly's ship does, an allusion to the stereotype of masculine technology's domination of feminized nature; thus while Jolly is stranded, Warudoc can come to his rescue by towing his ship in to shore. Warudoc also exhibits his dominance by taking advantage of the situation and demanding half of Jolly's treasure in exchange for the towing. These events clearly portray Warudoc as the active party in this encounter, whereas Jolly is passive. Warudoc's actions in this segment of the story are, like his appearance, evidence of Luna's participation in the *Pop'n Music* fandom. Although he is the protagonist with whom readers are meant to sympathize, his behavior is in character with his portrayal in the art book as a boastful, greedy, "evil" pirate.

Yet, by the end of the story, the characters' roles have been changed; Jolly is in control of the situation and Warudoc is made vulnerable. Luna begins to effect this change about halfway through the story when Jolly offers to buy dinner for Warudoc:

> "Come to the city with me tonight and I'll see that ye get the finest seafood dinner that gold can buy, ahaha!" He clapped Warudoc on the back powerfully, almost making him stumble. "Nary a pirate around who hates seafood, even if ye don't have the smarts to carry it around!"
> "I — what?" Warudoc said shakily, getting to his feet again. "Well, er —"
> "Then it's settled!" Jolly laughed. "I'll tell ye ... pirates with sympathy, we're a dying breed!"

In this short passage, there are three indications that Warudoc is losing dominance and Jolly is gaining it: (1) Jolly offers to pay for dinner, a traditionally "masculine" role; (2) he physically shakes Warudoc when clapping him on the back, again a "masculine" gesture; and (3) Warudoc falters in his response to Jolly's offer, leading Jolly to assume acceptance. With this dialogue, Luna starts to interrupt *Pop'n Music*'s depiction of a dominant, masculine Warudoc and instead portrays him as hesitant and under Jolly's power.

Luna's interruption of Warudoc's dominance culminates in the hot spring scene at the end of "Married to the Sea." The hook replacing Warudoc's missing hand makes it difficult for him to bathe, and Jolly offers to wash his back. Warudoc leans against Jolly, observing that Jolly "seemed to just tower over him." Eventually Warudoc nearly falls asleep, giving Jolly the opportunity to kiss him. Throughout the scene, Luna emphasizes Warudoc's lack of control over the situation; he is the passive party while Jolly performs the actions of bathing, towering over, and kissing him. Luna's description of how the two pirates leave the hot springs sums up the direction their relationship has taken: "Jolly pulled him along, like Warudoc had barely any weight to him." At the climax of the story, Warudoc completely relinquishes his dominance by admitting his affection for Jolly.

Luna thus *participates* in the *Pop'n Music* fandom through her research and efforts to prove her knowledge to other fans as seen in her author's note, yet she also *interrupts* the fandom by rewriting both the games' setting and the masculinist character of Warudoc. This gives her an opportunity to reshape the fandom into one more satisfactory to her and to share this rewritten fandom with other fans online. Luna's participation in and interruptions to the fandom speak to the benefits of fan fiction described by Jenkins and Kustritz, for they allow her to fully "exploit" and "elaborate" on the world and characters of *Pop'n Music* in a way that makes her own voice — that of a young, adult, female slash author — heard.

By applying these strategies of participation and interruption in the classroom, students (and instructors) can both better comprehend assigned texts and make their own voices heard regarding academic writing. Researchers such as Jenkins and Angela Thomas understand the value of fan fiction in a curricular setting; as Jenkins suggests, there are "powerful opportunities for learning" inherent in the "informal learning cultures" created by fan fiction (*Convergence* 177). That such opportunities exist is evident in the amount of research Luna put into her composition of "Married to the Sea": she willingly engaged with a non–English text, working with her peers in order to understand it, for the purpose of developing the character of Warudoc for her fan fiction. In addition, she makes continuous references to her research throughout "Married to the Sea," successfully integrating her findings into the story. If Luna is willing to expend such effort to comprehend the fandoms about which she writes, it follows that her comprehension of academic texts could benefit from fan fiction as well. Thomas notes that instructors "are recognising the importance of including the texts of popular culture into the English curriculum as valid and significant texts for study" (229). As an example of this recognition, Luna's instructor could construct an assignment requiring that the students write a fan fiction story for a text read for class. Just as Luna participates in the fandom of *Pop'n Music* by researching it in order to write accurate fan fiction for her own enjoyment, she would then participate in this academic text through similar research of it conducted to compose fan fiction for class.

Luna's participation in a fandom through interruption is as important as her research of that fandom. She countered a masculinist narrative — Warudoc's possession of women — by interrupting the fandom and rewriting it in a way that repaired its faults as she sees them. Similarly, curricular fan fiction can encourage marginalized students to rewrite the academic texts which previously silenced members of their groups. For the hypothetical assignment described above, Luna might interrupt a canonical academic text with a masculinist message and rescript it into a narrative which corrects what she perceives as its faults. Thus, the participatory nature of fan fiction can enable its authors to protest, correct, and rescript the texts we encounter whether they are in the domain of pop culture or the academic canon. In short, fan fiction lets us make our voices heard.

*I wish to thank Madam Luna for generously sharing her writing and her thoughts on fan fiction with me. I also owe much gratitude to Kevin Roozen, Michelle Sidler, and Isabelle Thompson for their assistance in my research, and to Pierre Cyr for his help in the composition of this chapter.*

## NOTES

1. Throughout this chapter, I use the term "text" to refer to visual- and audio-based artifacts such as films and videogames as well as print-based artifacts such as books.

2. The term "fandom" is a combination of the words "fan" and "kingdom," while the term "slash" originates from the early days of *Star Trek* fan fiction when authors used the phrase "Kirk/Spock" to describe stories featuring a pairing between the two characters (Kustritz 371–72).

3. AU stands for "alternate universe," which denotes a story that could not logically take place within the canon text due to the fan fiction author's changes to the characters or setting.

## WORKS CITED

Hellekson, Karen, and Kristina Busse. *Fan Fiction and Fan Communities in the Age of the Internet.* Jefferson, NC: McFarland, 2006.

Jenkins, Henry. *Convergence Culture: Where Old and New Media Collide.* New York: New York University Press, 2006.

_____. *Fans, Bloggers, and Gamers: Exploring Participatory Culture.* New York: New York University Press, 2006.

_____. *Textual Poachers: Television Fans & Participatory Culture.* New York: Routledge, 1992.

Kustritz, Anne. "Slashing the Romance Narrative." *The Journal of American Culture* 26.3 (2003): 371–384.

"Madam Luna." "Married to the Sea." *FanFiction.net.* 5 Apr. 2007. <http://www.fanfic tion.net/s/3425511/1/>.

_____. Personal interview. 5 Mar. 2007.

_____. Personal interview. 7 Apr. 2007.

Reynolds, Nedra. "Interrupting Our Way to Agency: Feminist Cultural Studies and Composition." *Feminism and Composition Studies: In Other Words.* New York: MLA, 1998. 58–73.

Thomas, Angela. "Fan Fiction Online: Engagement, Critical Response and Affective Play through Writing." *Australian Journal of Language and Literacy* 29.3 (2006): 226–239.

# 10

# *Dungeons and Dragons* for Jocks: Trash Talking and Viewing Habits of Fantasy Football League Participants

*Julie L. Rowse*

I've always been a sports fan. My dad waited ten years for a son but saw no reason to not teach his three daughters about sports. The few memories that remain of my early years on a California Air Force Base include learning how to catch a fly ball so that I could replicate the skill in Little League games and learning the rules of professional baseball and college football. My memories of becoming a sports fan become clearer with our family's move to Nebraska in 1981. My parents sprang for cable, which of course meant access to the Turner Broadcasting Station. Suddenly, the Atlanta Braves became our team to watch, and with ESPN in our channel lineup, I could view highlights from all avenues of American sport. By the time I turned twelve, I discovered that talking about sports with boys was a great equalizer; being conversant in sports alleviated my anxiety around the opposite sex. But talking to boys was a tangential reason for watching sports by that point. I was a true fan. My dad struck a healthy balance between being a fan of a team (the Atlanta Braves, the Dallas Cowboys, BYU college football) and being a fan of sports. So even when "our" teams lost, he would point out the spectacular plays made by the opposing team. When I tell people I am a sports fan, it is hard to convey that I am not simply a fan of certain teams; I am a fan of sports.

So it was the natural order of things, years later, that I had no trouble immersing myself in the world of fantasy sports when one of my high school journalism students asked me to join a fantasy football league because he was short members for the 2003 season. I knew the basic concept behind fantasy sports but had never played them. Fantasy football encourages fans to create their ultimate team — to maximize the real-world talents of individual athletes in a virtual world of competitive sport. A fan picks who he thinks are the best football players, and competes against another person's idea of who are the best football players. I figured it would be a nice Sunday afternoon activity and would give me a chance to maintain and develop friendships with people who were also interested in sports. One of the things I've noticed, though, since I started playing, was how casual I am in my preparation and playing of fantasy football in comparison to most people in my leagues. My fellow players invested in print magazines that ranked the athletes; some even paid for premium online services that emailed injury reports and gave up-to-the-minute updates prior to games. They watched *SportsCenter* religiously, as well as other news programs that focused on NFL players. They scrutinized their (and their opponents') rosters, analyzed statistics, and made well-informed decisions on which players to play each week. I, on the other hand, consulted no outside sources in print or online. Saturday nights I glanced at who was successful the previous week, who was injured or suspended, and then set my roster. Perhaps that casual attitude is gender-related (but that is a topic for a different paper).

Just prior to the 2006 season, I was invited to play in three different fantasy football leagues. Each league had different rules and different ways of scoring, as well as different levels of "trash-talking." I was fascinated by these differences and decided to conduct an inventory of fantasy football player habits. My methodology for the project was simple: I emailed a ten question survey to thirty people. Twelve people responded — admittedly, a small sample. My initial intent with this project was to conduct an ethnographic study of fans who participate in fantasy football Leagues and try to develop a theory as to whether or not online leagues function as a community. Therefore, while my survey asked general interest questions regarding community, I wanted to know three main things from the respondents. First, I wanted to know how important it was to them to be in leagues with people they knew; second, how they defined trash talking in fantasy football leagues and whether or not trash talking was vital to their overall experience; and third, how playing fantasy football had changed their football viewing habits. This chapter explores the results of that survey.

As I analyzed my data, it became clear that, for my respondents, knowing people in an online league was not important. In fact, some respondents enjoyed the anonymity of joining random leagues and viewed it as an opportunity to take bigger risks with certain players. The themes from my survey that received the most discussion were that of trash talking and viewing habits; thus, these topics became the focal points of this chapter. First, I describe each league's rules and general operational style. Then I move into the respondents' answers to my survey and attempt to extrapolate from those responses a theory regarding whether or not fantasy football leagues could be considered online communities. But before I offer my data analysis, I provide a brief overview of the popularity of fantasy sports in general.

While the exact origin of fantasy football is disputed, some track it as far back as the mid–1960s. Before the Internet, fantasy sports were played at the local bar or in someone's home (using chalkboards), scoring was done completely by hand, and results were shared over the phone or at specified gatherings. In the early days of fantasy football, league participants had to know each other in some way, and had to live in the same area, since league business was conducted in person as opposed to online. The Internet made leagues much easier to manage, as the drafting of players and weekly scoring are done with the help of sites like ESPN.com, cbssportsline.com, and Yahoo! Sports. Furthermore, many people are involved in more than one league each season, live in different states, and may participate in completely random leagues in which they know no one. According to the Fantasy Sports Trade Association (yes, it is an industry that warrants its own association), "Over 15 million U.S. adults play fantasy sports ... about 90% [of those] gear up for football season" (Holahan). Online fantasy sports outlets grow 20 percent–25 percent every year, and revenues total between $1 and $2 billion (Holahan).

Fantasy football — and other fantasy sports — grows in popularity each year. Prizes for the winners range from money (all participants pay entry fees which are doled out to the winners at the end of the season) to virtual trophies. One of my friends has five virtual trophies from participating in Yahoo! Sports leagues since 2003. Another friend has won eight virtual trophies since 2002. The leagues I participate in do not involve money, but the prize at the end is equally valuable: bragging rights.

## League #1—The Survivor League

Three years ago, a friend of mine suggested we begin a "survivor" league, inspired by the popular reality television program *Survivor*. The idea behind this league was that each participant would pick who he or she thought was the best at each position, and stick with those players for the entire season. There would be no trades and no substitutions for injuries; thus there would be no cause for real interaction among league members. Every person in our league picked two quarterbacks, two running backs, two wide receivers, one defense/special teams, and a backup defense/special teams to cover for bye weeks.[1] Each player was not only assigned positive point values based on yards acquired and touchdowns scored, but was also assigned negative point values for missteps like fumbles and interceptions. Whichever league member had the most points at the end of the week won immunity for the next week and could not be eliminated from the league. Because there were no trades or substitutions, there was no real reason to engage the other members of the league in conversation. However, the league commissioner would email a limerick every Sunday evening to give hints as to who might be ousted after Monday night's game. Following are two of the limericks he sent out:

> There once was a man in Week 5
> Whose top scores kept him alive
> Twice topping the list
> He created a TWIST
> Now two people will not survive...!

> Each week brings a new twist of fate
> The stats sometimes keep me up late
> But it's worth all the time
> Creating a rhyme
> To warn you that now there's just EIGHT!!!

The Survivor league did not provide a sense of community, as league members did not communicate with each other during the season. As someone who was knocked out after Week 4, I stopped reading the emails to see who was still alive in the competition. Only the league commissioner seemed to communicate with the league.

## League #2—The Yahoo! League

Another fantasy football league in which I regularly participate is comprised mostly of a group of my former high school students and their friends. We use Yahoo! Sports as our fantasy football outlet. In this league, most of the banter takes place in August as the league is initially set up and the live draft approaches. Emails are sent to invite people to the league and much communication takes place to ensure all league members can be online for the live draft. Participants in this league live in several different states across two different time zones.

Each member manages a team with fifteen slots, which are filled every week with one quarterback, three wide receivers, two running backs, one tight end, one kicker, and one defense. The remaining six slots are filled with football players who might not be all-stars, but are good enough to spell any starters with injuries or bye weeks. Once the league is set up, communication between league members occurs via a message board, but in this league, most board communication takes place between the brothers who created the league. In the 2006 season, there were twelve participants in this league but only four people used the message board.

## League #3 — The Email League

The third, and most intriguing, league was run entirely by email. This league, set up by the same person who ran the Survivor league, had eight participants and had the strongest sense of community of the three leagues. Each participant knew the league commissioner, but not all participants knew each other. Out of the eight people, I knew three — the commissioner, his wife, and her brother. His wife was a late addition to the league, a topic I will address later.

To set up this league, we had an email draft that took two weeks to complete. The final rosters were the same size as the rosters in the Yahoo! league, but each week instead of playing three wide receivers, we played only two. There was also a limit on how many wide receivers and running backs we could have on our roster. This way, one person could not be six deep at running back, leaving all others in the league to search the dregs of third strings to find decent players. In this league, all scoring was done in Microsoft Excel by each participant, and then the spreadsheet was emailed to all eight participants. Prior to the start of the season, the commissioner sent scoring rules and playing rules to all participants, so everyone would understand the unique nature of playing in a league that was not mediated by an online provider. Incidentally, when I tried to explain this league's standard operating procedures to my sister (who is not a sports fan), she noted dryly, "Fantasy football is like *Dungeons and Dragons* for jocks. The only difference is you don't have dice."

## The Results — Trash Talking

Of the people who responded to my survey, half were in more than one league, and most were in at least one league in which they did not know their competition personally. Their reasons for joining random leagues are fairly uniform. They wanted to experiment with different scoring formats, they wanted to draft a completely different roster and see how it fared, and most interestingly, they did not care about losing to strangers. One 19-year-old male responded that "[it's] still a chance to beat other people at something, but if I lost to strangers, there are no negative repercussions. I just forget about it." A 35-year-old responded similarly: "I joined a public league just to have a couple of teams where if I won, it was objective, but if I lost, I didn't have to hear it from people I know. In other words, no penalty on a personal level for not doing well." Admittedly, I am using a rather small sample, but I wondered if their reasons for playing against people they do not know implied that they do not trash talk in these random leagues. It seems that trash talking is an online activity reserved for people they know.

Most respondents agreed that trash talking is an important part of fantasy football. One 21-year-old male defined trash talking as "making fun of people who don't do very well, or who make really dumb decisions. It's usually not mean-spirited, but some of my brother's friends annoy me, so I give them a harder time. Also, I make fun of any Eagles fans by reminding them of any losses." For him, trash talking is not just for his weekly opponents, but includes ribbing fans of teams he does not like, while another respondent (a 19-year-old male) saw entertainment in the trash talking of fantasy leagues: "I think trash talking is a fun way to communicate between players in the league. I think in fun leagues, where you are friends with others in the league, it's important to keep things interesting and [it] provides added entertainment on Sundays when you can see if the person talking trash is winning or not." In contrast, a 23-year-old male recognized the importance of trash talking, but was reluctant to engage in it: "I have only talked trash in response to another person starting it. My goal was to defend my team. I never initiate the trash talking because I'm really just not good at it." This comment suggests that not only is the competition taking place between different fantasy teams, but also there is competition in players' ability to talk trash — and an inability to be clever might invite more scrutiny.

The previously quoted limericks were the closest thing to trash talking in the Survivor league. The only other example of trash talking in that league was the way the commissioner alerted the players as to who was "off the island." Each email with the week's standings would also include commentary and a personal message to the person in last place, ending with: "You are the weakest link. GOODBYE!" But all trash talking in this league began and ended with the league commissioner. Individual players did not respond to his taunting.

In truth, most inter-player communication in each of my leagues was minimal during the 2006 season, until Week 12. Week 12 (at the beginning of November) is an interesting time for most leagues. Since the National Football League starts playoffs in January, most fantasy leagues have their playoffs in December, when all pro teams are still playing football. This way, even if a player has Marty Booker, a wide receiver for the Miami Dolphins, on her fantasy team, she is not penalized in January when Miami's season is a memory. Consequently, Week 12 is when participants start looking more closely at their chances for making fantasy playoffs.

In one league, shortly after the Week 12 standings were sent, the most fervent trash talking took place. The first place participant (#1) — who had not played fantasy football before that season — lost to the eighth place participant in the league, and the commissioner sent an email to the league that he was formulating some searing trash talk for #1. What resulted follows:

> **League Commissioner to #1**: Did you win this week? No? Wow. There for a second I thought you might actually have the right to say something.
>
> Making fun of other people's victories while ignoring your own miserable loss to — who? — the league cellar dweller? It's sort of...well, pathetic. I mean they won. I say "they" meaning "not you."
>
> Let's focus on the one relevant point in this exchange. I laid a 35 point whipping down on you in Week 7, which means I own you. Your license plate should read "O-W-N-3-D." I understand, it's a rookie mistake...it happens. It takes a while to know when to talk smack and when to just clam your ugly pork hole. Bow down, grasshopper. Kiss the ring. Mercy shall be yours.

> **#1 to League Commissioner**: Wow! You've been smoking too many bongs, King Yahoo. Big dog? Big dog? I thought a big dog is actually in first place. Are you in first place Chief Yahoo? No, your wife, the Girly Girls are, who just whipped you a couple of weeks ago by 60 points! You need to bow to her! But, be careful bowing in your dress, don't want to embarrass yourself. As far as who owns who, if you think you own me because you beat me by 35 points, the Girlies beat you by 60 points, so I think the Head Yahoo is owned and branded by the Girlies. I'll bet that Girlies tattoo looks good on you! And since you are owned and branded by the Girlies, I think your license plate should read "1GIRL"!
>
> As far as losing to the "league cellar dweller," I don't mind losing to [him], whose team put up a very respectable 137 points. How about you? You beat [your opponent] without even breaking 100 points. If you had played me, you would have lost, little Yahoo.
>
> Funny as to how you made the schedule up so you only had to play me once during the season (afraid of the rook?). But that's OK, I'll get my rematch in the playoffs, and then we will see who bows down, kisses the ring, owns who, blah, blah, blah...

> **League Commissioner to #1**: PS The schedule was generated randomly, Sen. McCarthy. But it's a good thing you only had to lose to me once this year. Not enough Prozac in the world to handle that kind of humiliation, so count your blessings. Last thing I need is more spam from the underprivileged after another bloody loss. You know, at least my 6-year-old son knows that when his older brother is sitting on top of him, it's best to cease and desist the yap trap. I guess some people never learn. Where's Darwin when you need him?

This exchange is rather advanced as far as trash talking is concerned, but it demonstrates that to be a good trash talker, it is not enough to say simply, "My team is better than your team. Ha Ha Ha." This particular exchange could be parsed for any number of subtexts: emasculation, incompetency due to drug use, mental illness. Additionally, the league commissioner is assuming that the victim — and the rest of the league — have a basic knowledge of history, science, and even popular culture to understand some of his references.

Sometimes trash talking is more basic, however, the result of hurt feelings with repercussions for the entire league. In the email league, one participant was upset over a scoring decision that caused him to lose in Week 7. It is important to remember that the rules and scoring were shared with league members prior to the start of the season, and feedback was requested, something that the league commissioner was not obligated to do. However, being fair, he wanted input from those who would be playing. The offended player had an opportunity to question this scoring rule prior to the start of the season but did not. During the season, then, his grievance was shared with the league, and according to the league rules, each player voted on the outcome. The offended player lost the vote, and sent this email to the entire league:

> Had I known that this scoring system was so FUBAR'd I would not have agreed to join in such a league. I have played FFB probably longer than most of you have combined and a defensive TD scored via INT, FUMBLE RECOVERY, BALL THROWN BY A HEAD COACH ONTO THE FIELD ACCIDENTALLY HAS NEVER NEVER NEVER BEEN COUNTED AGAINST A DEFENSE. However I will make this decision easy for everyone so that you guys can fight it out amongst you all.

He then announced he was dropping his entire team and would no longer be a member of our league. The league commissioner emailed the league, letting us know that the losing participant had indeed quit, and he warned us to "remove [his] email address from future league correspondence He made it abundantly clear that he wants no part in our affairs." I asked the league commissioner if I could still send the losing participant a survey, and he advised against it. We needed someone to take over the team that had been dropped, so the league commissioner's wife (who does know quite a bit about sports) volunteered to step in and manage the team.

## The Results — Viewing Habits

The second major focus of my survey was to find out how playing fantasy football influenced player viewing habits. For me, playing fantasy football has definitely changed how I watch football — I actually watch NFL games now. I was raised on a healthy diet of college football, and was taught that college football was more esteemed than professional football because college athletes really wanted to play. It was not just a job for college athletes, nor was it about money. There are many ways to challenge that line of thinking, of course, and now that I am older, I recognize that college football (at least Division I) is not a bastion of the "we play for the love of the game" mentality. But even after I lost my college football innocence, I still shied away from the NFL. I never lived in a city with an NFL team, so there was no geographically-induced loyalty. Sometimes I would watch a team to follow a college athlete who had been drafted, but Sunday afternoons just were not big football days in my home growing up.

Fantasy football has made me more of an NFL fan, but each season I am a fan of different players — the players on my fantasy roster. My respondents shared some interesting insights into their own football viewing habits and the unique relationship one develops with players as opposed to teams. One 35 year-old male responded:

> I used to root for two teams: the Chiefs and the Redskins. No, not because of my Early American Anthropology class. Because I was born in Kansas City and grew up in Northern Virginia ... then the salary cap came along and free agency became the name of the game. Loyalty to an NFL team changed fundamentally as players shopped for the best deal. Jerry Rice is a good example. The guy WAS the 49ers. He was there under Joe Montana and Steve Young. But then he shopped around in his waning years and [was] sent to Seattle and Denver before retiring. This is what gave fantasy football its wings. If the salary cap was the death of player loyalty in the NFL, Terrell Owens was the Angel of Death.

Terrell Owens is a prime example of how fantasy football has changed the way people watch football. Owens has had a few behavior problems in the past several years. A gifted wide receiver, he clashed with management in the San Francisco 49ers organization and languished on the bench for a season (that was my first fantasy season and someone had advised me to grab Owens during my draft — a move that did me absolutely no good). Owens was dealt to Philadelphia, and fantasy players drooled over the numbers he would likely post with Donovan McNabb as the Eagles' quarterback. Owens did not disappoint that year, but felt his performance warranted more money than his contract allowed. Owens griped for another year in Philadelphia, a repeat performance of his San Francisco tantrum, and was eventually sent to Dallas. During the 2006 season, he caught for 1180 yards and 13 touchdowns, delighting his legions of fantasy owners (NFL.com). Even if those owners despised the Dallas Cowboys, they hoped every pass from Dallas quarterback Tony Romo landed in Owens' outstretched arms.

Loyalty, for a fantasy football player, changes every year, and is not usually aligned with a specific NFL team. As a 45-year-old respondent noted, "The one downside in fantasy football is that now I watch players more than I watch teams.... I never pick players from the Denver Broncos because I am loyal to that team. I wouldn't want to change the way I watch them." A 21-year-old respondent echoed that sentiment: "When I draft players who go up against the Cowboys, it makes it hard to know which team to root for ... essentially, fantasy football has changed my focus from a team-based interest to a player-based interest." Playing fantasy football does not only change whom people root for during games, but according to a 19-year-old male respondent, it changes what people do during games as well:

> I would never consider watching a San Francisco/Minnesota game unless I was completely bored, but with fantasy football, I suddenly have a stake in the game, so I watch actively. While I'm watching football, I'll generally scan the bottom line or be online at the same time to check stats on my fantasy players — keep up with how they're doing. I can't change anything about my roster by then, but I still do it compulsively. Fantasy football can even make me root for players and teams that I hate, simply because I want a big performance out of my fantasy squad. I try to draft players that I like on teams that I like, but sometimes I'm forced to go with an Eagle or Redskin. That's how the game works.

In addition to watching teams he likes, he watches games he wouldn't normally watch. Perhaps more interesting are his activities during the games. While a game is on television, he will check online scores and statistics to see how his fantasy players are performing in games that are not shown in his area. NFL.com updates statistics every 75 seconds and has complete play-by-play coverage of every game, so keeping up is quite simple. On some Sundays, I myself have spent hours at my computer tracking games, because no games of interest were carried on my local television stations.

## Conclusions

The topic of fantasy football has received little academic attention. Yet with so many participants and so much money tied up in the industry, there is much work to be done. For example, how important is gender to fantasy football participants? How do professional athletes feel about fans that do not necessarily care if teams win or lose? What is the difference between fans who play for money and fans who play for bragging rights? Furthermore, considering the small sample I used for this project, I know I have not garnered the depth of data requisite to draw many solid conclusions, but it is a place to start.

When I started this project, I set out to show that fantasy football leagues functioned as communities. As I analyzed league communication in the three leagues I participated in, and as the surveys rolled in, I was proven wrong. The Survivor league and the Yahoo league participants hardly communicated with each other. The email league, by its nature, required players to communicate somewhat, as rosters were emailed back and forth, and scoring was done by hand. It seems that the advent of Internet fantasy sports has, in some cases, created some rather solipsistic behaviors in football fans. Today, for some people, watching football games is simply a way to track statistics, which takes away from the popular American ritual of just "hanging out with the guys" to watch a good game. Instead of gathering at a neighbor's home to conduct a fantasy draft, computers are used. Instead of taunting a buddy sitting on the couch, well-thought-out barbs are lobbed about cyberspace. Instead of cheering for the Indianapolis Colts, people are cheering for Peyton Manning. But the picture need not be entirely bleak: fantasy players who live in cities or states without professional teams may find a team to "adopt," through selecting players who perform well. Also, fans of sports might discover an interest in additional sports through the fantasy sports vehicle. Yahoo! Sports, in addition to fantasy football, offers Fantasy Baseball, Basketball, Hockey, Golf, and even Auto Racing. While I did not see compelling evidence that fantasy football leagues shared a similar community aesthetic to other online venues, the leagues I participated in did keep me connected to friends across the country. We may not have communicated every week about our personal lives, but participating in this online activity served as enough contact to maintain our relationships during the busy fall season. Furthermore, perhaps fantasy football gives sports fans another venue in which to revel in their fandom by providing an additional way of consuming the sport.

## Notes

1. Every NFL team has a bye week (when they do not play a game) at some point.

## Works Cited

Holahan, Catherine. "Fantasy Football 2.0." *Business Week Online*. 1 Sept. 2006.
"NFL.com — Terrell Owens." 9 Dec. 2006. National Football League. 9 Dec. 2006 <http://www.nfl.com/players/playerpage>.

# 11

# Alternate Universes on Video: Ficvid and the Future of Narrative

## Kim Middleton

It seems appropriate to begin this chapter by narrating the way I stumbled upon a small subset of fan production, as the story gestures at the ways in which these products — short pieces I'd like to call ficvids — set themselves apart from other kinds of fan video and in doing so, signal emerging priorities and literacies for the digital generation. Like many cult television fans and a surprising number of academics,[1] I am a bit obsessed with the now-defunct TV show *Buffy the Vampire Slayer*. A supernatural television drama sprung from the ashes of an unsuccessful film, *Buffy* follows the adventures of a Southern Californian teenage girl who is also, as the first season's introduction tells us, "a chosen one ... [with] the strength and skill needed to fight the vampires, demons, and the forces of darkness, stopping the swell of their numbers and the spread of their evil" ("Welcome"). Despite the fact that the show ended in 2003, and its spin-off, *Angel the Series*, was cancelled in 2005, the scholarly and fan production surrounding the show continues almost unabated. In addition to a teeming network of fan fiction stories, multiple sites, and LiveJournal communities, the advent of streaming video has allowed fans access to an enormous array of Buffyverse material: clips from both series; outtakes and bloopers; interviews with cast members, writers and directors; dailies footage; and an increasing number of videos made by fans from the contents of this public archive.

In the fall of 2007, I had only just discovered the wealth of *Buffy* stuff to be had on YouTube. The site's rather primitive search function lends itself better to browsing the gamut than to finding a distinct unit,[2] and so I was distractedly surfing the 9,000 or so items within the "BTVS" tag when the title of a particular video caught my eye: "Out of My Mind AU Spuffy." In the tradition of fan videos, the first clause, "Out of My Mind," immediately signifies the title of the song to which the video is set. And to an informed *Buffy* participant, the "Spuffy" term is clear — it's a contraction categorizing content that supports a controversial relationship between Buffy and the character Spike.[3] I was pulled up short by the middle term, however, which belongs to a distinctly different medium. "AU" is an acronym that stands for "alternate universe." A generic fan *fiction* designation, "AU" categorizes narratives that involve characters from a given fan text, but places them in situations that run far afield of the events and/or the cosmic laws of the show itself (e.g., Buffy is the warden at a prison, Harry Potter is a pirate).

True to its title, "Out of My Mind" is indeed a video that represents a relationship between Buffy and Spike, and imagines that relationship in a universe unfamiliar to the show's viewers. Sara, the video's composer, utilizes the first paragraph of an extensive set of notes to describe the plot of her AU film: "Spike works for Liam and Drusilla Angelus, and one day they have a new job for him, to kill Buffy Summers who is the daughter of one of their rivals." Here, Sara redacts any otherworldly context and rearranges the familial, romantic, and professional relationships among existing characters. In the video itself, she edits together scenes from multiple seasons of the television show, selects those with the same setting to maintain continuity, creates the appearance of new shot sequences to establish conversation and character intent, and even maintains and repurposes some existing dialogue to reinforce the AU plot. Almost an afterthought, the song Sara chooses to score the video works to set the tone and to speak to Spike's state of mind, but doesn't appear to lyrically match the action at any given moment. In short, "Out of My Mind" is an elegant jerry-rigged machine; using the same footage fans recognize from the show and painstaking editing, it tells a radically different story about the characters in *Buffy the Vampire Slayer*.

Of the approximately 9,000 YouTube videos with the "BTVS" tag, only 121 include an "alternate universe" designation as of June 2008. As a subset of the overall participatory investment in *Buffy the Vampire Slayer*, then, this type of video represents but a small fraction of production and/or posting within this particular fandom.[4] Still, this emergent genre of amateur media composition signifies some surprising new literacies among its producers, and I argue here that these differentiate them from the earlier generation of "vidders," and perhaps even their contemporaries, in three important ways. First and foremost, ficvidders are concerned with narrative: they illustrate the ways in which existing footage from a show can be wrenched loose from its story and made to serve fans' creative endeavors. Second, ficvidders add an important set of technical skills to those traditionally used by fan vidders. Both groups demonstrate a facility with the complexities of new editing technologies; but the former depends on the cut/splice/match aesthetic of montage music video, while ficvidders deploy the formal components of narrative cinema throughout their work. Finally, ficvidders utilize technological and social protocols to differentiate among the variety of audiences to whom they hope to expose their work and from whom they hope to conceal it, based upon their evaluation of Buffyverse competency and communal trust. In short, ficvid may be a tiny subgenre of amateur production within the field of digital media, but it's one that complicates current cultural fears about "kids nowadays."

Recent studies of our online practices document an almost-meteoric rise in users' involvement with video sharing sites. A Pew Research report from January 2008 states, "The audience for YouTube and other internet video sites has risen sharply the past year. Nearly half of online adults now say they have visited such sites. On a typical day at the end of 2007, the share of internet users going to video sites was nearly twice as large as it had been at the end of 2006" (Rainie 1). While the consumer side of video sharing evinces the greatest increase in use, the production side is also growing by leaps and bounds. The same study notes that the number of people who have posted videos online has tripled since 2006 (Rainie 3). Engaging with others via digital video and the internet, then, is quickly becoming an important form of social interaction. In addition, the sites that allow for interaction in and around video incite scholars' declarations of a seismic cultural shift. Lucas Hildebrand notes, "YouTube has contributed to a culture of the clip," while *New York Times* columnist Virginia Heffernan calls the site "neither a nascent art form nor a video library but a recently unearthed civilization" (2). Digital video sites are fast becoming crucial arenas where we engage with the culture and those who make it.

I lay out this brief overview of the ficvid genre and composing processes, then, in the hopes that it will reveal an emergent means of participating in the video-sharing phenomenon that has caught the attention of mainstream media. At the same time, I note here the ways in which ficvid literacies are not sui generis, but rather illustrate ties to a multitude of other practices and communal interactions: amateur video production, social networks, fan communities and fan fiction protocols, and a surprising affiliation and attachment to complex narratives. Film and video have long been the bogeymen of "mass deception," responsible for the death of autonomous thought most often associated with reading — and more specifically, reading "literature." The National Endowment for the Arts 2004 study, "Reading at Risk," defined its terminological parameters by focusing solely on reader's engagement with poetry, novels, short stories, and plays. As late as July 2008, the NEA chairman Dana Gioia stated, "Whatever the benefits of newer electronic media they provide no measurable substitute for the intellectual and personal development initiated and sustained by frequent reading" (Rich 1). At a time when digital technologies as a whole, and film and video in particular, are vilified for luring young people away from the benefits of reading literature, it's important to recognize the digital generation's deep attachment to narrative, both as consumers and producers. As a genre, ficvid highlights the fact that this cultural attachment to narrative remains, and exemplifies the new literacies that are necessary to participate in its circulation.

Henry Jenkins' landmark work *Textual Poachers: Television Fans and Participatory Culture* documents a panoply of participatory media that allow fans to engage in satisfying ways with their show (or shows) of choice: 'zines, art, fiction, music, and video. Published in 1992, *Textual Poachers* describes a bygone era of amateur video production, in which fans recorded and re-edited videotapes of television broadcasts as a way to create new meanings within the scope of their most-beloved series: "Fan music video is ... a unique form, ideally suited to demands of fan culture, depending for its significance upon the careful welding of words and images to comment on the series narrative" (225). By combining the emotive and lyric content of popular music with carefully chosen scenes and sequences from televised episodes, the medium of video allowed tech-savvy fans the singular opportunity to maintain the original source material while revising its context and meaning. The "welded" aesthetic of fan videos, then, supports a host of possibilities that includes, Jenkins cites, its ability to "represent subtexts [the series] normally represses" (228); its potential to reconsider the affect of scenes or series' tropes (231–32); and to give voice to a character's unspoken desires (235–60).

Jenkins's study is fundamental to understanding how and why video circulates in fan communities; yet the specific practices he notes have undergone radical changes with respect to the technologies currently being used. *Textual Poachers* describes the painstaking process of video editing at the time (a particular VCR's tendency to rewind a few seconds before it records, for instance), which adept vidders had to master in order to create their texts. Once assembled on an individual machine, the products were copied and then distributed to viewers either by hand or mail. Since then, of course, producing fan video has become considerably less labor-intensive. Fans no longer have to record episodes when they air; favorite programs are available, in their entirety, on DVD or online. Video-editing programs are now bundled with consumer-grade operating systems, and some (like Apple's iMovie) come standard with any computer purchase. These programs enable seamless and exacting editing, in which footage can be cut by fractions of a second. Likewise, distribution practices have shifted radically, as the Pew report shows: thousands of people post videos to the Internet daily, and millions watch, not only via sites like YouTube and GoogleVideo, but also throughout the blogosphere and online communities. Fan video is a small subset of the torrent of videos made, posted, consumed, and commented upon everyday, but new technologies have made it possible for more amateur vidders to participate and for more vids to be available to a range of audiences.

Considerations of narrative have been a component of fan video since Jenkins's early study. In his desire to differentiate vidders' multi-layered work from MTV's commercial, iconographic aesthetic, Jenkins asserts: "fan video is first and foremost a narrative art" (233). His analysis goes on to characterize the aesthetic strategies vidders employ as distinct from the MTV approaches, as they strive to meaningfully match song and moving images. Chief among these are the "word-image connections" (244) in which affect-laden scenes (well-known to fans) are placed, montage-fashion, into sequences that echo the lyrics to the song and, as such, visually signal a theme cherished by fans — a characters' unspoken thoughts (236) or a subtextual relationship. In her 2008 article "Reframing Fan Videos," Angelina Karpovich concurs with Jenkins's claim about the narrative work of fan video, going so far as to list the various types of narrative intervention:

> A vid can focus on a secondary character ... it can dramatically juxtapose the characters' actions with the lyrics of the song, reframing the characters and their relationships and thus altering their significance; or it can bring together characters from multiple sources.... A vid can explore "alternative universes," where, for example, characters who were killed off in the source text are still alive and still part of the ongoing narrative. A popular genre is the "ship" (shortened version of "relationship") vid in which footage of two characters who may or may not be romantically involved in the source texts is edited to suggest a romantic relationship between them [19].

Like Jenkins, Karpovich details the numerous narrative options available within this genre; unlike him, however she lists these in order to highlight and thus reclaim the influence of the MTV aesthetic on fan videos, and call attention to the intertextual audiovisual media landscape in which vidders work. Her excavation of multimedia influences on contemporary fan video speaks to the increasing sophistication of amateur video artists. They bring to bear a host of techniques from a broad array of genres that may inevitably exceed those found in their specific fan source text.

For both Jenkins and Karpovich, fan video is a product of complex cognitive processes: the amplification of subtexts via "mode-matching" (Sorapure), the intensification of bonds within a social network of fans, and the replication of intertextual multimedia aesthetics that engender those subtexts and social bonds. The origin of these processes, they contend, lies in the careful construction of a meaningful relationship between the music and the visuals at any given moment in the video. While both scholars mention a narrative function of this genre, they defer an analysis of the narrative structure and craft itself in fan videos. These characteristics, I'd argue, in cooperation with the "welded aesthetic" both Jenkins and Karpovich highlight, present a challenging undertaking with specific artistic and social implications.

Few authors or filmmakers would dispute that the development of a coherent alternative narrative comprised solely of pre-existing elements counts as a complicated aesthetic endeavor, both functionally and cognitively. Ficvid, like fan fiction, shares a certain amount of intellectual and creative terrain with the canonical narrative arts. The success of both, for instance, rests on the characteristics we consistently associate with compelling stories in print and in movies. Roberta Pearson makes the structural connections among fan production, literature, and cult film and television explicit:

> Fan fiction follows the conventions of the nineteenth century realist novel and the classical Hollywood cinema, attempting to construct fully realised, psychologically convincing characters who resemble their television templates.... The collective episodes of the original text have themselves established a metaverse rich with spatial/temporal narrative settings and character possibilities; fans can, if they wish, indulge in an imaginative extension of the metaverse that conforms in spirit, if not to the letter, to the "canon." Cult television fans can revel in the development of characters and long, complex narrative arcs.

Here, Pearson maps a system of reciprocal influences among the original media text, the fan production inspired by it, and modern narrative genres, a constellation that orbits a core of common investments in character depth and story arc. In addition, she notes that fan engagement with a given source text is often categorically and creatively aligned with particular cosmologies set forth in the show itself, as well as commonly-lauded aesthetic forms. Deborah Kaplan's "Construction of Fan Fiction Character Through Narrative" offers examples of lengthy fan fictions that weave the narrative conventions of a given source text with those of nineteenth century literature and utilize literary techniques familiar to scholars. Fan fiction, then, has been recognized by some as an enterprise that learns its best practices from literary genres and conventions in order to attend to audience expectations for complex and satisfying narratives.

Ficvid is no different in these respects, with one significant exception: its appropriation from the source text is discretely bound by the exigency of the existing footage. In other words, much of the primary source material is immutable. Consider this comparison. Even under the strictest conditions, a fan fiction author can revise the narrative of a well-known episode by crafting interior monologues for various characters that represent surrogate motives for existing dialogue. She can imagine scenes that occur "off stage" or outside the televised footage; she can devise an alternate ending to an event while still maintaining fans' expectations of appropriate and believable characterization. A ficvidder, on the other hand, can only use existing footage to revise the narrative of an episode; thus, she must locate scenes from elsewhere in the source text or related materials that can indicate variant character reactions, interactions, or events and juxtapose them in such a way as to both rupture the familiar order of the shots and indicate a new set of relationships and divergent emplotment.[5]

Thus, at the heart of the ficvid enterprise is a reciprocal process that revolves around the original context in the source materials. In order to craft an AU narrative, vidders must first decontextualize particular shots and scenes from the plot or characterization work they currently perform in given episodes. As they edit the raw footage, vidders reverse the process, syntactically building new contexts for those same shots and scenes to construct the AU narrative and thus attempt to invest them with new meaning. Narrative decontextualization and recontextualization, however, are far from hermetic processes that obliterate one another. Rather, the two together construct a palimpsest of meaning that can heighten the effect of the ficvid.[6] Jim Collins notes a roughly-parallel phenomenon in films and graphic novels of the 1990's: "hyper-conscious popular narrative adopts or appropriates diverse semantic units which, by this point in the development of popular culture, are always already encrusted with one or more sets of syntactic associations that are inseparable from those individual units" (178). In Collins' reading, auteurs like Alan Moore and Tim Burton, in working with a figure like Batman, acknowledge narrative elements that are loaded with associations for fans and other viewerships, and purposefully activate those in their new superhero origin stories. Ficvidders, I'd argue, participate in a similar aesthetic process: consciously or not, they use iconic and affect-laden shots and scenes in their AU narratives. These individual units bring with them a series of "encrustations" and harness them for the new ficvid story. In other words, they bring their baggage with them into a new story.

The ficvid "Dust to Dust," created by Holly Gilmore, features several examples of such encrustations and their effects. A 10-minute magnum opus, "Dust to Dust" follows a relatively simple narrative line that imagines an alternate ending to the controversial season six plot in which Buffy returns from the dead. In Gilmore's rendition, Buffy's unhappiness at her resurrection (a theme that occupies a good portion of the televised episodes) is allayed by Spike turning her into a vampire. Thus freed from responsibility and morality (and perhaps her soul), she and Spike run amok until another vampire slayer, Faith, arrives to kill both of them. "Dust to Dust" employs hundreds of cuts and four different songs, and I can't hope to do justice to it in its entirety. One small scene, however, speaks to the ways the ficvid genre utilizes the simultaneous deployment of decontextualization and recontextualization, trading on activating viewers' memories of the scene's original associations and then combining them with the new ones that the ficvidder is building via the AU narrative. At the climax of her video, Gilmore uses a fight scene between Buffy and Faith, clipped from the season four episode "Who Are You," in which Faith switches bodies — and thus lives — with Buffy via magical means; in the scene, they beat each other bloody on the dais of an empty church. In the source text, Faith has always been the bad girl to Buffy's good. At the end of season three, for example, Faith participates in a plot to allow a demon to take over the town and attempts to kill Buffy's boyfriend. This particular fight scene, then, in its original incarnation, encapsulates a complex matrix in the minds of viewers. Buffy is really Faith and Faith Buffy; Buffy has been wronged by Faith, thus drawing our sympathies, and yet the episode also plays up what Faith has learned by literally walking in Buffy's shoes: the responsibilities and benefits endemic to Slayerhood and relationships with friends, boyfriends, and parents. Critics, in fact, see this scene as a crucial point of self-discovery in Faith's narrative arc; her battle with Buffy is transmogrified, via the body-switch, into a desire to destroy herself for her previous sins.[7] The scene ends with a reaction shot of Faith, put back in her own body. The medium close up reveals consternation and guilt as she flees the church, and can provoke an empathetic response from viewers.

A complicated play of sympathy and morality, then, surrounds the footage of this Buffy/Faith fight scene. Gilmore, however, repurposes this scene for her own narrative, staging it as the final showdown between now-vampire Buffy and slayer Faith. In "Dust to Dust," no indication of body-switching is given; thus, the fight we witness does not require the constant "who is who" identity calculus of the original narrative. Since many of the previous scenes highlight Buffy's sorrow and subsequent joy at being turned into a vampire, our sympathies are trained on her as Gilmore's heroine. These feelings are intensified by the consequent event: a quick cut to black during the fight scene, followed by Faith's reaction shot (described above), indicates that she's killed Buffy (this is reinforced by the next scene, in which a battered Spike weeps — originally the season-five scene that immediately follows Buffy's death).

On its own, "Dust to Dust" features Buffy as the wronged and eventually mourned party. But for fans who carry the source-text attachments and identifications with both characters into their viewing of this video, the narrative incites a vertiginous set of questions that interrogate their reactions to the characters. "Dust to Dust" characterizes Faith solely as Buffy's murderer, one who deserves punishment (the final scene of the video shows Faith taken away by the police with Spike looking on). Yet this so strongly conflicts with the ethos of the original episode that it produces a deep ambivalence; the savvy *Buffy* viewer experiences the ficvid's portrayal and that of the source text simultaneously. Likewise, while the audience may mourn Buffy's death in "Dust to Dust" (like our emotive surrogate Spike), it can't help but censure many of her violent or sexualized actions qua vampire in the video, particularly because they are coded as Faith's in the source text. The lingering fascination with this ficvid, then, rests in its uneasy settling place for our judgments of characters and their actions, as we encounter the encrusted associations with the footage in its original context and in its new narrative, simultaneously.

As a genre, many ficvids activate this hyperconscious narrative style vis-à-vis the deep visual and emotive memories of fans. This activation requires comprehensive knowledge of the source text: a significant familiarity with particular scenes and their import over the course of scores of episodes and across a number of plot lines. Arguably, this dedication to a lengthy narrative requires incredible focus and attention prior to video production.[8] In order to create and distribute the hyperconscious narratives discussed above, however, ficvidders must also achieve a fluency with the complexities of editing software and the unique interactive features of a variety of video sharing sites. It's tempting to categorize these competencies as simple technical dexterity. In *Multiliteracies for a Digital Age*, however, Stuart Selber rejects this reductive view, introducing the term "functional literacy" to describe the complex skills required for interaction with computer software and within online environments. Selber urges teachers of writing and communication to see functional literacy as a comprehensive achievement that includes technical facility and at least two additional skill sets: first, a fluency with specialized discourses endemic to digital media; and second, proficiency with social conventions and the localized knowledge required to practice these (51–61). In both their production and effective circulation, fan videos — and ficvids in particular — make both of these components of functional literacy visible.

Any contemporary fan video, ficvid or otherwise, is composed by way of software,[9] and thus vidders shape their creative visions within the taxonomy of possible operations a given program offers. A constitutive element of any video-editing interface is the ability to layer visuals and sound to create the aesthetic welding outlined by Jenkins and Karpovich. Thus, composing a fan video requires a base level of technical facility — i.e., the skills to import footage and music to a program and then to select relevant footage and match it to the song in order to create meaning. In and of itself, this facility indicates a familiarity with the specialized discourse of the editing interface and its particular commands and affordances. Ficvidders are conversant with this same discourse, but add an additional layer of discursive fluency to shape their texts: the language of narrative cinema. In her book *Closely-Watched Films: An Introduction to the Art of Narrative Film Technique*, Marilyn Fabe analyzes the work of thirteen auteurs and their respective contributions to the development of the genre. She notes, for instance, the overall effect of D. W. Griffith's use of match cuts and point-of-view shots: "Griffith succeeded in breaking down the action of his narratives into a number of separate shots, creating dramatic emphasis, without drawing attention to the medium or confusing his audience" (6). Later, she discusses Orson Welles's work in *Citizen Kane*, which exemplifies temporal complexity (through the use of flashback) and unreliable narration (resulting from the multiple points of view) (83).

Evidence of formal elements such as these abounds in ficvid. In "Dust to Dust," for example, Gilmore utilizes a directional match cut in a scene that depicts Spike biting Buffy. Piecing together a scene with Spike (from season six) and a scene from the episode "Graduation Day, Part One" (season three) in which Buffy is bitten by her boyfriend Angel, Gilmore carefully selects footage where Spike's movement across the screen, from right to left, matches that of Angel's. In addition, she edits out much of the close-up on Angel's face, leading to a near seamless transition between the two. Other ficvidders use eyeline matches to indicate one character's interest in another. The "Soulmates" video, by Marie (Spikesredqueen), creates a faux shot-reverse-shot sequence: footage of Angel gazing right, at a slight downward angle into the foreground, alternates with that of the character Willow looking up and left. By matching the direction and angle of their gazes, the sequence signifies a romantic relationship between them that only exists within the AU. In addition, Marie extracts Angel's monologue of obsession with Buffy from season two's "Passion" and layers it over these matches, thus repurposing an audio track to establish a hyperconscious narrative (wherein viewers apply the associations of danger in the source text to this new narrative).

A comprehensive study of ficvids would reveal the density of narrative cinema techniques. In addition to those mentioned here, many vidders apply a black and white effect to particular scenes to code them as the past or flashbacks; some use a slow motion effect over footage to lend it special emphasis. In many ways, this array of conventions is the set of tools that makes AU stories possible. The specialized discourse of narrative film serves as the grammar through which the audience grasps temporality and character motivations, and, as such, the elements that allow them to perceive an alternate narrative to the one it knows. The language of narrative cinema, then, is the ficvidder's discursive instrument for the process of recontextualization, crucial to their own narrative developments.

If technical and cinematic skills account for one component of ficvidders' functional literacy, the circulation of the finished texts most clearly exposes the second: the performance of appropriate social conventions. When it comes to displaying their work, vidders choose from a dizzying number of options. As Karpovich writes, "[C]ompleted videos are made available in a range of ways: via peer-to-peer networks, as direct downloads from the vidders' personal websites, as files uploaded to online vidding communities and archives, and as files shared on free video hosting sites such as YouTube.com" (20). Each of these distribution options comes with its own etiquette, specific to the community (or communities) that reside at a given site. Citing historian Lisa Gitelman in his most recent work, Jenkins calls these "a set of associated 'protocols' or social and cultural practices that have grown up around that technology" (*Convergence* 14). While the *technologies* that engender video sharing are similar across widely-divergent sites, the *protocols* specific to these differ significantly based on the options allowed by various interfaces (e.g., commenting, linking, video responses) and the audiences who converge at the site. Video producers and audience members, then, create patterns of behavior and interaction particular to the site's affordances and participants' preferences.

A number of scholars have begun to study the protocols of sites like YouTube, above and beyond their ostensible purpose of video sharing. Patricia Lange analyzes the ways in which users manipulate the channel and tagging functions in order to calibrate the visibility of their videos. She writes, "Beyond profile-based friendship connections, the analysis showed how video sharing can become an important way for participants to negotiate membership in social networks" (16). Danah Boyd casts a broad net over a number of social network sites and deems them "networked publics" that allow users to develop and practice important individual and civic skills: "social network sites are providing teens with a space to work out identity and status, make sense of cultural cues and negotiate public life" (2). Thus, learning to make and upload a video are but the first steps in achieving a comprehensive functional literacy; additional experience interacting with digital others is required as well. In order to make her work visible to a receptive audience, a user must enter (or already participate in) a particular community, shape a digital self within that space, and communicate with respect to the conventions of the network.

If true functional literacy for video sharing requires fluency with site functions and community protocols, then the subset of ficvidders takes on an additional responsibility as contributors prepare their work for their peers: the performance of deep knowledge about the source texts. Karen Hellekson and Kristina Busse explain the high stakes in online fan communities (as opposed to the wider public of YouTube):

> Most important to treatments of fan texts are understandings of canon, the events presented in the media source that provide the universe, setting, and characters, and fanon, the events created by the fan community in a particular fandom and repeated pervasively throughout the fantext.... An understanding of canon is particularly important for the creators of fan texts because they are judged on how well they stick to or depart from canon [10].

Like fan fiction writers, ficvidders must acknowledge their familiarity with the source texts and the history of contributions made by other fandom participants. They need to be cognizant of the cultural cues particular to fan communities: the way that their own text is positioned vis-à-vis the fanon and the appropriate tags describing it with reference to the relevant genres and relationships.

Canon and fanon function, at least initially, as the central anchor for communities of participants, and thus provide an integral means for vidders to develop their identities and social bonds. In essence, ficvidders must decide how best to reach their audience, with respect to the protocols specific to various sites. Online fan communities' requirement of specialized knowledge of canon and fanon is the very same function that guarantees an audience well-versed in the source text. A more public site (YouTube or GoogleVideo) allows for a wider audience, but risks untutored, and perhaps critical, viewers. Making these finely-weighted decisions cement the ficvidders' functional literacy with regards to informed social interaction.

As an emergent genre, then, ficvid reveals surprising complexities of sustained narrative involvement, production, and distribution. While it remains a minute portion of the torrent of digital video that uses source texts to intervene in a larger cultural conversation, ficvid's dedication to, and deployment of, narrative counters much of the apocalyptic discourse characterizing the digital generation. Ficvids attest to a deep and abiding focus on lengthy, complex narratives. It may be easy to dismiss these as stories that appear in a degraded pop form, yet vidders' own texts feature elements from literature and classic cinema (many, in fact, depend on these for the coherence). In their spare time and for pleasure, vidders engage in time-consuming and cognitively-challenging acts of composing. They build relationships in a variety of online spaces with those whose interests mirror their own, and thus help to shape new communities dedicated to careful assessment of new narratives in light of their source texts and the panoply of related fan production surrounding them. In short, the processes involved in and the protocols surrounding ficvid evince an emergent culture of readers/writers/producers who are invested in the future of narrative, and who are at the forefront of developing the literacies necessary to sustain that future.

## NOTES

1. See the online journal *Slayage*, as well as the 2007 collection *Undead TV: Essays on* Buffy the Vampire Slayer for a snapshot of the ongoing scholarly investment in the series.

2. In a response to Alan McKee's *In Media Res* Request for Comment regarding *Buffy's* opening sequence, Jonathan Gray writes: "Certainly, that intro plays a large role in Buffy fandom: a while back, I tried to get the Buffy intro on YouTube and had to first wade through about 50 fan-made intros" (Gray).

3. See Derek Johnson's analysis of the politics and implications of this relationship in "Fan-Tagonism: Factions, Institutions, and Constitutive Hegemonies of Fandom."

4. In comparison, there are 217,000 videos posted with the Harry Potter tag, only 917 of which feature "AU" (and a minute number of these appear in the search because they use the word "Australia"). Thus, AU vids in various fandoms represent a very small portion of the overall production. The Buffyverse has a far larger proportion of this kind of video production than many of its fandom counterparts.

5. In the interest of full disclosure, it should be noted that a common paratextual element of ficvids is the use of extended notes — 50–100 words — that describe the setting, plot, and important relationships that comprise the AU. These notes, however, function primarily as short summaries or teasers, as in the notes for "Out of My Mind." A generous critic might compare them to the summary paragraphs that sometimes precede chapters in Victorian novels.

6. Jenkins describes the frisson imparted by decontextualization: "Part of the pleasure [for fans] ... would reside in the challenge of quickly identifying the shots and recalling their original contexts" (238).

7. See Gregory Stevenson, *Televised Morality: The Case of Buffy the Vampire Slayer*, and J. Michael Richardson and J. Douglas Rabb, "Buffy, Faith and Bad Faith: Choosing to be the Chosen One."

8. In some instances, it's also the case that ficvidders' knowledge extends beyond the source text into additional sources that offer new visual resources. For example, a number of Buffyverse AU videos integrate footage from films with Sarah Michelle Gellar (the actress who plays Buffy), or from the television series *Bones*, which features *Buffy* and *Angel* cast member David Boreanaz.

9. At the most basic level, a fan video requires its maker to effectively use at least two programs to compose: 1) one of any number of programs that disables DVD encryption, and thus allows footage to be copied into an editing program, OR one that allows them to download and save streaming clips from the web; and 2) one of a number of video editing programs, all of which feature tools that allow selection, rearrangement, and layering of various media in addition to other diachronic and syntagmatic features.

## WORKS CITED

Boyd, Danah. "Why Youth (Heart) Social Network Sites: The Role of Networked Publics in Teenage Social Life." *MacArthur Foundation Series on Digital Learning — Youth, Identity, and Digital Media Volume.* Ed. David Buckingham. Cambridge, MA: MIT Press, 2007. 119–42.

Collins, Jim. "Batman: The Movie, The Narrative, The Hyperconscious." *The Many Lives of the Batman.* Ed. Roberta E. Pearson and William Uricchio. London: BFI, 1991. 164–81.

Fabe, Marilyn. *Closely Watched Films: An Introduction to the Art of Narrative Film Technique.* Berkeley: University of California Press, 2004.

Gilmore, Holly. "Dust to Dust, Buffy AU." *YouTube*. 2007. 3 March 2008. <http://www.youtube.com/watch?v=gLpaZIJfy5o>.

Gray, Jonathan. "Even Buffy's Regular..." Comment. 25 Feb. 2007. "Previously on Buffy." Alan McKee. *In Media Res: A Media Commons Project*. <http://mediacommons.futureofthebook.org/videos/2007/02/23/previously-on-buffy/>.

Heffernan, Virginia. "Pixels at an Exhibition." *The New York Times* 18 May 2008. 27 Jul 2008 <http://www.nytimes.com/2008/05/18/magazine/18wwln-medium-t.html?pagewanted=1>.

Hellekson, Karen, and Kristina Busse. *Fan Fiction and Fan Communities in the Age of the Internet*. Jefferson, NC: McFarland, 2006.

Hildebrand, Lucas. "YouTube: Where Cultural Memory and Copyright Converge." *Film Quarterly* 61.1 (2007): 48–57.

Jenkins, Henry. *Convergence Culture: Where Old and New Media Collide*. New York: New York University Press, 2006.

_____. *Textual Poachers: Television Fans and Participatory Culture*. New York: Routledge, 1992.

Johnson, Derek. "Fan-Tagonism: Factions, Institutions, and Constitutive Hegemonies of Fandom." *Fandom: Identities and Communities in a Mediated World*. Ed. Jonathan Gray, Cornel Sandvoss, and C. Lee Harrington. New York: New York University Press, 2007. 285–300.

Kaplan, Deborah. "Construction of Fan Fiction Character Through Narrative." *Fan Fiction and Fan Communities in the Age of the Internet*. Ed. Karen Hellekson and Kristina Busse. Jefferson, NC: McFarland, 2006. 134–152.

Karpovich, Angelina. "Reframing Fan Videos." *Music, Sound and Multimedia: From the Live to the Virtual*. Ed. Jamie Sexton. Edinburgh: Edinburgh University Press, 2008. 17–28.

Lange, Patricia. "Publicly Private and Privately Public: Social Networking on YouTube." *Journal of Computer-Mediated Communication* 13.1 (2007). Article 18. <http://jcmc.indiana.edu/vol13/issue1/lange.html>.

Levine, Elana, and Lisa Parks. *Undead TV: Essays on Buffy the Vampire Slayer*. Durham: Duke University Press, 2007.

Marie (Spikesredqueen). "Soulmates." 5 March 2008. <http://www.bloodqueen.com/buffy vids.php>.

National Endowment for the Arts. *Reading at Risk: A Survey of Literary Reading in America*. Research Division Report #46. Washington: NEA, 2004.

Pearson, Roberta E. "Kings of Infinite Space: Cult Television Characters and Narrative Possibilities." *Scope: An Online Journal of Film and TV Studies* Nov. 2008. 12 May 2008 <http://www.scope.nottingham.ac.uk/article.php?issue=nov2003&id=262&section=article.>.

Rainie, Lee. "Pew Internet Project Data Memo: Video Sharing Websites." *Pew Internet and American Life Project*. 9 Jan. 2008. <http://www.pewinternet.org/PPF/r/219/report_display.asp>.

Rich, Motoko. "Literacy Debate: Online, R U Really Reading?" *The New York Times* 27 July 2008. 27 July 2008 <http://www.nytimes.com/2008/07/27/books/27reading.html?pagewanted=1&_r=1&hp>.

Richardson, Michael J., and J. Douglass Rabb. "Buffy, Faith and Bad Faith: Choosing to Be the Chosen One." *Slayage* 6.3 (2007). 15 May 2008. <http://slayageonline.com/essays/slayage23/Richardson_Rabb.htm>.

Sara. "Out of My Mind — AU Spuffy." *YouTube*. 2007. 26 March 2008 <http://www.youtube.com/watch?v=fpi4eA32K3Y>.

Selber, Stuart. *Multiliteracies for a Digital Age*. Carbondale: Southern Illinois University Press, 2004.

*Slayage: The Online International Journal of Buffy Studies.* <http://slayageonline.com>.

Sorapure, Madeleine. "Between Modes: Assessing Student New Media Compositions." *Kairos* 10.2 (2006). 15 Nov. 2007 <http://kairos.technorhetoric.net/10.2/binder2.html ?coverweb/sorapure/index.html>.

Stevenson, Gregory. *Televised Morality: The Case of Buffy the Vampire Slayer.* Lanham, MD: Hamilton Books, 2004.

"Welcome to the Hellmouth/The Harvest." *Buffy the Vampire Slayer — Collector's Set.* Dir. Joss Whedon. WB 1997. 10 March 1997. DVD. 20th Century–Fox 2007.

# 12

# Dean, Mal and Snape
# Walk into a Bar:
# Lessons in Crossing Over

*Julie Flynn*

I find it difficult, if not impossible, to divorce my fannish and scholarly selves. Both worlds color the way I read any given text and each sphere influences the way I act in the other. The larger community that is Fandom, as opposed to one small fandom centered on a particular narrative, provides a way in which to consume narrative that incorporates unique rhetorical and exegetical strategies. While most fans will enter Fandom through one gateway text, once they have learned the methods and etiquette of Fandom at large, they will usually apply those to other texts. Fan fiction, as I have mentioned in some of my other work, is an interpretative act that operates on many levels providing different types of readings. These interpretations are akin to scholarly writing in terms of the issues explored but divergent in its narrative construct ("Fanon or Canon"). A scholar does not learn the methodology of her field and only apply it to one text or author and neither does a fan. With the skills of Fandom firmly in hand, a fan might attempt the next step and produce the fannish equivalent of comparative literature — the crossover.

The crossover is a type of fan fiction that involves combining one or more elements from two or more source texts into one narrative. These stories come from the natural question that fans often find themselves asking: "Who would win in a fight, Superman or Batman?" We wonder what beloved characters would do if faced with the situations other characters must go through in their narratives. What would Robert Chase do if he found out he was a mutant (Npkedit)? What would Connor's life have been like if he had been placed with the Bluths instead of the Reillys ("Five Families")? Could it be that Petunia hates magic because she could never see Aslan (Mirkat)?

In order to answer questions such as these and write an effective crossover, fan writers must take into account the competing narrative realities of the source texts. For example, the rules for vampire behavior are different in *Buffy the Vampire Slayer, Supernatural, The Vampire Chronicles,* and Marvel Comics. If fan writers choose to ignore the discrepancies, they run the risk of alienating readers who are experts on and zealots about those rules. If they acknowledge the divergent elements, they also run the risk of alienating readers, but can make these differences work as conflicts within the narrative. Victoria P, a.k.a. musesfool, does just this with a fic entitled "Fifteen Percent Concentrated Power of Will," wherein the characters of *Supernatural* repeatedly run into Faith from *Buffy.* The story melds the worlds not by negotiating the rules, but by expressly not blending them. *Supernatural's* reality is one of the Buffyverse's many parallel worlds.

Other writers have merged the worlds by setting up one character as the proxy. In "Cohen (& Moody)," *The O.C.'s* Seth Cohen expresses his dismay when his girlfriend leaves him to be, although it is not explicit, a slayer by taking in *Harry Potter's* Mad-eye Moody as a roommate. Seth's confusion is what makes the story both believable and humorous because fics where the characters just accept or exposit the differences rarely work. Despite the palpable fictionality of the narratives, there must be some form of realism to make them believable.

What all this really boils down to is that I love crossovers. I have written a few, and will never fail to click on a link when I see a promising (or even not so promising) summary. In fact, the first fic I ever read was a crossover between the television shows *Pretender* and *Highlander, the Series.* While I might now have some reservations about how certain rules were thrown out in that particular crossover, I have to admit that there was enough of a spark to suck me into Fandom. As I have grown as a scholar, I have also grown as a fan. I see little difference in the underlying methods of how academics and fen study texts, even though the differences in terms of form and legitimacy are self-evident. Even more, I maintain that we can learn from the crossover as scholars and as teachers.

For the past three years, I have worked in test prep. Many hopeful sixteen and seventeen year olds have come to me for help with a standardized test. While I do cover all sections of these tests in my work, I believe that my students benefit the most from the help I give them on their essays. The SAT presents a prompt that asks students a general question about one of a few standard topics to which they must respond in twenty-five minutes. In tutoring sessions, I ask my students to think of two examples, drawn from their interests, that apply to the topic. They make the essays work around the common theme found in both examples and in the prompt.

I use these same techniques in the introductory literature courses I teach as an adjunct instructor, this time by asking my students to make connections to other texts. "Does this story/poem/play/character remind you of anything else?" Making these connections allows my largely non–English major students to see the benefit and profundity of literature. Applying John Donne to Kanye West demonstrates the former's continued relevancy. Reading "Do Not Go Gentle into that Good Night" through John McCain or Hugh Heffner highlights the poem's message in a way that many twenty-year-olds would have trouble coming to on their own.

The crossover provides this same advantage and insight. It is a way of connecting texts with similar themes, of testing the limits of a fandom, or of reading the mores of one narrative through those of another. It is a natural and common instinct and one which educators can use to our advantage. Besides, everyone knows Octavian would beat both Batman and Superman.

## WORKS CITED

Flynn, Julie. "Is this Fanon or Canon: Fanfiction as Narratorial Exegesis." Prophecy 2007: From Hero to Legend. Sheraton Centre Hotel, Toronto, ON. 3 Aug. 2008.

_____. "'There Should Be Fic for That': Interpretive Strategies in Fan Fiction." NeMLA Conference. Buffalo Hyatt Regency, Buffalo, NY. 11 Apr. 2008.

_____. "'We Owe It to Each Other to Tell Stories': Neil Gaiman and Polyphonic Narrative." Thesis. Drew University, 2006.

Kovsky, Anna. "Cohen (& Moody)." *the speed of glaciers, maybe*. 10 Apr 2005. 30 June 2008. <http://www.annakovsky.com/cohenmoody.html>.

_____. "Five Families Connor Was Not Magically Squeezed Into After His Real Vampire Dad Slit His Throat." *the speed of glaciers, maybe*. 21 Jan. 2006. 30 June 2008. <http://www.annakovsky.com/connor.html>.

Mirkat. "The Made-Up Things." Weblog entry. *I worshipped dead men for their strength...* 31 Mar. 2005. 30 June 2008. <http://fire-and-a-rose.livejournal.com/335567.html.>.

Npkedit. "Mind Over Matter." Weblog entry. *npkedit's Journal*. 21 Oct. 2006. 30 June 2008. <http://npkedit.livejournal.com/74775.html.>.

P., Victoria. "Fifteen Percent Concentrated Power of Will." *Achromatic*. 16 Jan. 2007. 30 June 2008. <http://www.unfitforsociety.net/musesfool/15percent.htm.>.

# 13

# Stars of a Different Variety:
# Stealth Teaching Through Fanfic

*Kristine Larsen*

Let's be honest — the thought of an astrophysicist writing fanfic might seem oxymoronic at best, painful at worst. After all, why would an ivory tower stargazer who naturally communicates in the language of mathematics lower her gaze to the earthly (and sometimes very earthly) world of fantasy/sci-fi fanfic? What kind of turgid, stilted prose and plotlines might such fanfic entail? And more importantly, would anyone actually read it? First, let me attempt to convince you that writing fanfic has far more in common with my "night job" than one might initially suspect.

Surprisingly, writing high quality fanfic is actually an application of the scientific method. A writer comes up with a burning question that needs to be answered; for example, just how did Methos become one of the Four Horsemen in the Bronze Age? Next, a rational hypothesis is developed, and a 'thought experiment'— a story — is conducted to test this hypothesis to see how it stands up to scrutiny. As with any hypothesis and experiment, the laws of nature — the canon in the case of fanfic — must be adhered to, and any exceptions are to be carefully examined with a skeptical eye. Finally, the results of the experiment are submitted for peer review — the beta readers — and if deemed acceptable, published and afterwards remain open to public criticism.

If the above analogy seems a tad tongue-in-cheek, it is only very slightly so. As a faculty member, I am always on the hunt for "teachable moments," both inside and outside the classroom. I am also always searching for "learnable moments," opportunities to deepen my own understanding, both of topics I have long been interested in, and those which I accidentally stumble across in the course of casual reading. Equally important is the opportunity to hone my communication skills, especially for a nontechnical audience. Over the years, I have found that writing fanfic affords me unique opportunities to fulfill all these personal goals.

It will come as no surprise that my fanfic contains a plethora of astronomical references. However, this is a more natural fit with the genre than one might at first suspect. From planetary alignments to constellations, eclipses to lunar cycles, auroras to meteor showers, the night sky permeates the historical imagination. As the oldest science, astronomy ties together all human cultures across all times, be they factual or fictional. Therefore using astronomical phenomena as plot points or backdrops within a fanfic story is not as strange or artificial as it might seem. How different is this than Tolkien using the phases of the moon to drive the chronology of the travels of the Fellowship in *The Lord of the Rings*? The *Chronicles of Narnia* are replete with dying red giant stars, astrological alignments, and multiple universes. Phillip Pullman's *His Dark Materials* series draws heavily upon astronomy, including auroras, dark matter, parallel universes, and even a special telescope, the *Amber Spyglass*. *Heroes* uses the image of a total solar eclipse as its official icon, and *Lost* has certainly taught its viewers more about the potential dangers of time travel than any physics textbook or lecture by Stephen Hawking. As a scientist, I not only use scientific motifs and motivations in a canonical and natural way, but unlike many television writers and literary authors, I always make sure they are used correctly in my fanfic.

But looking beyond my primary field of knowledge, writing fanfic has given me an excuse to research a wide variety of fascinating topics that I would not have otherwise taken the time to study. For example, in writing a series of stories based on the major arcana of the tarot, I had to research such eclectic topics as the street layout in Pompeii, mountains in Washington State, progeria, the Dead Sea Scrolls, millennialism, and the Vietnam War. A novel-length fanfic work necessitated acquiring a rudimentary knowledge of proto–Indo-European language, medieval monasteries in Turkey, Akkadian monarchs, albinism, hermaphrodites, Egyptian pyramids, Bronze Age geological catastrophes, poisonous snakes, posttraumatic stress disorder, tuberculosis, and red tide, among many other topics.

In writing fanfic, I have come to the undeniable conclusion that I am, above all else, an unabashed research whore. As a result, my stories are known for their extensive bibliographies and footnotes, which readers surprisingly appear to appreciate. For example, the novel described above had over 600 difference references in its bibliography. But rather than intimidate potential readers, this attention to detail has only seemed to further attract an audience. I have received numerous emails from readers who have actually taken the time to read one or more of the references listed at the end of a particular story, and thanked me for motivating them to learn more about a particular subject. Fanfic has become for me the ultimate method of "stealth teaching" outside the formal classroom.

Writing fanfic has one further personal benefit. Canon-based fanfic is only as good as the author's knowledge of the canon. In researching background information for Tolkien-based stories, I have increased my knowledge of the primary text tenfold, and have come across myriad obscure references to astronomical phenomena which I have parlayed into serious scholarly research papers and conference presentations. Whether this is a case of the sublime or the profane directly affecting the mundane I will leave to the reader to ponder. What I can say without a doubt is that writing fanfic has not only allowed me to entertain myself and others, but to educate us all as well, and although they do not know it, my professional colleagues (in both the scientific and literary spheres) have been learning along the way as well.

At the end of the day, isn't that the real role of college professors, regardless of our department or specialty?

# III

*Re-Create:*
*Creating Narratives within*
*Established Frames*

# 14

# Writing and Rhetoric for a Ludic Democracy: YouTube, Fandom, and Participatory Pleasure

*Diane Penrod*

In his book *Ground Zero*, French theorist Paul Virilio proposed that at some point in the future, a "synchronization of opinion" would give rise to a "public image of a system of conditioning in which the *optically correct* would succeed the *politically correct*" (31). Virilio argues that such a system is more than a "genuine virtual democracy"; it is a "ludic democracy," (31) where playfulness and parody stand in tandem with other information forms. Nowhere do we see Virilio's claim hold as true as with the rise of YouTube, a site where users' visual and verbal video play often supersedes the intended, official versions of a text. As YouTube combines with specific aspects of agency found in fandom (Sandvoss 4), Virilio's future synchronization of opinion and the formation of a ludic democracy are happening now.

What we see on YouTube is optical correctness succeeding political correctness, as fans play with public images to generate new content and forms of knowledge. YouTube's optical correctness is most apparent in the fandom sites, where loyal followers of programs and films like *Star Trek*, *Battlestar Galactica*, and *Star Wars* generate short video streams that frequently mash-up (blend or remix) real events with parody or construct new public images for other fans to comment. Fandom's participatory culture, so eloquently described in detail since Henry Jenkins' work in 1990s, has matured beyond conventions, gaming, and branding research to the point where essay collections like this one propose there are significant affective and cognitive dimensions to aficionados' behaviors. Certainly the rise in new media technologies has contributed to an academic interest in learning more about participatory culture and participatory pleasure.

On YouTube, fans are not pathological or dysfunctional cult followers, nor are they eroticized groupies or misfits; rather, these individuals maintain a complex relationship to targeted programs and films that transcends one's identity ("I am a Trekkie," for instance) and their short clips frequently address "the very substance, premises and consequences of contemporary life" (Sandvoss 4) as seen through the lens of a particular program or film. Those fans who generate YouTube videos "negotiate and appropriate their object of fandom," becoming textually productive in that they "create new objects of fandom" for others (Sandvoss 30).

While many fan-constructed YouTube videos are laudatory, just as many demonstrate disappointment or resentment toward the original source. What transpires with regard to fan-based YouTube videos is a high degree of participatory culture in that there is an emotional and intellectual investment not only in watching these programs, but also in assembling various forms of short films.

Participatory pleasure arises through the display, proliferation, and ephermerality of fan-generated videos, as both creator and viewer share in mutual cultural production and consumption of these texts. The pleasure evolves as viewers become absorbed in the YouTube narratives. Consequently, these fans are not merely fans of a program or film; many are or become supporters of those who compose the YouTubes.

Such maneuvers, then, change the ways we need to understand the rhetoric of fandom — particularly fandom's visual rhetoric — toward viewers acting as participant-observers rather than distanced as observers. Participatory pleasure in YouTube depends upon multiple levels of agency for both the producer and the consumers of the short narratives. YouTube shows all of us, scholars, fans, and students alike, that we "can never step outside the system and look upon it from above" (Sandvoss 5). Because we are always already participants in the system, knowledgeable about these popular cultural references, each of us understands the optical correctness of these user-made videos. Furthermore, when the videos cross into ludic democracy, as will be shown in a later section, YouTube viewers engage in participatory pleasure that often undermines political correctness or academic propriety.

Therefore, this chapter examines three fan-driven spaces on YouTube — *Star Trek*, *Battlestar Galactica*, and *Star Wars*— in terms of their fans' participatory pleasure in creating various types of YouTube video streams. These three sites were selected for the following reasons:

- Science fiction frequently uses political themes to create situations, which allows for fans to use optical correctness to displace political correctness in YouTube videos.

- The raw materials from the original storylines are crucial in developing the YouTube videos, which as Jenkins suggests, provides "instructions for a preferred reading, but do not necessarily overpower and subdue" the viewer and permits the remixes to be read "against the grain" of the original (*Textual Poachers* 63).
- These three productions have huge fan bases that reach across multiple demographic metrics, which takes these titles out of the realm of cult status and into the mainstream.
- The YouTube videos highlight creativity in writing and visual rhetoric and demonstrate wide-ranging levels of fan participation; quite simply, most of these videos are really cool to watch.
- Each space highlights contemporary rhetorical elements in fandom and in ludic democracy, such as camp, parody, homage, trucage, and satire.

## Cool and Cultish or Smart and Satirical? Fan-Based YouTube Videos and Participatory Pleasure

This section begins on a note of personal disclosure: I love YouTube videos, especially YouTube videos that playfully acknowledge TV programs or movies that I enjoy watching on a regular basis. I find it fascinating to look at re-mediated YouTube videos driven by scenes and characters or images from earlier programs and see how fans mash-up past content to form new narratives. These changed textual spaces become highly interesting places for learning how people share information through humor.

Many academics (and probably far too many parents) view YouTube as a location for what is often snarkily described as "cool and cultish." Those of us who find YouTube to be something more than a place for classroom examples are often considered to be co-opted by consumer or media culture. In other words, these individuals find YouTube little more than a receptacle for trivial stuff that appeals to youth culture with little redeeming intellectual value. But how wrong those people are. Fan-based YouTube videos are generally smart and satirical, mixing pleasure with consumption, devotion, *jouissance*, and a dialogue with others. Many fan-constructed YouTube videos illustrate Matt Hills' point that fans frequently possess a good deal of intellectual capital — not just about a particular program or film, but about society as well. This is what makes studying the rhetoric of fans' participatory pleasure on YouTube both fun and germane to Paul Virilio's remarks in this chapter's introduction.

Careful viewing of fan-generated YouTube videos illustrates six contemporary rhetorical strategies that dominate reading and writing in new media spaces: camp, parody, homage, *trucage*, filking, and satire. For those unfamiliar with the differences across these strategies, here is a short set of operational terms:

- Camp: Items that are frivolous, banal, filled with artifice, or play with the boundaries of middle class pretentiousness.
- Parody: Work that mocks, comments on, or spoofs an original text, actor, or author.
- Homage: Work that repeats a scene, a stylistic element, or an image from an original text to show respect for the creator.
- *Trucage*: Christian Metz's term to theorize the technical skill needed to help viewers enjoy the illusions of special effects while still maintaining a deep interest for the implications of a narrative.
- Filking: Creating fan-based content to comment on and provide a fan's perspective to political or social issues of the day.
- Satire: Work that contains an angry humor or edgy sarcasm directed toward a topic or a person, which usually becomes covert cultural criticism.

So, as we watch fan-generated YouTubes, it becomes important for us to read these videos with an eye toward rhetorical strategies like those named above. These strategies complement new media texts, and these elements enhance one's viewing pleasure by allowing us to participate in the construction of new narratives. Moreover, on YouTube, these strategies are generally haptic and verbal to capture the characters' or scenes' essences that appeal to hardcore fans, so there is an additional aspect of optical correctness that outweighs political correctness.

The contemporary rhetoric of fandom is, as Cornel Sandvoss, Jenkins, Hills, and others have noted, far more complex and sophisticated than in the past. Fans no longer simply take in and worship content produced by a corporate entity; they generate their own content, sometimes remixing older material with new contexts, and ask that others play along.

## Camp, Parody, Homage, Trucage, Filking, Satire ... or a Mash-Up of Everything but the Kitchen TV? Three Case Studies of Contemporary Fandom YouTube Sites

YouTube videos can be read along multiple lines — as being narcissistic, as textual poaching, as generating cultural or subcultural capital, as representing transitional objects, or as creating self-reflexive statements — a point that Sandvoss (123) makes clear. One might also consider the possibility of YouTube videos encapsulating an emotional or sentimental set of experiences, as Jenkins (*Textual Poachers* 24) suggests. In the three case studies that follow, all of Sandvoss's and Jenkins's reading options are available to us for analysis. However, what is also apparent is that these video streams adopt the six rhetorical strategies outlined in the earlier section.

## Star Trek

One of the reasons I selected *Star Trek* for inclusion is that the entire series (1966–2005) affected multiple generations of fans as well as provided fuel for some of the more derisive and stereotypical comments on fan behavior in both the mainstream media and in academic culture. That said, some of the funniest parodies, campiest outtakes, and cleverest satires on YouTube occur when *Star Trek* is involved. Whether we read these particular YouTubes as textual poaching or transitional objects across generations of viewers, what becomes apparent is that *Star Trek* YouTubes frequently demonstrate a sentimental set of cross-generational experiences.

An excellent example of the point I am trying to make can be found in the YouTube titled "Star Trek — The Fourth of July Is Hotter in Space" created by folks at CBS. While one might not think of a rival television network generating fan videos, the cultural influence of *Star Trek* transcends the usual pettiness and conformity found in network programming wars. In this send-up, the original cast of *Star Trek* (an NBC network program in 1966) loves eating space chicken on July 4th and rockin' out to a parodied version of 1976's "Blitzkrieg Bop" by the Ramones. The sentimental experiences come from culturally-shared understandings of July 4th barbeques and the intergenerational recognition of the beat found in "Blitzkrieg Bop."

A classic mash-up parody of the original *Star Trek* series and the later series *Star Trek Voyager* occurs in "Star Trek Parody Coffee Commercial" by DiRRRty Flip in August 2007. This video illustrates how spoof works to comment upon the coffee generation. In this short clip, Sulu has been re-mixed with the Voyager crew as they've spilled their last cup of coffee and must return to base for more. The subtle reference to Juan Valdez parodies the Columbian coffee growers' longtime spokesperson as well as the current need for people's caffeine fixes.

Homage in YouTube depends upon a fan's special technical skills and publicly expressed respect for both the fan's ability to generate optical correctness and for the program or the film itself. Generally, on YouTube I have found homage is paired with *trucage*. For hard-core TV science fiction fans,

FireWarlock's YouTube "Star Trek vs. Babylon 5 Space Battle" (June 2007) offers incredible running commentary from viewers who know the arcane references and offer technical discussions on seeming minutiae of Galaxy class ships being in battle with Constitution class warships. This particular video demonstrates both homage and *trucage* at two distinct levels, as these fans — save for minor technical quibbles — acknowledge the creator's ability with quotes like "freaking amazing video" and "awesome!" as well as tremendous respect for the two television programs.

These three examples illustrate how Jenkins' "grassroots convergence" (*Fans* 155) unfolds on YouTube. Through digital media, fans are empowered to shape "the production, distribution, and reception of media content" (*Fans* 155) around the world and across generations. Through the proliferation of *Star Trek* YouTube videos, we see Jenkins's point about fan culture in action: It is "dialogic rather than disruptive, affective more than ideological and collaborative more than confrontational" (*Fans* 150).

## Battlestar Galactica

*Battlestar Galactica* offers both an interesting intergenerational fan history and a narrative that moved from its earlier campy premise to a darker storyline in the remake. Why the program is important for this discussion, however, is that the evolution of the series as well as the fan-based YouTube videos clearly demonstrates the idea of textual poaching.

The original 1978 *Battlestar Galactica* exemplifies Michel de Certeau's concept of textual poaching in that the storyline blends ideas from the Book of Mormon with a contemporary film, *Chariots of the Gods*, to move beyond the primary textual boundaries of both items. Intentionally or not, the 1978 *Galactica* was campy; episodes were often banal, filled with artifice. Additionally, the selection of actor Lorne Greene as Commander Adama gave rise to many disdainfully calling the program "Ponderosa in Space," a reference to Greene's long-running role as Pa Cartwright in the 1960s television western, *Bonanza*. Consequently, many viewers in the late 1970s saw the original *Galactica* as simply a silly action-adventure.

Clearly "camp" does not describe the 2003–2009 version of *Galactica*. The revised *Battlestar Galactica* departs from the older series in that the storyline is edgier and the characters more flawed than in 1978. There is, however, significant textual poaching, as historical and contemporary allegories of insurgency, religion, and political upheaval abound in the storyline. Textual poaching is a critical maneuver in fan rhetoric because, as Jenkins notes, this is how "texts become real" (*Textual Poachers* 50). By appropriating various programs' or films' scenes and sequences, fans not only "direct attention to the meanings texts accumulate through their use," but also rework "borrowed materials to fit them into the context of [the fans'] lived experience" (*Textual Poachers* 51, brackets mine).

Many of the *Galactica* YouTube fan videos center on textual poaching as remixes of episodes or seasons. Often the mash-ups attempt to provide a catalyst for discussion or debate about the most recent episode or season. However, there are several homage-like *Galactica* videos available that poach and examine stylistic elements like the language and images used on the program through *trucage*. Two fine examples of this strategy are found in Vogt48's "The Sounds of Cylons — Battlestar Galactica" and Pizzicotta's "Battlestar Galactica — Frak Compilation 1." These YouTubes offer insight into how fans use a program's discourse or images as transitional objects by finding and taking these existing clips and creating something new. Transitional objects are items that take the place of an affective bond; in this case, the program's language or repeated images represent the connection viewers have with both the program, its characters, and with each other. Matt Hills, writing in his book *Fan Cultures*, suggests that every human draws "on cultural artifacts as 'transitional objects'" (106) throughout life. When these objects are compiled into various YouTubes, a space is created where, as Hills offers, "a cultural repertoire which 'holds' the interest of the fan and constitutes the subject's symbolic project of self" (109) emerges.

Both Vogt48 and Pizzicotta's works demonstrate this idea quite well. In "The Sounds of Cylons — Battlestar Galactica," Vogt48 remixes scenes from the revised *Galactica* series to Simon and Garfunkel's "The Sounds of Silence." While watching the video, the images are suggestive enough to believe that Simon and Garfunkel are singing "the sounds of cylons" as the refrain. And the song itself amplifies the images Vogt48 selected from the four seasons of Galactica. Such a point is made by several fans, who offer props to Vogt48 for his skill in combining optical correctness with the song's lyrics. For viewers, Vogt48's YouTube offers a range of editing techniques that demonstrates *trucage* as a way to heighten rhetorical effect on a narrative. Similarly, Pizzicotta's "Frak Compilation 1" splices scenes from the first season of the updated *Battlestar Galactica* to highlight the word "frak," a Galactican substitute for a similar, commonly vulgar English term. The amplification of "frak" is in many ways genuine *trucage*, as Pizzicotta uses jump cut techniques to frame the selected dialogue and scenes to create rhetorical effect.

Pizzicotta's video spawned a series of "frak" videos on YouTube, from Ianchen886's 2007 video "FRAK!" to the dozens of remakes of Scifistorm's March 2008 video "What the Frak" Galactica retrospective. Each of these frak videos address the range of word play that exists in the 2003 series. The "What the Frak" retrospective in particular presents multiple puns in the narrative that connect to the episodes in a maneuver that can be read as both *trucage* and camp. In each of these short films, the word "frak" becomes a transitional object that establishes a bond between fans and with the series.

For *Galactica* fans in particular, language becomes an affective element. The word "frak" defines the world as they construct it. As such, "FRAK!" uses the story's language in a very traditional manner — as a social and public process of making meaning. Through *trucage* in combination with either homage or camp, the idea is to create fan YouTube videos that build an illusion of community rather than foster parody or satire. In those videos, viewers find a space that appears physical, habitable, and itinerant — just like the program proposes to be.

## Star Wars

*Star Wars* might be the location on YouTube where the campiest, most parodic, and most satirical fan-created videos reside. There are thousands of *Star Wars* YouTubes, far more than this paper can address. There are gangsta *Star Wars* videos, Lego *Star Wars* videos, and *Star Wars* spoof videos where the characters fight everyone from Monty Python and Benny Hill to sports fans. There is even the "Chad Vader Training Video Series," in which Darth Vader's unsuccessful brother, Chad, offers tips for those interested in rising to the top of grocery store management.

Historically, these comic or satirical approaches fit in the film's timeline. *Star Wars* has always spawned a type of campiness in fandom; the fan-created classic 1977 spoof *Hardware Wars* and the Mel Brooks' 1987 parody *Spaceballs* are but two of the early attempts to offer audiences participatory pleasure. Mockumentaries like George Lucas' own *Return of the Ewok* in 1982 and *R2 D2: Beneath the Dome* (2002) allow audiences to see the *Star Wars* franchise from very different perspectives. So, even the creator of the *Star Wars* saga recognizes the value of camp, parody, and humor in the narrative.

Furthermore, the *Star Wars* saga has been constructed as an endlessly deferred narrative, what Hills calls an "*unfinished and focused* narrative expanse" that begs to be *hyperdiegetic* (137). That is, the story entreats audiences to see it as a "vast and detailed narrative space," a "fraction of which is ever directly seen or encountered" (137) that implores others to offer re-readings and new readings of these tales. Consequently, the volume of YouTube videos proffers a range of readings and re-readings for the *Star Wars* community.

Rhetorically, *Star Wars* YouTube fan videos are prime examples of Jenkins's description of filking. Filking is the process of wide-ranging textual poaching and creating cultural content for a particular fandom community.

As Jenkins writes, filking provides "a spontaneous and ongoing process of popular creation, one which builds upon community traditions but which is continually open to individual contribution and innovation" ("Filking" 221). So fan filks on YouTube may be campy, parodic, satirical, or homage — sometimes a blend of all of the above. Particularly with the *Star Wars* YouTubes, the filks depend upon *trucage* to innovate and to create a larger cultural logic within the fan community.

## I Almost Forgot.... They Did Throw in the Kitchen TV!

Of course, YouTube provides everything and the kitchen TV when it comes to fan videos. I would be remiss in not discussing a classic fan-generated YouTube that incorporates filking, *trucage*, a little camp, plus some parody and satire to produce one of the great homage videos to TV science fiction: Stanz510's *Battlestar Galactica vs. Star Wars vs. Star Trek vs. Babylon 5*. A mash-up of battle scenes from each of these programs set to a *Star Wars* soundtrack, the video ends with everyone heading back to Earth in an impressive display. Hyperdiegesis aside, at the end of the day, so it seems, all good space explorers and their fans simply want to return home.

## YouTube as Ludic Democracy and the Implications for Teaching Writing

Ludic democracy, with its strong sense of play, offers us different types of citizenship and knowledge to discover. Studying fan-generated YouTube videos helps us learn more about how various communities are formed or organized and the types of knowledge these groups value. Examining a body of fandom videos exposes scholars and students to the ways individuals create a sense of identification along short, medium, and long-term goals or ideas. For teaching rhetoric and writing, such opportunities allow us to explore multiple cultural logics and uses for language, which can only benefit those who live in a multi-media, multi-sensory era.

Whether ludic democracy is, as Virilio suggested, a virtual democracy designed for "infantilized tele-citizens" (31) is unclear. Certainly more people each day sign on to YouTube and contribute short films for others to enjoy. And there are always moments of pleasure — participatory pleasure — within any genuine democracy. But does an outlet like YouTube keep citizens from maturing, keep individuals from focusing solely on a field of play or the endless search for pleasure rather than musing on critical issues of the day? On that point I am not so sanguine. It may be that YouTube videos enhance our ability to become informed tele-citizens, particularly if compositionists use rhetorical strategies to help students deconstruct filks to learn more about the world around them.

As I tried to explain using three major fan sites on YouTube, there are rhetorical strategies and techniques at work that not only provide participatory pleasure, they also demonstrate larger social issues at play in society. Students who learn how to incorporate these newer rhetorical principles into their thinking processes reduce the chances of becoming or remaining one of Virilio's infantilized tele-citizens. Fandom's participatory pleasure need not be looked at as trivial or as mindless pursuits. There is knowledge and meaning made through play on YouTube, as those spaces proffer opportunities for agency, action, and interaction. One does not have to merely engage in an acceptance of or acceptable read of the filks. The implications for writing, then, become clear: If play allows us to interpret and make meaning from our daily recreational experience, then YouTube makes available the prospect of writing about fandom videos an occasion for constructing and negotiating a range of civic ideas.

Even for those who feel it necessary to imbue their writing instruction with some gravitas, let me suggest that fandom YouTubes can provide an academic seriousness that parallel anything found in a traditional composition textbook. Rhetorically, we can examine these filks as representing various types of power relationships (in terms of viewer rankings and commentaries), the sorts of identities constructed through fandom, the exclusions of some storyline ideas or concepts in favor of others, and the host of opposing ethical principles present in the videos and in the making of the videos. Certainly by estranging the familiar worlds of fan culture via YouTube videos, instructors can discuss the finer points of rhetoric and visual rhetorical strategies in ways that students can grasp.

Because an exploration of fandom is also often an ethnographic (or autoethnographic) process, writing instruction takes on a decidedly qualitative, social science approach. Students must become participants in their own research and examine their own fan behaviors in light of what they discover on YouTube. While autoethnography may be controversial for some, there is little doubt that genuine autoethnography provides insight into issues that are frequently overlooked in society. Even if a more structured research methodology, such as oral history, is proposed, students discover intangible cultural heritages about contemporary items that engender mutual respect across communities and individuals. Such approaches help students become more literate about the world-at-large.

I have argued elsewhere that pleasure and play should not be excluded from the writing process, particularly when the topics center on popular culture. Scholars and students alike are fans of specific types of popular culture; however, what differentiates the two groups in their fandom is that scholars need to be able to address the arbitrary nature of what makes a text "popular" and what sustains the text(s) popularity. So much of fandom and popular culture are bound by cultural taste—both our own and the larger social domain. Discussing which popular topics give us pleasure opens opportunities for studying what makes people happy or provides them with gratification. Therefore, damn those who condemn ludic democracy as being "less than" other forms of participatory culture—fire up the starboard engines, set phasers on "stun," and get the frak on YouTube to find what fan filks have value for the classroom.

## WORKS CITED

deCerteau, Michel. *The Practice of Everyday Life*. Berkeley: University of California Press, 1984.
Hills, Matt. *Fan Cultures*. New York: Routledge, 2002.
Jenkins, Henry. *Fans, Bloggers, and Gamers*. New York: New York University Press, 2006.
_____. "'Strangers No More, We Sing': Filking and the Social Construction of the Science Fiction Community." *The Adoring Audience: Fan Culture and Popular Media*. Ed. Lisa A. Lewis. New York: Routledge, 1992. 208–36.
_____. *Textual Poachers: Television, Fans & Participatory Culture*. New York: Routledge, 1992.
Lewis, Lisa A. *The Adoring Audience: Fan Culture and Popular Media*. New York: Routledge, 1992.
Metz, Christian. "Trucage and the Film." Trans. Françoise Meltzer. *Critical Enquiry* 3 (1977): 657–75.
Penrod, Diane. *Miss Grundy Doesn't Teach Here Anymore: Popular Culture in the Composition Classroom*. Portsmouth, NH: Heinemann/Boynton-Cook, 1997.
_____. "The Trouble with Harry: A Reason for Teaching Media Literacy to Young Adults." *The Writing Instructor* (Dec. 2001). Jul. 2008 <http://www.writinginstructor.com/penrod.html>.
Sandvoss, Cornel. *Fans*. Cambridge, UK: Polity Press, 2005.
Virilio, Paul. *Ground Zero*. New York: Verso, 2002.

# 15

# World of Rhetcraft: Rhetorical Production and Raiding in *World of Warcraft*

*Christopher Paul*

Massively multiplayer online games (MMOGs), like *World of Warcraft* (*WoW*), are distinct from other videogames due to a number of design elements that promote social interaction and rhetorical production. MMOGs are typically played in persistent, dynamic worlds that are regularly updated and shaped by the actions of both the company designing the game and the players within the game. An extension of the early multi-user dungeons (MUDs), game designers and scholars have addressed both the many different players who inhabit these games and their motivations for playing them (see Bartle; Yee; Williams et al.). What is often left unmentioned, however, is the wealth of rhetorical activity that occurs within and surrounds MMOGs, including one of the richest inspirations for extra-game texts: the dynamics of "raiding" in *WoW*.

Raiding, one of the many *WoW* activities for players to engage in, generally consists of gathering substantial numbers of people, from ten to forty or more, and battling computer-controlled enemies in large-scale, carefully managed combat. Relative skills and success in managing large groups frequently determines the success of raids, as groups who communicate well are more likely to be victorious. Raids generally last for multiple hours, with the most active players raiding for forty or more hours a week and more casual players raiding closer to ten hours a week; previous research has indicated that a third of *WoW* players participate in at least some raiding activities (Duchenault et al. 310; Williams et al. 345). Among the many fascinating things about raiding as a gaming practice is the immense rhetorical activity of the raiders, especially the amount of rhetorical production developed outside of the game; raiders are constantly writing and developing texts to better master the "game" they chose to play.

I have played *WoW* since its launch and, over the past two years, I have raided with a guild that ranks among the top ten percent in the world.[1] I am immersed in the constant rhetorical renegotiation of the canon of player-created texts surrounding *WoW*, and in order to convey the intricate connection between raiders and the processes of reading and writing, a discussion is needed of the typical dynamics of MMOGs, as well as an overview of how raiding developed and plays out in practice and examples of the kinds of texts *WoW* raiders have produced. Instead of pushing people away from practices of reading and writing, raiding virtually requires players to debate and master dozens of sets of complicated instructions adapted for their particular groups. Thus the role of rhetoric, particularly the production and consumption of various texts, in raiding makes literacy a fundamental component of being a "good" raider, just as essential as mastery of one's in-game skills or access to a stable internet connection.[2]

## *MMOGs and Raiding*

The nature of game worlds like *WoW* distinguish MMOGs from many other kinds of games in two key ways: it is frequently updated and persistent. Regular updates mean that both the rules of the game and its content can be changed or altered by game designers after its release. New areas can be added to the game, new monsters can be patched in and battled, and rules of the game can be changed midstream. As a result, the instructions for these games must be substantively different from those for the early arcade game, *Pong*, which sufficed with "avoid missing ball for high score." The dynamism of the game world means that any attempt to summarize rules or expectations in a permanent, lasting form is deficient the moment the game changes. Unlike sophisticated console and PC games that may come with lengthy instruction manuals, a typical MMOG instruction manual may be short in comparison, as the printed words found there are likely already out of date. At least partially driven by the dynamic changes of game worlds, MMOG players, especially raiders, often generate their own instructions and compendiums of information online, on websites that can be regularly updated to respond to changes in the game. The malleability of the contexts of online worlds often results in player-created online guides that are far superior to the instructions provided by an MMOG's publisher.

The second way in which the game world of MMOGs is different than other videogames is that these worlds do not stop when players leave them;

the world continues on with whoever remains, even if all players are logged off. Games like *WoW* feature these persistent worlds, where the action only stops when the game's servers are offline. When persistence is combined with features that encourage working together, players must juggle real world events and activities to meet others online. As a result, to play together MMOG players must not only coordinate schedules, as one might for a bowling league or a *Quake* team, but are also subject to the events that unfold in the game world when they are offline. In many online games, this dynamic requires players to negotiate access to scarce resources, compete for accomplishments in real-time, and ultimately, persistence forces interaction with other players.

Within these two key distinguishing features of MMOGs, raiding can be seen as an activity that grew out of the combination of a dynamic game that could be changed and as an adaptation to the persistence of the online world. The raiding that occurs within *WoW* can be most clearly traced to a set of emergent behaviors in the MMOG *Everquest*. Raiding was not designed as an initial feature of *Everquest*, but it emerged as a practice from within the player base and designers, leveraging the dynamic nature of MMOGs, added tools to support raiding within *Everquest* as the game developed and it eventually became "a central component of the game" (Taylor *Play* 41). Raiding is now considered a key design element of many large-scale MMOGs, as the players who raid tend to be quite invested in their game of choice because of the time required to build relationships with others, which often means they are less likely to cancel their subscription than other players. Raiding is viewed by many as the top of the MMOG food chain, as those who raid are also likely to have some of the best equipment and most elegantly designed gear.

Raiding is best defined as a particular set of practices within MMOGs that requires the coordination of dozens of people's real world schedules to attempt, and ideally win, massive online battles. For those who do not raid, however, the practices of raiders seem almost alien as T.L. Taylor describes when she relates a discussion with a pair of raiders in which, for the first time, she "felt out of my element in an *Everquest* conversation. Despite some paltry attempts at joining in, I was essentially unable to relate to their experience of the game" (*Play* 68). Raiders are constantly developing linguistic practices that are just as foreign to non-raiding players as the language of the average MMOG player would be to someone who has never played the game. Raiders frequently play more often, in more structured time blocks, than the normal MMOG player, which results in fundamentally different gaming experiences.

The drive to raid is largely derived from two key game design elements. First, those who raid are able to experience parts of the game that others can only see secondhand through online videos. Furthermore, raiders receive rewards from their successful battles that demarcate their victories to everyone they meet in the game world. If Julian Dibbell is correct in his assertion that a primary drive in online games is "to own and not be owned," raiders are often in a position to "own" all challengers (7). Rewards from raiding vary from strictly cosmetic items that can only be attained via raiding, like a special bear to ride, to powerful equipment that makes many other aspects of the game easier while also making in-game avatars quite impressive to behold. As a result of these factors, successful raiders stand out from others and I personally have frequently received out of the blue remarks from other players to express their appreciation, awe, or envy about what my character was wearing. However, raiding comes at a substantial cost. Successful raiding requires many hours a week of game play and often the acceptance of a general sublimation of self within the game, as members of a raiding guild[3] are generally expected to "help out the guild and its members whenever possible" (Taylor *Play* 48). Raiders can skip sleep, defer time with family and friends, call in sick for work, and often schedule their real world lives to facilitate their raiding.[4] Because the game world will persist without a player, the compulsion for raiders to log on and help their guild can range from a substantial personal desire to a condition of their membership in a particular raiding guild. To this end, in the competition for a recent first in the world accomplishment within *WoW*, members of a leading guild took multiple days of vacation time to aid their effort to be the first to slay the demon Kil'Jaeden (Csulok).

There are many elements of raiding, from showing up at a specified time to carrying out sophisticated and complicated instructions with a couple dozen other people, but one of the key pieces to successfully raiding is reading and producing rhetorical texts that analyze and address specific elements of the game. Although a primary element of raiding is pressing the right buttons at the right times to make online avatars perform desired tasks at key moments, in the long run, this is only a small part of raiding. In addition to "playing the game," coordinating up to thirty-nine other people requires careful and exacting rhetorical production to ensure that a group works together. Much like any other group activity, raiding depends on developing instructions and planning for dynamic events. In-game rhetorical production is only a small part of raiding, however, as raiders frequently turn to out-of-game rhetorical artifacts to more fully discuss events that are or will be occurring in-game.

A number of out-of-game texts illustrate the fundamental connection between rhetorical activity and raiding. To beat the difficult encounters found in raiding, players have created extensive community forums to supplement what is offered by Blizzard, the game studio that develops *WoW*. Other sites publish tactical guides and instructional videos are uploaded to YouTube and other video hosting services. Individual raiding guilds typically have guild forums to coordinate adaptation of strategies for their group and to discuss recent raids. All these are composed about the game from outside the game, indicating that raiding "play" in *World of Warcraft* is far more complicated than simply logging on to a game; it is also a collection of rhetorical processes. Raiders, with little incentive other than recognition, are reading and writing lengthy texts about what they are doing in the game and about the decisions made by game designers. In these texts, it is easy to see how rhetorical activity is *required* to raid successfully.

## *Rhetorics of* WoW

The relationship between rhetoric and raiding is likely clearest in the out of game texts. These public web sites offer those who do not play *WoW* a glimpse of the mountains of rhetorical texts that aid raiders in successfully completing some of *WoW*'s most difficult tasks. Three primary resources will be discussed in this chapter, although there are many other online resources that further establish the rhetorical production and consumption of raiders in *WoW*. Bosskillers (www.bosskillers.com) is primarily a strategy resource that offers links to multiple guides on how different battles work, with accompanying strategies that guilds can employ in their raids. A *WoW* guild, Elitist Jerks, runs a public section of their forums that addresses *WoW*-related topics in general (http://elitistjerks.com/forums.php), but many of the users reading and posting on the forums actively raid in *WoW*, which makes their forums an excellent example of the rhetorics of raiding. Finally, World of Raids (http://www.worldofraids.com/) is a growing online resource that is starting to compile elements of the first two texts along with a variety of other information that keeps raiders up to date on changes made to *WoW*.

Bosskillers offers non-raiders an informative glimpse of the kinds of rhetorical texts intimately tied to raiding in games like *WoW*. Because raiding in *WoW* is comprised of a series of battles, or encounters, against computer-controlled enemies that act in predictable, definable ways, players frequently compose strategy guides that outline the special abilities or dynamics of a particular fight and suggest a plan of attack or recommended strategy (frequently shortened to "strat") for how to defeat a given enemy or "boss." Bosskillers is a compendium of these strategies, as the site offers small cash awards to solicit guides to certain encounters and offers raiders a central site to find at least one way in which a battle can be won. Bosskillers is a good starting point for a discussion of the role rhetoric plays within raiding, as it demonstrates rhetorical production and consumption in a straightforward manner that offers a clear locus from which to view a rhetoric of raiding for those unfamiliar with *WoW*.

Raiding encounters are generally organized by game designers in some form of progressive manner, from relatively easy to more complicated, difficult fights. The rewards for defeating enemies generally scale accordingly, with the introductory fights offering both the game-playing lessons and equipment to defeat future bosses. One of the introductory encounters in the recent expansion of *WoW* takes place in the citadel Karazhan against Attumen the Huntsman and his horse Midnight. This is a simple fight that only involves ten players and introduces players to what a raid can be like. There are two parts, or phases, to the fight and the Bosskillers guide fully explains its dynamics in 758 words and one diagram (Airfoam). This encounter is straightforward enough that players may not need the guide, as many players could simply show up and win the battle through trial and error.

While the Attumen guide offers a perspective on arguably the simplest end of raiding in *WoW*, the guide for Kael'thas Sunstrider, the final boss in the floating fortress Tempest Keep, demonstrates how raiding in *WoW* hinges on rhetorical engagement. The Kael'thas fight is comprised of five phases, each of which presents distinct challenges for the twenty-five people fighting the boss. In addition to fighting Kael'thas, the group must vanquish his team of four advisors and several legendary weapons, which must then be equipped and used in specific ways in the subsequent battle with Kael'thas himself. Groups that simply show up and expect to learn by trial and error are likely in for a long process of learning, which can be substantially shortened by looking outside of *WoW* for guides and discussion about how to defeat Kael'thas. In this case, the Bosskillers guide is 6,244 words long and incorporates five different diagrams to depict various phases of the fight (mko818). Simply learning how to defeat Kael'thas's four advisors is a task more daunting than vanquishing Attumen and it necessitates moving beyond mere button pushing to rhetorical engagement with texts like Bosskillers guides to make one's button pushing more successful. Even if a guild chooses not to consult prewritten guides, they must develop and test their own approach, a task that requires just as much application of argumentation and debate as it does traditional conceptions of game-playing. With more than a dozen fights that are closer to Kael'thas in complexity than to Attumen, Bosskillers introduces some of the connections between raiding and rhetoric, as good raiders must both play the game well and actively participate in the consumption of texts about the game.

The Elitist Jerks forums (http://elitistjerks.com/forums.php) take the strategies presented on sites like Bosskillers and make them dynamic, by taking advantage of the discussion framework enabled by Web-based forums. Bosskillers works well as a starting point both for discussing the rhetorical implications of raiding, and also for raiders, but the one-size-fits-all strategies presented there frequently need to be adapted or changed based on the composition of various groups or the relative strengths and weaknesses of particular guilds. Much like the one-size-fits-all approach does not work for those who do not fit within the expected norms of a piece of clothing, the same can be true for a raiding guild, should the group have an atypical distribution of players or if there is a large variance in the relative abilities of some of the group members. Forums, like the Elitist Jerks' discussion boards, offer the opportunity to engage in a dialogue about how specific dynamics of an encounter work or how a group can best adapt a strategy to suit their abilities.

Similar to the Bosskillers' guide for each encounter, Elitist Jerks offer a thread for most bosses and several for general discussion about other elements of the game, although they do not usually have discussions about the "easier" bosses in the game. The threads are generally started shortly after the most advanced guilds in the world begin attempting the encounter, but last for a substantial period of time as new groups progress to the point where they can engage the boss. The typical arc of the discussion moves from outlining the overarching structure of the fight to discussing particular elements of the fight and how they can be dealt with by various groups to an eventually emergent dialogue among players, with those yet to defeat the encounter asking questions about how to address a particular issue and more experienced players offering potential answers. Frequently, those who ask questions return later to post of their success and detail how they were finally triumphant, by extension offering a victorious case study for those who are still striving for victory.

The interactive dialogue that typifies the rhetorical dimension of Elitist Jerks is demonstrated in both their Kael'thas thread, which spans sixty-eight pages and almost a year of posting as of this writing, and in their Illidan Stormrage thread, which is thirty-one pages long and was begun in August 2007 (tr33hugger). What makes these discussions different than many others is that they are heavily moderated and the expectation of quality discussion is high. The guild that hosts the forums is rated as one of the top-twenty raiding guilds in the world (see http://wowjutsu.com/world/) and they actively monitor and police discussions to ensure productive dialogue. In the introductory thread, the lead moderator warns that constructive discussion is expected on their forums and that, instead of merely asking questions, "The best way to learn is to do your own research — search and read. And read. And read. Yes, we know that some of the threads are daunting, but that's a sign that it contains LOTS of information and that there's a VERY good chance your question has been answered already" (Kaubel). By removing posts that violate this fundamental rule and banning those that detract from the quality of discussion, Elitist Jerks offer a substantial resource to those who play *WoW*. However, utilizing that resource demands that users are able to engage in constructive discussion and, should their rhetorical abilities not match their skills in *WoW*, they are quickly removed from the group that can actively participate on the Elitist Jerks boards.[5]

A final place to see the rhetorical activity that goes into raiding in *WoW* is World of Raids (http://www.worldofraids.com/). In many ways, World of Raids seeks to combine the attributes of Bosskillers and Elitist Jerks into a single site, while adding some original material to make it an even more valuable resource. World of Raids has a discussion board, although the level of discussion rarely matches that of Elitist Jerks. Guides to various boss fights are also being integrated into the site, although it is not nearly as complete as the material available on Bosskillers. What World of Raids does offer to raiders is consistently updated news about the game and events tied to *WoW*. For players raiding in *WoW*, staying on top of developments in the game is instructive as it alerts them to changes in the consistently updated structure of the game and information about the social events in the game as well. World of Raids culls information from Blizzard employee's postings on various internet sites (Teza, "Kil'jaeden") and offers things like transcripts of recent Blizzard podcasts as they relate to *WoW* (Teza, "Blizzcast"). The site also posts information on the latest news about developments in the raiding scene of *WoW*, like first-time boss kills or information about one of the top guilds in the game disbanding (Teza, "EU"). All of this information adds context and depth to the rhetorical scene of *WoW*. The news situates changes and developments in the game and constructs a backdrop within which raiding occurs. World of Raids helps raiders manage the massive amounts of information that is produced in a persistent game being played by almost eleven million people around the world. Instead of having to seek out information from a variety of sources, World of Raids compiles the information and players only have to make a single stop to stay on top of recent *WoW*-related news. Should their guides and forums develop to the degree that Bosskillers and Elitist Jerks have, perhaps World of Raids will have an even bigger role in the World of Rhetcraft.

## *Implications of Rhetcraft*

Online games are just one more of the many ways in which social interaction is becoming increasingly digitally mediated. MMOGs stand as excellent examples of the dependence of such games on rhetorical production and consumption. No longer simply limited to what "comes out of the box," these games are regularly updated, persistent worlds inhabited by millions of people who are encouraged to interact with each other. Raiding is one way in which players have chosen to play MMOGs and raiding, as a practice, is fundamentally rooted in reading and writing.

Bosskillers, Elitist Jerks, and World of Raids all demonstrate pieces of what it takes to raid in *WoW*. However, these three sites only demonstrate parts of the writing produced about raiding. In addition to this kind of material, which is freely available online and easy for those who do not raid to see, there are private discussion boards that are typical of every raiding guild in the game, voluminous in-game communication that often occurs in text-based chat and voice-based discussion, and instructional videos that are widely available on video-sharing sites like YouTube. All of these pieces are examples of how the discourse of gaming is changed and shaped by emergent practices like raiding. Raiders are doing more than simply "playing" a game; they are engaged in a constant process of rewriting and rearticulating what it means to be a member of a digital generation.

## NOTES

1. I play as the human mage Alruna, a member of the Brave Companions, on the Draka server of *WoW*. Our current level of progression and world ranking can be found at http://www.wowjutsu.com.

2. For a discussion of the role of language fluency within *WoW* and as a part of the application process for guilds, see T.L. Taylor's "Does *WoW* Change Everything?"

3. Guilds are a primary social organizing structure standard in most MMOGs that typically gives members a common chat channel and a collective group of people with whom to work. For a deeper discussion of guilds, see Williams et al.

4. For a sometimes humorous, sometimes scary account of raiders offline sacrifices to make raids see: http://elitistjerks.com/f33/t14808-what_lengths_have_you_gone_make_raid/.

5. The one area in which the malleability of the rules is often displayed is in the proper use of English. As the boards are a worldwide resource, many members of the community do not speak English as their primary language. Although these boards are exclusively in English, those that make a good faith effort to speak English are not sanctioned, while those who refuse to rely on internet shorthand (u for you, PLZ for please, etc.) find their posting privileges revoked.

## WORKS CITED

Airfoam. "Attumen the Huntsman & Midnight Strategy Guide." *Bosskillers*. 23 Feb. 2007. 22 June 2008 <http://www.bosskillers.com/cgi-bin/bbguild/index.cgi?action=view_guide&guide_id=23>.

Bartle, Richard. "Hearts, Clubs, Diamonds, Spades: Players Who Suit MUDS." *Mud.co.uk*. 22 June 2008 <http://www.mud.co.uk/richard/hcds.htm>.

*Bosskillers*. 22 June 2008 <http://www.bosskillers.com>.

Csulok. "SK-Gaming Interview." *World of Raids*. 25 May 2008. 22 June 2008 <http://www.worldofraids.com/news/109.html>.

Dibell, Julian. *Play Money: Or, How I Quit My Day Job and Made Millions Trading Virtual Loot*. New York: Basic Books, 2006.

Duchenault, Nicolas, et al. "Building an MMO With Mass Appeal: A Look at Gameplay in *World of Warcraft*." *Games and Culture* 1.4 (2006): 281–317.

*Elitist Jerks*. 22 June 2008 <http://elitistjerks.com/forums.php>.

Kaubel. "READ AND COMPREHEND THESE BEFORE POSTING." *Elitist Jerks*. 31 Dec. 2006. 22 June 2008 <http://elitistjerks.com/f15/announcements.html>.

Kytarewn, et al. "What lengths have you gone to to make a raid?" *Elitist Jerks*. 13 Nov. 2007. 22 June 2008 <http://elitistjerks.com/f15/t14808-what_lengths_have_you_gone_make_raid/>.

LiteSabre, et al. "Kael'thas." *Elitist Jerks*. 18 June 2008. 22 June 2008 <http://elitistjerks.com/f15/t12839-kael_thas/>.

mko818. "Kael'thas Sunstrider Strategy Guide." *Bosskillers*. 30 May 2007. 22 June 2008 <http://www.bosskillers.com/cgi-bin/bbguild/index.cgi?action=view_guide&guide_id=86>.

Taylor, T.L. "Does WoW Change Everything? How a PvP Server, Multinational Player Base, and Surveillance Mod Scene Caused Me Panic." *Games and Culture* 1.4 (2006): 318–337.

_____. *Play Between Worlds: Exploring Online Game Culture*. Cambridge, Massachusetts: MIT Press, 2006.

Teza. "Blizzcast Episode 3 Now Available." *World of Raids*. 5 June 2008. 22 June 2008 <http://www.worldofraids.com/news/129.html>.

_____. "EU Guild Forte Disbands." *World of Raids*. 7 June 2008. 22 June 2008 <http://www.worldofraids.com/news/130.html>.

_____. "Kil'jaeden Hotfixed, WWI tickets, Daily Blue." *World of Raids*. 29 May 2008. 22 June 2008 <http://www.worldofraids.com/news/115.html>.

tr33hugger, et al. "The Illidan Thread (Was 'Flames of Azzinoth Question')." *Elitist Jerks*. 17 June 2008. 22 June 2008 <http://elitistjerks.com/f15/t15397-illidan_thread_flames_azzinoth_question/>.

Williams, Dmitri, et al. "From Tree House to Barracks: The Social Life of Guilds in *World of Warcraft*." *Games and Culture* 1.4 (2006): 338–361.

*World of Raids*. 22 June 2008 <http://www.worldofraids.com/>.

*WoWJutsu: World of Warcraft Guild Rankings*. 22 June 2008 <http://wowjutsu.com/world/>.

Yee, N. "The Demographics, Motivations and Derived Experiences of Massively Multi-User Online Graphical Environments." *PRESENCE: Teleoperators and Virtual Environments*. 15 (2006): 309–329.

# 16

# Rekindling Rhetoric: Oratory and Marketplace Culture in *Guild Wars*

*Matthew S. S. Johnson*

As has been well established by Jürgen Habermas (and other cultural theorists and historians), the marketplace, as traditionally conceived, has been a public space for much more than just commodity exchange. It has been a place for argumentation, political and religious oratory, entertainment, and overt displays of status or power. The exchange of goods, however, is often a prerequisite to these other marketplace activities: although I risk oversimplification, we can nevertheless understand that buying or selling material wares implies that one has some means (otherwise, such exchange is impossible, if one has nothing to trade), and the possession of material goods indicates at least some degree of leisure (otherwise, one's time is spent solely on survival). Means and leisure are in part what enables the *possibility* of political protest or the civic engagement characteristic of the traditional marketplace: means also show credibility; leisure clearly indicates that the agent has the time necessary to engage in public discourse; and means and leisure are prerequisites for the education necessary to develop the ability to engage others rhetorically, to persuade them of the plausibility, the credibility, the justice of some plan or principle. The marketplace as space that brings together those with goods to exchange and therefore the potential for rhetorical engagement eventually leads to coffee houses, salons, and other social gathering places for discussion, in addition to artistic displays, musical performances, and so forth.

The archetypal example of an environment that provided space for all of these activities is the marketplace of ancient Greece. In *The Structural Transformation of the Public Sphere*, Habermas discusses these central marketplaces, explaining that in the fully developed Greek city-state the sphere of the *polis*, which was common (*koine*) to the free citizens, was strictly separated from the sphere of the *oikos*; in the sphere of the *oikos*, each individual is in his own realm (*idia*). The public life, *bios politicos*, went on in the market place (*agora*), but of course this did not mean that it occurred necessarily only in this specific locale. The public sphere was constituted in discussion (*lexis*), which could also assume the forms of consultation and of sitting in the court of law, as well as in common action (*praxis*), be it the waging of war or competition in athletic games [3].

Habermas is succinctly describing here the centrality of the Greek city-state's public sphere, while offering a brief nod to the private sphere, the household or *oikos*, which, it certainly can be argued, served an equally important role in shaping public discourse, given that the individuals who participated in the marketplace's public activities were so heavily influenced by home life. The sort of public spaces of the ancient civilizations that Habermas describes—the *agora* of Greece or the *Forum Magnum* of Rome—and the breadth of activities that took place within them seem to have fallen out of favor somewhere (or somewhen) along the line. Certainly the marketplace for the selling of wares still exists: local farmers' markets, city squares dedicated on weekends to the selling of local produce or local arts and crafts (and a great many of us living in campus towns perhaps experience these events, these spaces, more often than the average American). There are even once-a-year marketplace events that share characteristics with the *agora* or *forum*: each June, for instance, Chicago's Dearborn Avenue, from Congress Parkway to Polk Street, is converted to the Printers Row Book Fair, where booksellers from the Midwest—and some fairly distantly beyond—gather to hawk their wares while authors deliver talks or give readings. Yet the authors generally speak in auditoriums in surrounding buildings, in closed rooms that require tickets available for purchase, often in advance. Thus, their oratory is usually delivered in comparatively private venues, a practice which establishes no new trend, for even by the Renaissance, "the baroque festival had already lost its public character" and "joust, dance and theater retreated from the public places into the enclosures of the park, from the streets into the rooms of the palace" (Habermas 9–10). As a result, these spaces are no longer places for public oration; even more so, they are no longer arenas for administering justice, recruiting apprentices, or bestowing honors to worthy citizens, as in the *agora* or *forum*. We have other arenas for these activities. We no longer see mongering, orating, recruiting, and entertaining happening simultaneously in the same public space. While there may be sound reasons that these public forums, with their varied activities, seem to be relegated to rhetorical history, along with politicians writing their own speeches or philosophers-academics-rhetors actually *orating* instead of *reading* (just attend any academic conference to see what I mean), now, however, the ancient marketplaces are experiencing resurgence.

The comparatively new electronic environments of massively multiplayer online games (MMOGs) (and more often than not fantasy-based role-playing games such as *Everquest, Ultima Online, World of Warcraft,* and *Guild Wars,* among others) heralds a rebirth of a rhetorical space largely lost in contemporary culture: the marketplace. Many MMOGs have what we might call "semi-virtual" marketplaces, spaces in which behaviors and actions identifiable to a particular environment "actually" take place, initiated by agents ("actual" people, as opposed to, say a computer program or mechanistic device), yet the environment itself is "merely" representative (often digital) rather than "authentic."[1] In these semi-virtual marketplaces, much more than the buying and selling of goods takes place; rather, commodity exchange serves merely as the common activity, the background noise behind significant rhetorical action. Ultimately, I argue that the parallel between Habermas's marketplaces and semi-virtual marketplaces is important precisely because they potentially could have the same general effect: If the ancient marketplace has "offspring" in the form of modern coffee houses and salons, and contemporary online discussion forums, all of which have the potential to effect real and far-reaching change, then MMOGs are strong candidates for serving as similar "training grounds" that have the potential to produce vigorous discourse.

## Economic Exchange the Guild Wars Marketplace

Edward Castronova who studies MMOGs (and whose PhD is in economics) realized while playing *Everquest* that "economic transactions between players were an incredibly important part of what was happening. Within the game, in the cities, people were constantly shouting offers to buy and sell goods and services" (15). The marketplaces in *Guild Wars* operate with similar energy, where "WTS [want to sell] naga pelts" and "WTB [want to buy] bolts of silk" are common enough cries.[2] It is clear why game economies would interest economists so thoroughly: even a cursory glance at the economy of *Guild Wars* reveals amazing complexity: It largely functions by a supply and demand system, where inflation is a problem and investments can be risky. "Gold sinks"— the "term applied to a game mechanic that removes currency from the in game economy and thus counteracts the effect of inflation" ("Official")— are necessary; some gold sinks take the form of crafters and merchants who require fees for dealing with goods, in addition to buying and selling them. According to the "Official *Guild Wars* Wiki," "Without the presence of gold sinks in the game, inflation would spiral out of control rendering it close to impossible for any new or casual player to trade with other players based on the money they obtain by playing" ("Official"). Commodity exchange may be the primary draw for participants in this arena, yet the marketplace's economic trade is frequently partner to an equally important motivator: discursive exchanges on which rhetorical affectivity can often be based.

What of politics, public action, the development of citizenry, and discussion? *Guild Wars*, in part to encourage these latter marketplace attributes, is programmed to specifically target trade-related discourse in order to preserve space for other discussion: "Using WTS or WTB in the local channel will automatically switch you to the trade channel. It is generally considered annoying to advertise wares in the local channel" ("Official"). Gamers' desire for a separate communications conduit for trading, in a space designed specifically for trading, is by itself evidence that something else is going on. And while there is ample trading, bartering, and hawking of wares, as these are necessary gameplay activities, what is more interesting is that *discussion* of trade simultaneously takes place in the same venue (even if on a different "channel"). The *Guild Wars* marketplace, as an arena for public discourse, enables commentary on and analysis of the very activity to which it seems to be primarily dedicated (in terms of gameplay), but in actuality functions as so much more. I overheard (read) one conversation in Kaineng center:

> "I'll give you up to 5K for two white [dyes]."
> "I'm investing my fortune into black dye."
> "I only have 6 blacks."
> "I'd rather invest my gold in something more stable — ecto used to be 15K."
> "How do you look it up? Is it online?"

White and black dyes are particularly valuable commodities in *Guild Wars*, not only because of their ability to color armor — clearly black is important to real *and* virtual fashion industries, making a statement in real and virtual cultures — but, like purchasing gold in the material world, are comparatively safe investments. These particular colors are rare enough that players convert excess gold — there are limits to how much currency a character can carry or store — into bottles of dye and other "material" goods. (The globs of ectoplasm to which one conversant refers is another highly-valued commodity because of its rarity.) The point here, though, is that players are *analyzing* their investment strategies and *sharing* information in order to invest wisely; in addition, the final comment brings attention to the websites — which function outside of the purview of the game itself— that are devoted to such discussion, reminding us of Habermas's other "specific locales" that also constitute segments of the larger public sphere, parts that are devoted to "discussion" and "consultation" (Habermas 3).

This brief passage of dialogue indicates the general camaraderie of gamers (the same gamers who are likely to also compete against each other), where one will freely offer advice to another; but not all trade is so benevolent, nor interactions so helpful. As in "real" marketplaces, *Guild Wars*'s suffers from less savory dealings. While the interface for trade between two players enables the ability to review trades before they are conducted and notifications are made when a particular deal has been altered by those involved in the exchange, nevertheless some players try to take advantage: quickly switching "100 platinum" to "10 platinum," claiming that the item for trade is in a bag (bags, used to increase the total number of objects a character can carry, can only be traded when empty), switching objects that appear similarly (the icon for rubies resembles that of lilac eyes, for instance), or simply claiming that a programming bug or Internet glitch occurred are all common enough scams. There is much advice offered on numerous *Guild Wars* websites on how to avoid being swindled, especially useful for players new to the game. The official wiki advises that gamers "look out for the signs" that are common to scammers, "ask on a public channel" if uncertain if a deal is genuine, and "if you catch a scammer in the act, be sure to let everyone around you know what he's up to and report it" ("Official"). All of the advice offered is specifically rhetorical in nature. Interpret and know the signs of the speaker (for instance, whether a deal seems "too good to be true"). Involve the public — everyone in the marketplace can see an announcement made in the public channel, which all can read. In fact, this involvement of the public will often bring swift and serious judgment on a player (the public, in-person delivery of justice in the marketplace was not uncommon in ancient Greece or Rome).

## The Performance of Status

The administering of justice in the marketplace complements other political activities — and those *not* related to trade — that once took place in the *agora* or *forum*. One inescapable element of the marketplace was the performance of class, of status. As Habermas explains, "The staging of publicity involved in representation was wedded to personal attributes such as insignia (badges and arms), dress (clothing and coiffure), demeanor (form of greeting and poise) and rhetoric (form of address and formal discourse in general)" (8). *Guild Wars*, as the name implies, involves guilds that are vying for dominance — not in terms of land, or even resources, *per se*, but rather *status*. Forming a guild requires minimal means — a mere 100 gold registration fee will do it. But then each member invitation also costs 100 gold. A guild cape will cost two platinum. A Guild Hall requires the purchase of a sigil or a win at the Hall of Heroes. And to fully staff a guild hall? That will be another 510 platinum, among other fees. Substantial funds are necessary to form and maintain a successful, significant (powerful, influential) guild. Once they procure membership, individual players want to display their guild associations, donning their capes to exhibit their ties, where the capes serve not only as guild markers, but also conspicuous individual status symbols.

Playing *Guild Wars Factions* on 23 February 2008, in the outpost titled "The Marketplace" (suitably enough for this essay), the guilds' recruiting agents were particularly lively:

> "Recruiting active loyal people."
> "Recruiting mature, loyal members — join our friendly guild today!"
> "Can I join a Luxon guild that is active?"
> "Recruiting new players! 13 guilds, Kurz and Lux, 1100+ members."[3]

"Active" and "loyal" are the operative terms here, indicating which guild characteristics are desirable when an individual is considering an offer to join a guild; what, after all, is the value of a non-participating member beyond a mere statistic? *Active participation* is what makes a member valuable. In addition, the number of players *already* members is a selling point for candidates, as is the guild's maintenance of a website apart from the game, for information exchanging, strategy planning, and socializing. Guilds with external websites continue their discursive activities beyond the border of the game itself, spilling into widely accessible electronic social environments.

Within guilds and, for that matter, for *Guild Wars'* equivalent of ronin, *individual* status displays are also important. A clear way to show status is by the quality and type of armor, because better armor becomes more readily available as a character advances in the game. More apparent, though, is the color of clothing. As I mentioned, certain dyes — and therefore colors, like medieval Europe's royal purple — are significantly more expensive than others; in addition, different dyes can be mixed to produce different colors. For instance, colors that have a metallic tone require more silver, an expensive dye, and so clearly show that a character has means. Means, of course, can manifest in different ways: a character might have significant exploration experience, indicating that the player has found dyes in travel; a character may have money, so that player can purchase dyes; and/or the player has shrewd trading abilities that she or he exercises in order to procure rarer colors, even without extensive journeying or funds.

Individual status is also communicated via public announcements that occur: when a character achieves a skill point (an award for completing some task or mission that also quite literally can increase an individual's power by enabling the acquisition of more effective spells or tactics, or enhancing a character's skill in abilities already learned), a statement is publicly broadcast: "so-and-so has received a skill point." Similarly, when a character achieves milestones of various kinds — such as exploring a certain percentage of the *Guild Wars'* realms — titles are obtained and publicly announced: "so-and-so has achieved the title Legendary Cartographer. The gods have extended their blessings."

The rhetorical display of status, "oral" and visual, communal and individual, clearly demonstrates the *Guild Wars* marketplace's existence as a hierarchical, semiotic domain where level, power, and status are put on display through multiple modalities and signs, while audiences are present to interpret their meanings. Avatars speak of their adventures, seek followers, and join guilds. They grandstand, they narrate their adventures. The game provides "emotes" — that is, the ability for avatars to *gesture* — to nod, to beg, to kneel, to clap, to flex, to moan, to salute, to yawn, to bow: all nonverbal rhetorical communication that illustrates a direct return to classical oration. They even play music and dance, which I mention merely to further demonstrate the parallels between the *agora* or *forum* and this new space, where entertainment reemerges from the "enclosures of the park" and the "rooms of the palace" back into the public marketplace. They do all of these things, all worthy of study. I dwell here on those rhetorical moves that serve to indicate *status*, though, because *those with it speak louder*. If the historical marketplace, in which public discourse was a given, can be seen as a precursor to the comparatively private coffee houses, whose participants intended their conversations to eventually reach public venues, then the volume at which its participants speak is significant.

The speeches made and conversations had largely promoted the free exchange of ideas and criticism of the ruling class. If indeed the marketplaces in online games have inherited any of these characteristics, then they certainly need to be considered spaces for significant public discourse, especially as they *seem* to be private (gamers in their own private spaces) and therefore promote free speech, but are rather public (a massive number of gamers reading participants' contributions and external websites onto which additional contributions overflow) and therefore the speech may have political effect. Discourse in any venue can have consequences, and these virtual marketplaces can serve as intriguing training grounds for an active citizenry. They may come to function, if they have not to some extent already done so, similarly to the "coffee-house discussions" for which "already in the 1670s the government had found itself compelled to issue proclamations that confronted the dangers [they] bred" given that "the coffee houses were considered seedbeds of political unrest" (Habermas 59).

## The Potential for Political Discourse in a Playful Space

Some may be skeptical of such a claim. Andrew Keen, in his popular *The Cult of the Amateur*, comments that "some argue that the Web 2.0, and the blogosphere in particular, represents a return to the vibrant democratic intellectual culture of the eighteenth-century London coffeehouse" (79); Keen is vehemently critical of such claims made directly or indirectly, for he is cynical of the anonymous or pseudonymous participation so common in online environments, especially when readers have so little ability to distinguish between reliable and comparatively unreliable sources. Keen may have a point — commercially invested companies plant positive reviews of their products, passing off such reviews as individually composed, while bloggers contribute to their own response sections (or those of competitors) using pseudonyms to generate participation and even controversy — but while MMOGs may function through pseudonymity, nevertheless gamers are invested wholly in their player-characters: it takes tens or hundreds of hours of gameplay to reach certain levels and objectives, and thereby achieve the means to procure sought-after items. The player-characters themselves — as other gamers have no access to their human counterparts — gain and lose reputation, becoming agents themselves: in other words, the pseudonyms act not as mere pseudonyms, but the very names that represent the inhabitants of the virtual worlds. From gamers' perspectives, all speeches and actions come from player-characters and are directed to them.[4] To be fair, Keen is not commenting specifically on MMOGs; but these games maintain the same sort of interactivity as Web 2.0 applications (about which Keen is critical), and for largely the same purposes: free communication exchange and collaboration.

Whether anonymous (or pseudonymous) or no, electronic social spaces offer relatively unregulated discursive exchange. What's more, like writers who address current controversial, social, political, and moral issues in the guise of science fiction (which for whatever reason *still* sometimes manages to avoid the censors to some extent), participants in massively multiplayer online games are potentially easy to pass off as "just playing a game." Yet we have seen instances of active, even potent, political discourse in non-gaming, online environments countless times before. On NPR's *All Things Considered* in January 2008, Andrea Seabrook reported on one major occurrence during her interview with Keith Lasop, who discussed "Distributed Denial of Service" (or "DDoS") attacks as a political tool. DDoS attacks are those in which an individual or group disrupts the services of Internet sites (the most common method is by flooding servers with so much traffic that sites cannot function, or their servers are forced to reset). Laslop, president of the Internet security firm Prolexic Technologies, recounted,

> One of the most prevalent ones [DDoS attacks] in the last six months has been the Russian elections. In Russia, these denial of services attacks are really almost used as a tool for cyber censorship. They use this as a tool to silence critics, to silence opposition parties. In fact, [Garry] Kasparov, the leader of the opposition [...] mentioned that the only way to get a political message out of Russia is actually through YouTube, because if you actually try to create your own opposition website and put a political message on that, they will actually take it offline [Seabrook].

The implications of this story are clear: widely accessible, communal access points on the Internet have in many ways provided *comparatively* safe places for which political and cultural criticism can be communicated, despite Keen's arguments. Of course, YouTube is not a game. True. But this example clearly illustrates a political outlet — a way around governmental censorship, a way to thwart the efforts of suppressive information control — that is *already established*. If the coffee house is an offspring of the marketplace, perhaps YouTube can be conceived as the offspring of the modem-based BBSs (Bulletin Board Systems) of the 1980s. And if so, such political activism may just as legitimately appear within games, accompanied by the predictable infiltration of interested government organizations, as evidenced by programs such as *Project Reynard*.

Ryan Singel from *Wired* reports that "having eliminated all terrorism in the real world, the U.S. intelligence community is working to develop software that will detect violent extremists infiltrating *World of Warcraft* and other massive multiplayer games, according to a data-mining report from the Director of National Intelligence." The report to which Singel refers reads,

> *Reynard* is a seedling effort to study the emerging phenomenon of social (particularly terrorist) dynamics in virtual worlds and large-scale online games and their implications for the Intelligence Community.... The cultural and behavioral norms of virtual worlds and gaming are generally unstudied. Therefore, *Reynard* will seek to identify the emerging social, behavioral and cultural norms in virtual worlds and gaming environments. The project would then apply the lessons learned to determine the feasibility of automatically detecting suspicious behavior and actions in the virtual world ["Data Mining" 5].

Part of me wants to let that stand on its own and just say, "Wow." Governments have long been aware of the potential impact of local, public, politically critical oratory, whether it is in support of or against a governing body, a candidate, a policy. Where is the *agora*, the *forum*, the marketplace — with all of their Habermasian characteristics, implications, and consequences — today? With an increasingly indifferent youth culture (if, perhaps, the majority of my undergraduates are any indication), and one that is not particularly politically active or perhaps even aware (and who can blame them? I have suffered the same *sense* of powerlessness in recent years, during which government is effectively split simply down party lines and all major issues are watered down by mainstream media — regardless of political affiliation — to simplistic binaries), is it not rather important that we have a marketplace? Perhaps, if my reading of *Guild Wars* and others' readings of the significance of gaming culture in general are at least partially accurate, we need only *locate* the contemporary marketplace. And we shall find one — an active, rhetorically savvy, hugely populated one — in massively multiplayer online games.[5]

We usually think of "technology" as something that proclaims the future, its innovators constantly looking ahead. Somewhat ironically, the comparatively new technology of online games challenges this conventional thinking. Virtual worlds (even while based on cutting-edge electronic technology that pushes the limits of Internet bandwidth and desktop computer capabilities) may reveal nostalgia for the past. Gamers have produced a healthy, functioning marketplace (a fantastic, even ideal version, perhaps, but still a historically recognizable one). What's more, the *forum*'s contemporary revision also has entertainment, commodity exchange, public oratory, and discussion, but it seems to have left behind some of its predecessor's less savory elements, such as punishment-as-spectacle and public fighting (in some online spaces, the result of the gamers' ludic spirits, in others, the game's programming parameters see to it). *Guild Wars* in particular and other massively multiplayer online role-playing games more generally serve as instances where brand new technology gives rise to old (but not dated) and productive community practice that has the potential to institute change — or at the very least, serve as an introduction to or even the training grounds for it.

## NOTES

1. The terms "real," "virtual," and "authentic" have been widely problematized; thus my liberal use of scare quotes. The relationship between the "real" and representations of it can be traced to classical rhetoric: Plato wrestles with philosophical truth and its communication, for instance (and how rhetoric itself has the potential to cloud our ability to reach truth, a claim that was especially damaging for the sophists). The relationship between language and reality, and language as representation can be seen in John Locke (for example, in *Essay Concerning Human Understanding*), Kenneth Burke (for example, in *Language as Symbolic Act*), Mikhail Bakhtin (for example, in *Marxism and the Philosophy of Language*), Jacques Derrida (multiple works) and many other theorists/philosophers who also interrogate this relationship, albeit in significantly different or nuanced ways. This conversation has occupied multimedia scholars/writers, especially with regard to online forums, e-living, MUDs, and later, avatars and video game personae (see Sherry Turkle, *Life on the Screen*; Julian Dibbell, *My Tiny Life*; Lisa Nakamura, *Race in Cyberspace*; and many others). In writing about online worlds, Edward Castronova — although he focuses on the

economies and commodities of them — definitively states, "I would argue that these processes of value creation have advanced so far, even at this early date, that almost everything known as a 'virtual' commodity — the gold piece, the magic helmets, the deadly spaceship, and so on — is now certifiably real. Indeed ... the term *virtual* is losing its meaning" (148). I prefer, too, "semi-virtual" (as opposed to "semi-real"), to emphasize the *partial* nature of virtuality, and the more *assumed* qualities of the real. Suffice it to say that this is a conversation covered much more thoroughly elsewhere, and is relevant — but not essential — to my argument here; we can therefore understand "semi-virtual" as a term that recognizes this complex history and understands online environments as maintaining characteristics of so-called real worlds *and* representations of them.

2. "Naga pelts" are the skins from a serpentine creature (traded and used much as reptilian hides are in the offline world). I say "cries" here precisely because they literally *aren't*. We automatically consider exclamations such as the ones I describe in verbal terms, and they are clearly intended in *Guild Wars* to approximate vocalizations insofar as it is possible to do so.

3. The Luxon and Kurzick peoples comprise different cultures with different ideologies, and guilds are often aligned with one or the other.

4. Or non-player-characters, to be accurate, but even NPCs, from the perspectives of gamers, are participants in MMOG societies.

5. Blogging is the new wunderkind techno-phenomenon. It has exploded. National news programs feature segments on the blogosphere, and sometimes these segments merely show reporters who are simply *reading* their computer screens to us (!). What I have said occurs in MMOGs also, to an extent, occurs in blogs. MMOGs have the semi-virtual qualities, however, unlike blogs — they are functioning worlds unto themselves. Conversation is also largely spontaneous and communication initiated via real time discussion. MMOGs preserve the sense of "speech" (as opposed to the still *written* character of the blog), even if the discourse exists as somewhat of a hybrid between writing and speaking, generally conceived. Where blogs might be public essays, MMOGs encourage speeches and public addresses, perhaps akin to a press release versus a press conference. While the significance of the blogsphere cannot, in my view, be overestimated, nevertheless it lies outside of the purview of this essay, even while it merits a nod here.

## Works Cited

Castronova, Edward. *Synthetic Worlds: The Business and Culture of Online Games.* Chicago: The University of Chicago Press, 2005.

"Data Mining Report." Office of the Director of National Intelligence. 15 Feb. 2008. Unclassified Government Data Mining Report. 27 June 2008. <http://www.fas.org/irp/dni/datamining.pdf>.

*Guild Wars.* CD-ROM (PC)/Massively-Multiplayer Online Game. NCSoft/ArenaNet. 26 Apr. 2005.

*Guild Wars Factions.* CD-ROM (PC)/Massively-Multiplayer Online Game. NCSoft/Arena Net. 28 Apr. 2006.

GuildWiki. 27 June 2008. <http://gw.gamewikis.org/wiki/Main_Page>

Habermas, Jürgen. *The Structural Transformation of the Public Sphere: An Inquiry into a Category of Bourgeois Society.* Trans. Thomas Burger. Cambridge, MA: MIT Press, 1998.

Keen, Andrew. *The Cult of the Amateur: How Today's Internet Is Killing Our Culture.* New York: Doubleday/Currency, 2007.

"Official *Guild Wars* Wiki." 27 June 2008. <http://wiki.guildwars.com/wiki/Main_Page>.

Seabrook, Andrea. "Hackers Target Scientology Web Sites." *All Things Considered*. NPR. 27 Jan. 2008.

Singel, Ryan. "U.S. Spies Want to Find Terrorists in *World of Warcraft*." 22 Feb. 2008. *Wired*. 27 June 2008. <http://blog.wired.com/27bstroke6/2008/02/nations-spies-w. html>.

# 17

# Virtual Guerrillas and a World of Extras: Shooting Machinima in Second Life

*Mark Pepper*

When the virtual world of Second Life launched in 2003, its first residents were largely early adopters and tech-savvy explorers. Then on the morning of October 18, 2006, a front page feature on Yahoo! brought more than 50,000 curious noobs into the world in a single day. This beginning of a subsequent popularity boom, though, never changed the basics of Second Life living. The world is still explored via an avatar — an infinitely customizable representation of the self that can walk, float, fly, or teleport across the world map. Everything a resident sees and interacts with is still user-generated content. Most importantly, there is still no publisher-imposed purposes or goals. After a brief tutorial of the control system, new residents are left with the freedom to figure out what their Second Lives will look like. However, continued press and popularity did expand the types of people interested in becoming residents. Among this still growing population are a group of curious educators forging new pedagogy and possibilities for virtual space.

By the Spring of 2007, I and three other such educators caught the Second Life (SL) buzz and set out to produce a machinima (muh-SHEEN-eh-mah) movie about educational possibilities in-world. We had all read numerous essays on education in SL but felt this research could not fully capture the excitement for skeptics and the uninitiated. Even though we were four composition teachers familiar with the merits of process over product, I must admit that initially our group constantly looked ahead to our finished movie. Only in hindsight do I agree with Leo Berkeley who believes the defining element of machinima is not within the finished product, but rather "occurs during the production process, where the user/filmmaker can interact with a programmed game environment that is sufficiently complex to have substantial elements of uncertainty and randomness" (66). In other words, machinima is in the doing and the embracing of the chaos that can come with approaching a virtual environment in untraditional ways.

This chapter is not about the technical aspects of making machinima. I am more interested in what it means to compose machinima in SL and how a rhetorical eye to cinematic presentation can deepen our senses of virtual identities. After a brief history of machinima, I discuss how the camera system plays an integral role in SL identity and narrative formation. In the subsequent sections, I build upon camera awareness to highlight machinima production in SL as a process of participatory composing. I also use examples from my own experience to encourage an approach that embraces sociality and interaction. As potential classroom practices, these tactics can play an integral part of pedagogies wishing to further problematize conceptions of what it means to compose a text in an increasingly collaborative and participatory world.

## What Is Machinima? Definitions and History

The Academy of Machinima Arts and Sciences defines machinima as "the convergence of filmmaking, animation and game development. Machinima is real-world filmmaking techniques applied within an interactive virtual space where characters and events can be either controlled by humans, scripts, or artificial intelligence" (Dellario and Marino). Berkeley defines machinima as "where 3D computer animation gameplay is recorded in real time as video footage and then used to produce traditional video narratives" (66). In another definition that highlights the hybridity of machinima, Katie Salen focuses on the genre as an example of emergent play consisting of "part theater, part film [and] part videogame" (99).

Despite subtle variations in definition, most people agree that machinima traces its roots to two influential videogames of the early 1990s: id Software's *Doom* and *Quake*. Besides pioneering the first-person shooter (FPS) genre, *Doom* broke new ground in game architecture and player customization. Gamers created thousands of player file mods (code that modifies the functionality of a base program) which could customize a single level or add elements that effectively alter the entire game. *Quake* proved even more groundbreaking. While previous games like *Wolfenstein 3D* and *Doom* used mathematical tricks to give an illusion of 3D space, *Quake* is widely regarded as the first truly 3D graphical game engine (Lowood 169). Further, the *Quake* engine constantly recorded a gamer's actions into data logs that played back real-time events. Circulation of these data logs amongst the *Quake* community showed other gamers play tactics or allowed bragging rights amongst gamers who pulled off amazing feats.

The popular player clan, The Rangers, released what is widely considered the first machinima with 1996's "Diary of a Camper." Not only did "DoaC" edit *Quake* replay files into a single-take narrative, but "an independent camera view framed the action," which broke the "independence of the spectator's view from that of any player/actor" (Lowood 178). *Quake* also spawned a series of early machinima videos known collectively as *"Quake Done Quick"* where players filmed themselves completing the game as quickly as possible. The "QDQ" films often altered the game's camera view and made the first use of postproduction techniques to give the movies a more cinematic feel.

By the 2000s, cinematic presentation took another leap forward as machinima makers began capturing images directly from the screen. With playback no longer dependant on running the movie through the game's engine, machinima films could be saved in file formats viewable by any media player. Films appeared online based on a variety of other game engines (most notably *Unreal* and *Half-Life*). Wider audiences brought the need for more creative tactics, leading to the split between what Michael Nitsche highlights as "inside-out" versus "outside-in" approaches to production. "Inside-out" production highlights how gamers play the game while "outside-in" approaches use the game as a virtual backlot to produce "stand-alone animation pieces" (Nitsche 1). The most (arguably) well-known series to utilize this "outside-in" approach is Rooster Teeth's *Red Vs Blue* which recasts the Spartan warriors of *Halo* into standard sitcom situations while simultaneously parodying FPS conventions.

However, *Red Vs Blue*'s familiar sitcom-like presentation is an element of machinima that Berkeley laments. After watching his first machinima films, he notes, "I was struck not by how new it seemed but rather how conservative and unadventurous the storytelling was" (67). Berkeley is partially correct and I would hesitate to suggest that my group's own machinima breaks any new ground. Berkeley is fair, though, in evoking Jay Bolter and Richard Grusin's work on remediation which suggests new media always "function in constant dialectic with earlier media, precisely as each earlier medium functioned when it was introduced" (Bolter and Grusin 50). For an infant form, it is not surprising that machinima reference both the visual and narrative conventions of more familiar entertainment.

If finished machinima look somewhat conservative, I argue their tweaking of traditional gameplay is much more radical. As Michel de Certeau writes, "Everyday life invents itself by poaching in countless ways on the property of others" (xii). Specifically in reference to cultural texts, the consumer is far from a passive absorber of their intended values or uses. Instead, the consumer integrates texts into the needs of their own lives and simultaneously takes "pleasure in getting around the rules of a constraining space" (18). In this sense, machinima represents the continuing deconstruction of producer/consumer binaries that have defined "culture industry" anxieties since the early twentieth-century. To make machinima is to engage videogames and virtual worlds on one's own terms and to dynamically participate in the shaping of cultural materials through boundary pushing play.

## Camera Positioning and Virtual Narratives

Currently, many videogames and virtual worlds come with screen capture technology built straight into the engines. In SL, simply clicking a button records footage straight to the hard drive. SL also contains a highly controllable 360-degree camera system. However, before a potential director makes that first click, merely living a SL involves constant rhetorical choices of a cinematic nature. These choices have implications for the virtual identity practices currently being employed by millions of virtual world residents and ultimately play an important role in machinima production and virtual pedagogy.

Camera control is not an unfamiliar experience for players of modern videogames. As early as the 1990s, games like Christophe de Dinechin's *Alpha Waves* were crafting true 3D environments (Dinechin 1). Games like 1996's *Mario 64* and 1998's *Banjo Kazooie* pioneered intelligent cameras that followed players through a 3D space and required occasional readjustment depending on the game's current objective. However, both games illustrate that camera freedom is somewhat illusionary. Players may control the camera positioning but accomplishing an objective usually depends on a best placement. By contrast, SL contains no pre-set objectives. The camera view is entirely dependent on wherever the resident decides is best placement. Therefore, camera POV is one of the seemingly endless rhetorical decisions a resident makes while living in-world.

All of which begs the question: what does a resident choose to look at? Or perhaps more importantly: how do these choices construct the identity of the avatar this camera is pointed at? The work of Mark C. Taylor is particularly useful for answering this question. In his book *The Moment of Complexity*, Taylor argues for a conception of knowing based on the complex world of network culture. As culture becomes a mix of words, images, sounds, and ideas, new ways to think about cognitive processes of understanding and meaning-making arise. Taylor suggests the metaphor of the screen: "a permeable membrane ... [that] does not simply divide but also joins by simultaneously keeping out and letting through" (199). If all subjects are screens, then knowing becomes a process of screening. Starting at a level below consciousness, humans screen noise and separate its currents into information and exformation (a concept Taylor adapts from Danish physicist Tor Norretranders). Information is whatever we find useful based on the restraints of any given situation. Exformation "is what is left out as information is formed from noise" (203); however, information and exformation are not predetermined. The same noise can be screened into either category depending on the rhetorical need.

This notion of screening is just as applicable to virtual worlds as meatspace, especially one like SL which can be densely populated by avatars, buildings, and other items. Add to this noise the occasional presence of voice chatter, streaming audio, or streaming video and SL can verge on the sensory overload of walking through any heavily populated area of the real world. In the real world, the able-bodied can easily move our heads around all over the environment. In SL, the view of a complex space is necessarily limited by camera framing. Seeing more requires a conscious choice to move the mouse or click a button.

Further, a screening notion of cognition does not include a purposeful agent. A complex system may contain patterns and organization; however, there is nothing intentionally performing this organization. Instead, "the mind is generated by complex interactions among patterns that emerge spontaneously. Insofar as human subjectivity or selfhood necessarily entails mental activity, the self is the result, rather than the presupposition of screening information" (Taylor 205). In other words, we do not make meaning of our surroundings based on notions of who we are or the existence of an a priori selfhood. The self is instead formed by a screening process that starts far below our consciousness on complexly affective levels (207). This notion is even easier to see at work in a virtual world. In real life we may still cling to a notion of stable self, but many people enter SL with very little idea of whom their virtual self will become. Some people try to mimic their real life selves in appearance, dialogue, and activities. Some try on radically different appearances and genders or engage proclivities that are repressed in their daily lives. Virtual identity is hardly a tabula rosa (it will always be partially informed by the previous experiences of the person behind the avatar) but radically new identities do have great freedom to form. Ultimately, becoming rhetorically aware of how the screening process is affected by camera positioning may play a fundamental role in forming the virtual identity.

I do not suggest that any specific camera positioning will have the same screening ramifications for everyone. However, I can offer my own experiences as a possible indicator of what can happen. For example, pressing the Escape key in SL enters a first-person POV where you see the world through your avatar's own eyes. Changing your view is accomplished through the mouse while the arrow keys still control bodily movement. This POV may technically offer the highest degree of immersion (or the feeling of being surrounded by a new virtual place). Without your own avatar on-screen the environment becomes the primary focus. However, screening the avatar out of view can potentially inhibit the transformative potential to shift shapes or identity. Since so much of virtual identity currently depends on avatar visuality, I doubt much connection is built with an avatar if he or she is rarely seen. No matter how immersive this view proves, there is no embodied presence through which to relate the surroundings and craft a narrative that makes sense out of the surrounding noise.

One of my most common camera habits directly addresses this lack of identification. I call it the "Star" view. This practice more closely mimics the camera of film, especially one with a big-budget "name" star whose presence is sometimes the selling point of the whole experience. I have found that centering and focusing the camera on my avatar (zooming in to check out facial features, inspect clothing, or watch animations) creates the closest connection between me and my virtual self. The Star View also enacts what James Gee calls "projective identity," described as the act of "seeing the virtual character as one's own project in the making, a creature whom I imbue with a certain trajectory through time defined by my aspirations for what I want that character to be and become" (55). With my avatar in focus, I effectively screen information and form a narrative about this identity based on any number of considerations I have put into forming it. My avatar becomes the "star" of my SL narrative(s), and I become keenly aware of my transformative potential.

Of course, to form information by framing the avatar is to also screen out exformation. Since the star view is often characterized by a zoomed in camera, much of the world's surroundings are removed from sight. Activities or people in the environment that could lead to interaction may be missed. I have also noticed that even when I have included other avatars in the frame, I feel less involved and integrally connected to the conversation or activity going on around me.

Most often, I employ what I call the "social-scene" view. This is the most camera-active practice and additionally mimics a lifetime's worth of consciously and subconsciously absorbing the camera work of television and film. In practice, the social-scene view involves a constant reframing of the principle actors and activity in an environment. Like the constantly moving camera of film, I constantly reframe the action from various angles. My avatar remains in frame; however, unlike the direct focus in star view, I pull the camera back wide enough to simultaneously frame other avatars. With my own hands actively positioning the camera (and the flow of chat dialogue partially dictating these choices), everything feels very movie scene like (albeit one that I have directorial and conversational roles in). My camera framing makes me keenly aware that I am inter/act/ing with a cast of other avatars, and the inclusion of my own avatar within the scene reminds me that my visual presence is appearing on their screens as well. Any information I derive about myself or the way I interact is based on a mixture of the noise generated by the other players in the scene. The narrative I construct will be formed by social interaction and I am reminded that I am merely a part of an ever morphing and dynamic scene.

Again, I am not suggesting that these are the only camera tactics. Nor would I suggest that other residents use them in similar ways for similar goals. However, I have attempted to show that camera positioning plays a crucial role in how a SL resident views what is happening on screen; and subsequently, these choices can affect a resident's sense of virtual identity. Will you be a disembodied being taking in maximum data at the cost of identification? Will you focus and project onto your virtual identity? Will you frame yourself with others and allow their noise contributions through your screen? In other words, careful where you place that camera — the choice may very well affect who you become.

## Participation and Disruption

If camera movement affects identity, then merely living in SL is already a cinematic performance. However, merely being in-world is obviously not yet machinima. Nothing is being filmed or preserved. Preservation of footage leads to the raw materials of a final machinima product, but shooting footage also changes the nature of one's agency and brings machinima into being. In the next sections, I explore this agency by shifting from everyday living in SL to the active process of filming. I additionally build off the camera implications of the previous section and highlight the possibilities for social participation and co-authorship.

As a director of a machinima project, I originally felt a desire to match our footage to the vision of our script. During our initial shoots, I found myself uncomfortably irritated when a pre-planned location proved full of avatars. They wanted to talk to us. They were distracting. Our IM windows filled with messages of interest. Other avatars walked in and out of (or even sat down in) a camera framing where the script did not need them. Our group of actors would pack up shop, find a new place, or plan to revisit the location later. This behavior was odd in hindsight, for I will usually talk to anyone in SL. However, while trying to film I felt their presences would only contradict or distract me from the narrative I was trying to shape.

Then during one shoot I entered into a great conversation with a curious onlooker. He had barely heard of machinima but seemed quite intrigued as I explained the concept. He was a history professor and we discussed the potential of SL for virtual historical recreation (and he is now a professional contact I still enjoy to this day). Something shifted. Soon my colleagues and I found ourselves talking with everyone. We started encouraging people to linger in the backgrounds of scenes, and we often borrowed their items and animations. I found myself pulling the camera back to find areas with the most potential for interaction. Our insular and highly-focused machinima crew had become a roving band of virtual guerrillas. However, where real life guerrilla directors often seek to disrupt an environment for the purposes of their film, we were actively disrupting the preconceived notions of our own filming process.

By the midway point of our shoot, my colleagues and I sensed we were not shooting footage for a soon-to-be machinima; in actuality, we had already made machinima by virtue of our intentions. Our real-time performativity felt so unlike any accustomed composing process that discounting the messy process felt potentially dangerous. No end product yet existed, but this was machinima — an active and social composing process that would never be fully witnessed by an audience. In some ways this absence will always haunt the finished product. However, a haunting is still a presence and in another sense our filming process will always show traces whenever someone watches our movie.

## Traces of Networked Authorship

Shooting on our machinima ended, and our group moved into recording voices and editing. As I sifted through footage, I was constantly struck by the traces of authorship from those who came before us. I may have chosen the camera positioning for each and every minute, but I would never exactly call the footage mine.

In his book *Rhetoric and Philosophy in Conflict*, Samuel Ijessling proposes the question "Who is actually speaking whenever something is said?" The answer may seem obvious. However, Ijessling evokes a post-structuralist approach to language to demonstrate how problematic the question really is. All utterances and texts are essentially a borrowing or rearranging of the language base and grow out of the previous conversational and textual encounters of the speaker or writer. Ijessling suggests that "speaking is always speaking before another and writing is always writing for another ... there must be some sort of invitation to speak and there is always the desire to find a hearing" (134). In other words, a text is always a response to a text that has come before. The one who claims authorship is always already a construction of the discourse that has come before. Although this summary is a simplification of the language philosophy involved, Ijessling's answer suggests territory already touched upon with Taylor's complexity theory. Ijessling writes, "It is better to define literary output, not as the work of an author, but as a web of meanings. On the one hand it results from a network of previous arguments and assertions and, on the other hand, it opens up unlimited possibilities for new arguments and texts" (132).

The world of SL is nothing if not a "web of meanings." Technically, even my own avatar has been constructed by someone else's prefab shape, skin, and clothes or constructed by me with the assistance of someone else's slider templates. Far from autonomously composing myself, I predominantly enter a network of other people's creations; I evoke an infinite rearranging of "textual" elements that have come before with only the illusion of any pure originality. Even the camera system is not my own creation; therefore, the system I have argued is so responsible for identity and narrative is ultimately based in someone else's previous construction.

This notion of using, poaching, or appropriating other people's texts is even more relevant when composing machinima. Any shot I frame is potentially "authored" by any number of people since everything in-world has been created by other residents. Let us suppose I choose to film a scene in someone's personal SL living space. A wide interior shot within the residence (which has been decorated with objects from numerous stores) could easily be authored by more than thirty to fifty different people. Each avatar in the space also contains traces of someone else's hand. Suppose I also choose to adjust the level of daylight coming through the window using the tools provided by a team of Linden Lab programmers. Add to these conditions that my chosen camera shots are in some way subconsciously absorbed from a lifetime of watching other directors' choices. If we consider this scene a co-authored text (in both composition and function), then it is a complex text that necessarily exists before I have any plans to incorporate it into a machinima. Further, when I choose to record, the pre-existing text has already in some way invited me; the text has called for and evoked a response. That response begins with the decision to choose that place over all others and to frame it in a specific manner. My ultimate recontextualizing of the scene in a machinima will necessarily only be a continuation of the narratives begun long ago when all things in the scene were created and found their way to their current placements.

Under these conditions, how can we truly suggest that a machinima has an author? The modernist sense of an autonomous and singularly directive author falls apart at every level. As Roland Barthes suggests, "to give a text an Author is to impose a limit on the text" (147), and I have strived to show that the SL machinima is in fact a limitless network of meanings and contributions. If we are desperate to hold onto a sense of traditional authorship at all, then perhaps it can be located in the person or people hitherto unmentioned — the eventual machinima audience. Barthes writes:

> A text is made up of multiple writings, drawn from many cultures and entering into mutual relations of dialogue, parody, contestation, but there is one place where this multiplicity is focused and that place is the reader, not, as was hitherto said, the author. The reader is the space on which all the quotations that make up writing are inscribed without any of them being lost; a text's unity lies not in its origin but in its destination [148].

The full depth of Barthes' assertion strikes me when I think about how an anonymous audience will never know the filming process that I have shared in this essay. But I ask myself: are these parts of the narrative really for them to know? Capturing the footage and editing a final machinima product is in some ways to let go of any illusions of a clear and unproblematic transfer of intention. The audience must ultimately make their meanings from what is presented to them on screen. This reality is yet another reason to embrace the chaos and randomness of shooting inside SL. If we approach machinima as a process where composing intentions will never fully manifest in the final product, there is little reason not to let social participation partially guide us. A distributed machinima is ultimately a repositioning of multiple narratives already begun and a long way off from ending. In fact, each object and avatar continues on in-world, fractured from (yet always playing a networked part in) the finished film.

## Machinima Redefined

Although Katie Salen's definition of machinima as "emergent play" moves the definition past mere technical aspects, it still does not account for the complexity of what ultimately ends up on screen. While the machinima video must be considered a multi-authored composition, the audience's viewing experience is framed by the director's camera and editing choices. I would still resist wanting to link these directorial choices to a notion of authorship. Consider this: my avatar makes an appearance on other people's screens, as do my actions and chat contributions. However, the way I look at the world through my camera is information that most often remains privy to only my eyes. If my camera positioning choices play such a fundamental role in virtual identity, then they must also be considered a central part of that identity itself. Therefore, it strikes me as odd that this central part of my identity is almost never shared with others.

Machinima, then, can be viewed not as the text of an author but as the interwoven texts of collaboratively offered identities. By letting others see the camera framing and screening that is usually hidden, the director offers a glimpse into an element of their virtual identity rarely seen. There is no guarantee of (or even a need for) the make-up of that identity to be interpreted correctly (as if such a thing even exists). What matters is the offering of perspective and the invitation to interpret at all. These implications suggest looking at machinima as an identity portrait that represents only one of potentially infinite points-of-view. By offering this point-of-view to an audience they are invited themselves to participate and add another layer to the complexly interpretive experience.

As a composition instructor, I remain surprised by my attitude at the start of our shoot. My behavior illustrates how unfamiliar ways of composing are always fraught with false starts and apprehension. Perhaps more appropriately, all composing is fraught with false starts and apprehension — but it takes moving into a new form to remember the creative possibilities of these feelings. Comfort often breeds stale contentment. Now when looking to have my own composition students experiment with machinima, I will certainly encourage them to approach the process as social cooperation and play. This orientation is likely the one students already bring to SL outside of the classroom, and I would warn against any pedagogical usage that somehow robs virtual worlds of these aspects. If participatory media is brought into the classroom, the pedagogy must highlight the skills students will need to live and thrive in a new media culture. These skills differ slightly according to whom you ask, but a starting list must necessarily include: basic technical literacy, openness to collaborative knowledge, ability to build a social network, negotiation of multicultural differences, and a playful explorative approach to problem solving. Machinima production offers all of these experiences and obviously more. The first step is taking control of our point-of-view, then letting go of control once our lenses are focused.

## WORKS CITED

Barthes, Roland. *Image Music Text*. New York: Hill & Wang, 1978.
Berkeley, Leo. "Situating Machinima in the New Mediascape." *Australian Journal of Emerging Technologies and Society* 4.2 (2006): 65–80.

Bolter, Jay David, and Richard Grusin. *Remediation: Understanding New Media.* Cambridge: MIT Press, 2000.

de Certeau, Michel. *The Practice of Everyday Life.* Trans. Steven Rendall. Berkeley: University of California Press, 1984.

Dellario, F., and P. Marino. "The Machinima FAQ." Academy of Machinima Arts and Sciences. 8 Mar. 2005. 17 Apr. 2008. <http://www.machinima.org/machinima-faq. html>.

Dinechin, Christophe de. "The Dawn of 3D Games." *Grenouille Bouille.* 9 Nov. 2007. 19 Apr. 2008. <http://grenouille-bouillie.blogspot.com/2007/10/dawn-of-3d-games. html>.

Gee, James Paul. *What Video Games Have to Teach Us About Learning and Literacy.* New York: Palgrave Macmillan, 2003.

Ijessling, Samuel. *Rhetoric and Philosophy in Conflict.* New York: Springer, 1976.

Lowood, Henry. "Found Technology: Players as Innovators in the Making of Machinima." *Digital Youth, Innovation, and the Unexpected.* Ed. Tara McPherson. Cambridge: MIT Press, 2008. 165–96.

Murray, Janet. *Hamlet on the Holodeck: The Future of Narrative in Cyberspace.* Cambridge: MIT Press, 1998.

Nitsche, Michael. "Claiming Its Space: Machinima." *Dichtung-Digital* 37 (2007). 17 Apr. 2008. <http://www.brown.edu/Research/dichtung-digital/>.

Salen, Katie. "Telefragging Monster Movies." *Game On: The History and Culture of Videogames.* Ed. L. King. London: Laurence King, 2002. 98–112.

Taylor, Mark C. *The Moment of Complexity: Emerging Network Culture.* Chicago: University of Chicago Press, 2001.

# 18

# Remix, Play, and Remediation: Undertheorized Composing Practices

*Andréa Davis, Suzanne Webb,*
*Dundee Lackey,* and *Dànielle Nicole DeVoss*

> Culture is remix ... remix is how we as humans live.— *Lessig, "Remix Culture"*
>
> We live in "a world that is both instantaneous and cumulative, in which all things (consumer goods and cultural products included) accumulate and crumple up endlessly. Everything ends up as odds and ends and debris to be glued back together, and thus begin anew."— *Boisvert*

Today is Thursday, June 5, 2008, and today's context is this:

- Around 11:00 P.M. EST on September 5, 2007, the English edition of Wikinews reached 10,000 news articles. As of 11:51 A.M. EST on June 5, 2008, there are almost 2.4 million articles included in the English-language area of Wikipedia.

- More than 150,000 new users are signing up daily on Facebook.com, opened to public user accounts in September 2007; Tom (the creator and Friend-in-Chief on MySpace) has 234,948,570 friends on MySpace — up from 195,407,675 less than nine months prior, meaning that Tom has made almost 39 million friends in less than thirty days. Friendster, launched in 2002, is considered near-defunct.

- As of 12:02 P.M. EST on June 5, 5,214 uploads had occurred in the last sixty seconds on Flickr; 71,248 things were tagged with "jump," 558,832 things were tagged with "urban," and 2.7 million things had been geotagged in the past 5 days.

- Blizzard Entertainment has launched a 2008 *World of Warcraft* Arena Tournament, and invited interested players to post feedback and strategies in tournament forums, which, as of 2:34 P.M. EST, hosted more than 1200 posts, which have been viewed more than 1.4 million times.

- As of 12:04 P.M. EST on YouTube, 309,686 users had viewed the 7-day-old video for Weezer's song "Pork & Beans," which features cameos and references to a range of Internet-famous work (e.g., "Shoes"; "Chocolate Rain," which itself had 23,982,338 views as of June 5, 2008; and the Diet Coke and Mentos experiments); 2,185 users had rated the video, and more than 1,600 had commented on the video.

These bits and bytes do not necessarily speak for themselves, but we do see them as compelling evidence of the ways in which writers and composers are remixing, rewriting, rescripting, and redelivering work in digital spaces. Importantly, these pieces show us, also, how people are remixing and composing across media differentials. Weezer, for instance, a top-selling, major-label-signed band, is drawing from what we might have in the past labeled "consumer-produced" media, which, in the recent past, would not have had a global audience, and perhaps would not have lived beyond the producer's video camera. Another popular YouTube video (not mentioned in the list above), Condilicious!, appropriates news footage, White House stills, and the identity of Condoleezza Rice, all set to the beat and music of Fergie's "Fergilicious." These bits and bytes remind us that the lines between media consumption and media production are porous in digital spaces; they illustrate, compellingly, today's digital media landscape, and we thus draw on them as departure points for discussing digital composing processes.

## What Is Digital Composing? What Is Remix?

That's how creativity happens. Artists collaborate over space and time, even if they lived centuries and continents apart. Profound creativity requires maximum exposure to others' works and liberal freedoms to reuse and reshape others' material.— *Vaidhynathan*

Writing happens across multiple modes of meaning-making. Computers and robust networks allow writers to choreograph audio, video, other visual elements, text, and more. Computers and robust networks allow writers to collaborate and co-author across space, time, and context. Computers and robust networks allow us to take the work of others, mix it, mash it, remix it, and send it further on down the digital line. This is all new. And its newness is profoundly important. Admittedly, some have been mixing media for years to create advertisements, movies, and CDs, for instance, but the range of access to these technologies is now accessible in ways we haven't seen before. Twenty years ago, the computer mouse was a clunky oddity. Eighteen years ago, in 1991, the web was relatively new, existing on only a few computers at a particle physics laboratory. Nine years ago, in 1999, the initial promises of web-based consumerism dissolved, and we faced a micro-depression created by withering venture capital and the collapse of many web-based businesses. Eight years ago, in 2000, the original version of iMovie was released. Less than three years ago, in February 2005, three developers created YouTube.

Many digital spaces propel us past the stereotypical image of the single author producing work in isolation, delivered in one-way fashion, to where we now have the possibilities for more distributed, shared views of author-ship — think of spaces like Wikipedia, for instance, where work and author-ial agency is attributed often in diverse, diffuse ways. Or spaces like those facilitated and supported by Creative Commons, where authors and artists can determine the ways in which they want to assert control over their work — and, in fact, rather than asserting control, most invite use, participation, and co-production. Remixing the words, images, and audio of others is not only fair game, but, in fact, commonplace, expected, and *valued*— it is part of the heart and fabric of the web. And it is, we would argue, a dominant compos-ing paradigm in digital space. Ownership is framed less by The Author and authorial claim and more by fair uses, open sharing, and community expec-tations and related motivations for writing — think of Blogger, LiveJournal, Facebook, or MySpace and the conventions that have been cultivated among these communities of writers. Typically, distribution is multi-point, nonlin-ear, rhizomatic, and often very interactive. In addition, the stories we tell throughout this chapter all contribute to how we are resituating notions of authorship, authority, ownership, and distribution. In the sections that fol-low, we present three stories that reflect more robust ways of thinking about writing in digital spaces, remixing in networked contexts, and resituating the author in a digital world. Three arguments unfold across the stories we tell:

1. Play and remix are crucial digital composing practices, yet are gener-ally understudied and undertheorized.
2. "New media" doesn't really exist, but we can identify a post-genre blur-ring and mashing of media and genres.
3. Consumption and analysis alone aren't enough to theorize play, remix, and new media — to address the ways in which writing practices shift in digital realms, we have to move toward production and reflection.

## Play as Learning (Sue)

Although we often revise when we write, I posit that revising through play is a more dynamic way for us to think of (and tackle) processes of revision. There is not much scholarship available (Costanzo, Sloan) on the notion of revision as play. By thinking of revision as play, I've managed to revise one piece into five formats, which serve (at least) that many different audiences: *Grand Theft Audio*, a Microsoft PowerPoint slideshow I wrote as a graduate student in fall 2006. *Grand Theft Audio* has morphed (not all by itself) into several different genres. It isn't a typical PowerPoint — it's more of a mini-movie, a multi-modal argument on copyright and Fair Use. It was fun to write, but it was, at times, a pain to craft. It's now a YouTube video (http://www.youtube.com/watch?v=_hN-IzWY3_E), the basis of an academic journal article, the foundation of an online conference keynote address, and a hyperlinked speech.

The original slideshow required approximately one hundred production hours. The many remixes of the original piece reflect another fifty hours for each of them. Some teachers and scholars assume that multimedia composing is easier or quicker than writing an alphabetic essay, but I disagree. I spent far more hours producing this slideshow than I would have typing up the same argument in the traditional academic essay format (in Times New Roman, 12 pt, double-spaced text). Because crafting the slideshow felt like play, I invested more time and more energy, and ended up with a product that is more compelling, and even fun, than an academic essay could ever be.

The original slideshow is a mixture of text, sound, images, and color that weaves together an informative report, U.S. intellectual property laws, a range of policies, popular culture, and metal music. This massive slideshow (ninety-nine slides) presents a blurring of production tools, each of which I had to *play with* in order to manipulate my argument into the mini-movie. It has a rich, loud soundtrack, with colorful logos and photos and a corresponding textual argument. During the one-hundred hours spent producing this mere ten-minute video, I was jumping across at least five different software applications, the web (for images and font faces), and iTunes (for the music). As I leapt from application to application, I blurred the lines between them. As I toggled across multiple modalities, I blurred the lines between what text can say, what images can show, and what music can convey. This playing taught me to push the boundaries of PowerPoint.

The multiple and layered messages in the movie speak to audiences in several ways: Although *Grand Theft Audio* helps viewers understand the complexities of copyright and Fair Use, it also demonstrates multimedia production concepts, including attention to graphic content, use of color, arrangement of screen space, overall layout, and font choice. I played with the text in the slideshow so that I'd have very little text on each screen; with the loud music in the background, the text had to stand out above the background noise. Piracy is a "dark" subject, so I played with the colors so they would reinforce the dark side of piracy. I played with words. I played with logos. I played with the timing. And then I played with what I'd already played with. I remixed my own work; I moved pieces; I mashed parts. I cut. I pasted. I merged. I morphed.

In the process of this playing, I hoped to export *GTA* to a YouTube-friendly format; I opened Windows Movie Maker and tried to import *Grand Theft Audio*. The ninety-nine slides crashed Movie Maker. Willing to play a bit longer, and wanting to push (back) at Movie Maker, I dragged each slide, individually, into Movie Maker and then recreated all of the transitions. These hours didn't feel much like play, and it changed the feel of the movie, but a .wmv file *will* load onto YouTube. Play (coupled with patience) taught me Movie Maker.

A few months later, I remixed *Grand Theft Audio* (yet again) into a textual piece. I wrote a discussion of the process of making *GTA* and transformed it into a manuscript for publication in a special issue of *Computers and Composition* on the subject of Media Convergence. Play got me published!

Other instructors have asked that I present *GTA* in their classrooms. So, to situate the movie for their students, I wrote a hyperlinked introduction (http://www.wordslingingwoman.com/GTAscript.pdf) that gives students context for the arguments the slideshow presents, discusses some of the graphic design techniques, and explains remix as a concept. When I guest lecture, I give an oral presentation to situate the movie, then I share a link with students so they can dig deeper into the myriad of composing practices I call *Grand Theft Audio*. My playing now teaches students.

## *Play as/and Genre Bending (Dundee)*

Those of us in rhetoric and composition interested in digital spaces, networked writing, distributed authorship, and play as inquiry want to teach students how to play with ideas, to consider research as a process of inquiry, and to make deliberate, rhetorical choices about forms, and styles. Too often, though, we have trouble doing this in our *own* work. Too often, our "choices" are something closer to habit. What I describe next is a project that set my habits off balance, and made me play — and learn, and rethink genre — long after I thought I had much left to learn about academic writing.

Before I began graduate study, I spent a brief period in a Mayan village in Guatemala as a volunteer teacher. Later, as part of my graduate work, I was assigned a literature review project for one of my courses. When I began, I had no idea that my choice and the specific genre of the literature review would ultimately lead so far away from the boundaries of the familiar (white pages; black text set at 12 pt; one-inch margins; etc.). Almost immediately, I began to ask myself: Why? Why do we choose to write in the genres and attendant forms we do, even when they don't match our purposes? It seems often our choices are based on the fact that there *are* established modes and genres — our choices are then simply habits that carry with them an implicit stamp of societal, disciplinary, and community approval. But sometimes, these choices work against us.

Take, for example, the case of Rigoberta Menchú—a Mayan woman who told the stories of violence against her people to anthropologist Elisabeth Burgos-Debray. The tapes eventually wound up being published in the form of a testimonio, *I, Rigoberta Menchú.* What would be the texture of the testimonio if it had been delivered via the original audiotapes? Or sketches? Or in some other mode or genre entirely than the print text? I began to wonder what this meant for my review of literature. Was I privileging something inadvertently, at the cost of something else, *simply by choosing this form?*

Ellen Cushman and Terese Monberg explain that "as composition scholars wrestle with ... questions of representation and authority, we are also experimenting with the conventional forms in which we (re)present our data and our interpretations" (168). Why shouldn't testimonio be (re)presented with cinematographic cues, especially considering Gunther Kress has said that "depiction is a better means of dealing with much in the world than writing or speech could be" and "the next generation of children actually [might be] more attuned to 'truth' through the specificity of depiction rather than the vagueness of the word" (Fortune 50)—why don't we *depict* at least as often as we *write*, especially in testimonio?

For my literature review, I wound up creating a web site (http://www. msu.edu/~lackeydu/guatemala) with the largest section devoted to a hypertextual political timeline, in which I attempted to use image, sound, and hyperlinked dissonant evidence to show the continuing and dividing nature of what happened in Guatemala (an idea gleaned from teaching Sean Williams' hypertext argument assignment). My web project is still essentially a review of literature and an information clearing house, but one approached aurally, visually, and emotionally. It is a space through which I demand much of the reader. I'm not doing, here, *all* the work of making sense for the reader, but providing instead an immersive experience, suggesting arguments through media items, through linking, and through some alphabetic text of my own. Almost all the images are links inviting readers to deeper inquiry. This site, then, is an exploration of a topic, but also a rhetorical exploration of and playing with genre—a mix of rhetorical analyses, travel and research notebook entries, and (visual) annotations that allowed me a space to learn, but also a place to consider the ways in which academics explore (or colonize), listen (or appropriate), or speak with (or for) the topics we study.

## Play as Production (Andréa)

The alarm on my cell phone goes off. It's 8:15 A.M. I didn't even go to bed until 2:30 A.M., but this is not uncommon. Still I rise. I feed the cat, start the coffee, plug in the cell phone to charge, and turn on the computer. My day has begun. While drinking the first of many cups of the day's coffee, I launch my web browser with its default three tabs — for Gmail and two other portal pages I use to check headlines, oil prices, weather, and of course, my horoscope. I start one of my instant messaging programs and say good morning to various people. I greet others on Google Talk, resident in my Gmail tab. I open a fourth tab in my web browser and log into Facebook, skimming newsfeeds and status messages. I compulsively return pokes and respond to invitations and comments. I go back to Gmail and click on the calendar link, opening a fifth tab, to see what my schedule is for the day. I think about the projects I'm working on — two manuscripts; my dissertation; a guidebook project for teaching assistants at Michigan State University, for which I am composing the section on teaching with technology; and several other projects. I open my word-processing software along with six different documents related to this very chapter while I continue sending instant messages back and forth to five different people. I return to Gmail to check on the three email accounts I access via Gmail; a new message has just arrived from the new section editors of *Kairos*, requesting verification that the current assistant editors (like me) wish to continue editing for the section. I reply in the affirmative. This reminds me that my portfolio site needs to be updated, so I launch an HTML editing and web development application and open the separate web page files and the CSS code for my website. I open a graphic-design program to play with an image I'm working on for the website, and then go back to the word-processing documents to re-read the proposal for this chapter. I toggle to my web browser and compulsively check each tab for new items, scanning RSS feeds as they periodically pop up to indicate updates on pages I've subscribed to. I open another email application and check mail on the six other email addresses through which I subscribe to at least a dozen different email lists, all of them professional or academic. I quickly scan subject lines, stopping to read only one or two of the messages. I open *World of Warcraft* to log on to my bank 'toon to check auctions. W00t! Most of my auctions have sold, and I just made 437 gold.

This hybrid of work and play — this mashing of technologies and genres, of socializing and writing, of multitasking and multimedia — is precisely the difference in composing practices we're talking about in this chapter. Composing in this digital landscape is a vastly different practice than the romanticized concept of the lone writer sequestered from the world's "intrusions" as s/he composes. I rarely, if ever, compose alone — my work, like my life, is networked and shared. Friends, colleagues, and people I've only ever known online through places like Second Life or *World of Warcraft* are all part of my composing process and spaces. In fact, it's not uncommon to meet with my co-editor in *World of Warcraft* to discuss our book in progress.

A crucial aspect of *play as production* is the social aspect of composing in these digital spaces and the relationship to multitasking that such a composing environment engages. The rich graphical interface of *World of Warcraft*, for instance, consists of many complicated layers of visual, textual, and audio elements that players seamlessly toggle between and across to manipulate their characters and interact with other players simultaneously. Such shifts between modes and across interfaces of in-game chat, character actions, and coordinated activities with other players is quite similar to the toggling with which I opened this section, describing my movement between computer applications, asynchronous communication, simultaneous conversations, textual production, and visual composing. While some research suggests that such toggling or multitasking may decrease student abilities to focus attention (Wallis), toggling as I described in my opening paragraphs is rapidly becoming normalized behavior. For members of the digital generations, it *is* the way to focus.

Equally as important in *play as production* is what it can produce. The "Leeroy Jenkins!" video is an apt illustration of *play as production* in these new composing practices and spaces. The short (just under 3 minutes) video packs in a rich visual argument employing humor, satire, rhetorical appeals, and archetypes. The video creators employ all the elements of a good academic argument, including an introduction that hooks the audience, an issue or problem for discussion, evidence to support the various assertions, and a satisfying conclusion that leaves the audience with a call to action. The video composers undoubtedly know their audience — other players of *World of Warcraft*, approximately the same age as themselves — and reveal this attention to audience through the in-game lingo they use and the tactics they discuss. The composers also take full advantage of the ethos provided through oratory and the timing of the event. Additionally, the purpose (to have fun and/or to promote the guild) is accomplished through the example of teamwork and humor. As Celia Pearce argues in her ethnographic research on productive game play, "the boundaries between play and production, between work and leisure, and between media consumption and media production are increasingly blurring"

(18). This is clearly the case for the composers of the "Leeroy Jenkins!" video, who use game play to create a rhetorically savvy and technologically sophisticated visual argument, and who show attention to both genre and their audience through appeals to ethos, pathos, logos, and kairos.

When we see students in class listening to iPods, instant messaging their friends, and updating their status messages in social networking spaces while they take notes or work on class projects, there is an implicit assumption that students are simply not paying attention. However, when we examine the way composing processes — perhaps especially for the digital generations — occur seamlessly in and across networks, media, and genres, we should question this assumption. As we argued earlier in this chapter, writing today means weaving text, images, sound, and video while working within and across multiple media, often for delivery within and across digital spaces. Writing in the digital landscapes in which students live and work means engaging collaboration and cooperation for invention and composition, and it means that what looks like play likely belies the rhetorically rich and complex processes at work. Play *is* production.

## Some Conclusions and Directions

According to Lawrence Lessig, remix culture is a culture of derivative works, a culture where everything and anything is up for grabs — to change, to integrate, to mix, and to mash. Certainly, the ability to do so has been accelerated by the personal computer and by digital networks, which allow us to more easily share, copy, download, and mix media. Bernard Schütze's work runs parallel with Lessig's characteristics of remix culture, but Schütze is more politically fervent in his declarations that remix culture "upholds the remix as an open challenge to a culture predicated on exclusive ownership, authorship, and controlled distribution." Schütze contextualizes remix culture as existing in a space where authority, ownership, and originality have been displaced: The Internet, where "the heap has reached the highest critical mass, permitting remix practices to Spread and Disseminate on a planetary scale. With its free-floating file sharing, splicing and sampling, and instant distribution of digital media, the Web has become an ideal ground for remix practices of all sorts." Worth1000 (www.worth1000.com), a daily image manipulation contest and gallery site, is an example of such a space of remix practices. Copying and imitating are common and effective strategies for learning, creating, and composing. They are valued methods of meaning-making. Important to the value of copying, however, is transformative value — the making of something new. This might come in the form of delivering a text into a new context; collecting the text with other texts to make a new compilation; adding additional text; taking a new stance toward the existing text; parodying the existing text; transforming an existing image to send a new meaning; etc.

Understanding writing-as-remix requires dramatically different approaches to authorship and ownership of texts — approaches that recognize and call attention to multiply-authored pieces, work that is written "collaboratively" with other artists and writers (living or dead, in physical proximity or across the globe), and work where ownership is shared across networks (of people and machines) and servers.

Play and remix are crucial digital composing practices, but these practices are generally understudied and undertheorized. We hope, through the situating discussion we've offered and the stories we've told, to have illustrated the ways in which play and remix are not just composing practices, but robust activities crucial to the lives we live as academics, students, citizens, and more. Remix happens; remix is a composing paradigm across digital networks and in virtual spaces. Play happens; play is a composing paradigm across digital networks and in virtual spaces. We do, however, need to be attentive to and extend the work of folks like Albert Rouzie and Lev Vygotsky, who help us understand play in innovative ways. Although Vygotsky is most known for his work in child development, subsequent research and the very essence of writing pedagogy situates writing as a space for learning and growing intellectually. Thus, many of the arguments Vygotsky posited regarding child development may also be said for writing development. Specifically, then, we should heed his advice to not "disregard the [writer's] needs — understood in the broadest sense to include everything that is a motive for action" — especially play (*Mind* 92). Vygotsky tells us that "play [is] a cognitive process" through which we find purpose and that, "superficially, play bears little resemblance to what it [can lead us] to" ("Play"). When we play — through our digital networks, in our virtual spaces, with our writing — we learn, we produce, we bend — we grow.

Each of us has faced a colleague, a parent, an administrator, or a student who has asked "what does *this* have to do with writing?" This question reminds us of the long-instilled habits of academe, and how we need to continually negotiate and renegotiate those habits. Composing in digital spaces, and writing framed by play and remix, need not be divorced from what we hold true as writing teachers. All of the elements of "good" composing practices carry into digital spaces. Further, we would argue that multimediated composing practices allow for a greater understanding of rhetorical practices than does work in traditional alphabetic modes alone. Writers wrestle with audio, with video, with still images, and with myriad other compositional elements, all requiring deep attention to rhetorical concerns.

We want to close with a few suggestions — ways in which we can integrate and value play in the writing classroom, and ways we can rethink genres and the work genres do, especially in digital contexts:

- Rework existing assignments to allow for and encourage play — our traditional beliefs about writing, reading, and learning are rich and flexible enough to migrate to different places. Digital movies have introductions. Web sites require details, description, and explanation. Blog entries require some sort of concluding statement or closure.

- Be patient. Be aware. Foster investment, and recognize investment. To integrate play, we must be willing to play, and playing — especially in digital spaces — takes time.

- Encourage media flexibility and transmediation. Encourage students to take genres and documents and move them into different media. Shifting asks for and requires play, and deeply analyzing both genres and the work genres do, and revision and the work revision does.

Challenging students to interrogate genres and forms, with attention to rhetorical concerns, and to make choices based on audience and purpose — rather than on our institutional habits or expectations — provides them with a rhetorical awareness that should equip them to think their way through any writing situation they may encounter. These lessons, however, require that we encourage students to think outside the box and beyond the default word-processing document. These lessons require us to be willing to do so ourselves, and to help develop the theories that explain how and why such works are created, what purposes they serve, and how working in more thoughtful, if unexpected, forms might be usefully taught and assessed in a writing curricula.

## WORKS CITED

Boisvert, Anne-Marie. "On Bricolage: Assembling Culture with Whatever Comes to Hand." Trans. Timothy Barnard. *HorizonZero* 8 (2003). 8 Feb. 2009 <http://www.horizonzero.ca/textsite/remix.php?is=8&file=4&tlang=0>.

Costanzo, William V. "Media, Metaphors, and Models." *The English Journal* 77.7 (1988): 28–32.

Cushman, Ellen, and Terese Guinsatao Monberg. "Re-Centering Authority: Social Reflexivity and Re-Positioning in Composition Research." *Under Construction: Working at the Intersections of Composition Theory, Research, and Practice.* Ed. Christine Farris and Christopher Anson. Logan: Utah State University Press, 1998. 166–80.

Davis, Andréa. "'Leeroy Jenkins!' What Digital Gamers Can Teach Us About Writing and Visual Arguments." *Play and Pedagogy: Videogames and Writing Instruction.* Ed. Doug Eyman, Andréa Davis, and Stewart Whittemore. (Forthcoming).

Fortune, Ron. "'You're not in Kansas anymore': Interactions Among Semiotic Modes in Multimodal Texts." *Computers and Composition* 22 (2005): 49–54.

Lessig, Lawrence. *Free Culture: How Big Media Uses Technology and the Law to Lock Down Culture and Control Creativity.* New York: Penguin Press, 2004.

_____. "Remix Culture." Conference on College Composition and Communication, San Francisco, CA, 2005.

Menchú, Rigoberta. *I, Rigoberta Menchú: An Indian Woman in Guatemala.* London: Verso, 1995.

PALS for Life. "Leeroy Jenkins!" YouTube. 8 Feb. 2009 <http://youtube.com/watch?v= Zll_jAKvarw>.

Pearce, Celia. "Productive Play: Game Culture from the Bottom Up." *Games and Culture* 1.1 (2006): 17–24.

Rouzie, Albert. *At Play in the Fields of Writing: A Serio-Ludic Rhetoric.* Cresskill, NJ: Hampton Press, 2005.

_____. "The Composition of Dramatic Experience: Play as Symbolic Action in Student Electronic Projects." *Computers and Composition* 17 (2000): 139–60.

_____. "Conversation and Carrying-on: Play, Conflict, and Serio-Ludic Discourse in Synchronous Computer Conferencing." *College Composition and Communication* 53 (2001): 251–99.

Schütze, Bernard. "Samples from the Heap: Notes on Recycling the Detritus of a Remixed Culture." *HorizonZero* 8 (2003). 8 Feb. 2009 <http://www.horizonzero.ca/textsite/ remix.php?tlang=0&is=8&file=5>.

Sloan, Gary. "Writing as Game." *The English Journal* 67.8 (1978): 44–7.

Vaidhyanathan, Siva. *Copyrights and Copywrongs: The Rise of Intellectual Property and How It Threatens Creativity.* New York: New York University Press, 2003.

Vygotsky, Lev. "Play and its Role in the Mental Development of the Child." Trans. Catherine Mulholland. Trans. of *Voprosy psikhologii* 6 (1966). Psychology and Marxism Internet Archive. 2002. 8 Feb 2009 <http://www.marxists.org/archive/vygotsky/works/ 1933/play.htm>.

_____. *Mind in Society: The Development of Higher Psychological Processes.* Ed. Michael Cole, Vera John-Steiner, Sylvia Scribner, and Ellen Souberman. Cambridge: Harvard University Press, 1978.

Wallis, Claudia. "The Multitasking Generation." *Time Magazine* 19 Mar. 2006: 48–55.

# 19

# Conf(us)(ess)ions of a
# Videogame Role-Player

*Zach Waggoner*

I have identity confusion. My name is Zach. I'm a Caucasian male college teacher. I like to play basketball and hike. I've been Zach for, well, all my life. However, in the past two years I've spent several hundred hours being someone else as well. Her name is Zaara. Zaara is a female Dark Elf rogue. Zaara likes to steal books from people's homes while they're away and kills orcs with savage glee. I have identity confusion.

Confusion: mental discomfiture and mental perturbation; putting to shame; perplexity; disorder (according to definitions 1, 2, 3, and 5 in the *Oxford English Dictionary*). At times, I do feel shameful and perplexed. This is mostly when I need to grade a set of papers, but Zaara is determined to find some Green Lichen, the final ingredient needed to complete the potion she is making. I might get lucky; Green Lichen might grow near the town where Zaara is currently searching. If so, I'll be grading in five minutes. But if Green Lichen can only be found on the top of a mountain on the other side of Vvardenfell, grading isn't going to happen for at least an hour or two. I am perturbed by the disorder this will cause in my grading schedule — but I just can't leave *Morrowind*.

*Morrowind* is a single-player fantasy video role-playing game. Nope, I'm not online, questing with virtual friends from around our global village. Other than the static and admittedly limited non-player characters (NPCs) that populate Vvardenfell, the island setting of *Morrowind*, I'm all alone. Or rather, Zaara is. But somehow, I'm never lonely within *Morrowind's* vast diegetic gameworld. Searching wizard towers for rare artifacts, bartering with shopkeepers for new weapons and armor, and teaching Zaara to pick locks more effectively all somehow matter a great deal to me. I want very badly for Zaara to have a meaningful life experience in Vvardenfell. But how did this happen? How does *Morrowind* persuade me to care about my avatar so much?

Mostly, it's the great freedom I have to create the type of avatar I want to play. *Morrowind* allows users to choose the avatar's name, sex, and race. Any name can be chosen, and NPCs refer to the avatar by name in text-based conversations. *Morrowind* offers users the opportunity to choose a male or female avatar from the ten different races that inhabit Vvardenfell. Several different facial features and hairstyles are available for each race and sex as well. *Morrowind* also allows users to choose the class of their avatar: this class identifies which of the twenty-seven skills available are most important to the avatar. These choices effectively define the avatar's way of life in the game-world.

How did I make these initial decisions for Zaara? Very, very carefully, drawing heavily on my (Zach's) personality and gaming preferences, refined over years of videogame role-playing. The name Zaara is a combination of my name and my partner's name, Sara. Dark Elves are strong, agile, and intelligent, and can become adept fighters, thieves, or wizards. This makes them an excellent racial choice for users who seek a balanced approach to diegetic problem-solving. I like balanced avatars; after all, I consider myself to be a balanced person in my non-virtual life (NVL). And why a female, you ask? Good question. In my NVL, I'm a strong-yet-silent feminist; somehow, it's more comfortable to overtly embrace this aspect of my identity through a female avatar. It feels "natural" to play a woman in *Morrowind*'s virtual space. In Vvardenfell, I can be whoever I want to be — and Zaara is infused with attributes that are essential to Zach's identity.

In *Morrowind*, I can be a great hero, if I choose to follow the epic central storyline. How big a hero? Think Frodo meets Luke Skywalker meets Neo. The denizens of Vvardenfell are relying on me to rid their world of a great evil. Will I? Maybe. It's tempting. But there is so much to do in the meantime. *Morrowind* is completely open-ended: Zaara is free to wander Vvardenfell at will, going anywhere at any time. The main quest need never even be uncovered. Many dozens of smaller stories and missions can be discovered and followed in random order. It's up to me. I can even be a great villain, killing *Morrowind*'s inhabitants (and even their gods). The possibilities feel endless for Zaara while moving through Vvardenfell.

Lately, I've been helping Zaara improve her accuracy with a long bow. Didn't I mention? The more avatars use a particular skill, the more adept they become in it. In this way the user's actions continually impact the skills and attributes of the avatar throughout the gaming experience. When I first began exploring Vvardenfell with Zaara, she was a terrible shot with the long bow, hitting her target only five percent of the time. But I've been practicing (and therefore so has Zaara). Now Zaara strikes her targets sixty-nine percent of the time. I can feel her skills and abilities evolving with each passing hour. Invariably, it brings a smile to my (inter)face.

So, who am I, when I'm in Vvardenfell? Am I Zach or am I Zaara? James P. Gee describes a three-pronged identity construct to help explain the confusion I feel: real-world identity, virtual identity, and projective identity. Through Gee's construct, Zach is my real-world identity (or the sum of my non-virtual identities). Zaara is my virtual identity, the diegetic avatar I control and shape in the gameworld. Projective identity is the liminal space between Zach and Zaara where the two identities are fused together. In other words, Zach's actions influence Zaara's actions, but Zach's diegetic choices for Zaara are also influenced by who Zaara is and what she's previously done in *Morrowind*. Confusing? Maybe. But nevertheless, Zach and Zaara are fused together in intimate ways, and I just can't seem to stop practicing with Zaara's expensive ebony bow.

Wait a minute. Zach and Zaara, fused together. Fused. Together. Confusion: the failure to distinguish; fusion together; mixture in which the distinction of the elements is lost by intimate intermingling (definitions 7 and 9, *Oxford English Dictionary*). I am Zach. I am Zaara. I have identity confusion. I have identity con-fusion, and I'm not ashamed.

## WORKS CITED

Gee, James Paul. *What Video Games Have to Teach Us About Learning and Literacy.* New York: Palgrave Macmillan, 2003.

# 20

# Born Again in a Fictional Universe: A Participant Portrait of *EVE Online*

*Harald Warmelink*

For a number of years, so many gamers have been lured to games of a massively multiplayer nature that over 16 million active subscribers worldwide participate in forty-five such games, with increasing growth since 1998 (Woodcock). As a player of online games, I came across *EVE Online* during a quest to find another game to try out. In particular, this short paragraph detailing the primary difference between *EVE* and other online games caught my attention:

> Most other MMORPGs [massively multiplayer online role-playing games] focus on a structured playing style with predictable outcomes and monotonous leveling. This seemingly innocent fact is why EVE is so different from almost all other MMORPGs, as the players have an incredible impact on how the game develops [CCP].

Struck by this specific quote, I decided to give *EVE* a go. From the get-go, it was clear that *EVE* is an elaborate fictional universe consisting of hundreds of solar systems, each with planets, suns, asteroid belts, as well as space stations. Each solar system has one or more jump gates that allow players to instantaneously "jump" into a neighboring solar system with their space ship. However, this construct is not the first thing that a player is confronted with when he or she logs into the game for the first time.

## Developing a Character

Logging in for the first time, I started reading the copious background information (or "lore") that sheds light on the construct of the fictional universe. I needed to create a character by choosing from four different races and subsequently three different classes. Each combination of race and class comes with its own background story detailing the struggles and advances that led to the status quo, as well as how that specific race and class relates to others.

Creating a character is complete after picking and mixing different character attributes, choosing an appearance, and entering a name. At the end of that process, I felt emotionally attached to this character, having spent at least an hour deciding who this character should actually be. Then I entered the universe in my first space ship feeling vulnerable and alone. The many available tutorials led me to choose skills my character would develop first, but I quickly found out that choosing skills to develop meant choosing who you want to be in *EVE*. As skill development takes significant time (hours, if not days), I needed to plan the process carefully, starting with finding out what could be done in this fictional universe.

I quickly discovered the ability to mine asteroid belts, explore solar systems, dock space stations, run various missions, and buy and sell goods, amongst many other things. All of this occurs in a Player-versus-Player construct, meaning that players can compete against or even fight each other. Yet, even after learning all of this, there was still much more to be discovered. As a player in this enormous construct, it was quite evident that play was not just about developing a character, but also about developing yourself as a player, trying to understand the complex construct of the *EVE* universe. This universe is too intricately detailed for a player to discover alone. After playing for a total of about thirty hours, I realized something crucial: I needed to socialize more.

## My First Corporation

Although I had interacted with other players already through various chat channels, social interaction can have a much more profound meaning in *EVE*. The construct of the universe actually encourages players to form organizations (called *corporations*) of all sorts. In December 2007, over 34,000 corporations were reported to exist (Guðmundsson). Taking the character I created and my play preferences into account, I browsed the profiles and websites of many corporations. Chatting to representatives looking for new members, I discovered how different each corporation is.

The biggest corporations offer the best benefits and protection. But I started to realize that not only would I have to plan my character's skill development, but I would also have to plan a corporate career. As the topnotch corporations were still well beyond reach, I decided to join a laid-back corporation with hardly any requirements. Instead, this corporation consisted of relatively new players looking to learn *EVE* collaboratively through regular meet-ups.

I learned the intricacies of the universe much faster by playing within a corporation but I also found myself having some obligations to the corporation as well. Every Friday, we met up to mine asteroid belts collectively so we could sell the harvested ore to fill the corporate bank account. This allowed us to pay the rent for our corporate headquarters in the space station we used as a base of operations. By fulfilling these obligations, I was able to reap the benefits of the corporation.

## Growing Up, Yet Again

Information is key when playing in *EVE*. To develop your character and reach your goals, you need to work both with and against other players. Players compete against each other directly as well as through the corporations they belong to. With more than 200,000 active players (Woodcock), it is important to keep track of what is going on. Fortunately, a number of players started online radio stations that allow players to easily keep track of the latest developments while playing. Still, getting to know the universe and its inhabitants is a continuous process of trial and error. Indeed, getting blown to bits by another player becomes more and more normal. Playing in *EVE* is not necessarily about successes. Instead I find the continuous development of my character as well as the corporations I can be a part of more important.

The *EVE* universe is mind boggling, considering all the solar systems and the corporations involved. I feel reborn in a place about which I still need to learn so much more. I wonder when I will have mastered the game. As the developer continues to expand the game extensively, I realize this may never be the case.

## WORKS CITED

CCP. "About *Eve Online*." 2008. *EVE Online Player Guide*. 29 May 2008. <http://www.eve-online.com/guide/en/>.

Guðmundsson, Eyjólfur. "Econ Dev Blog No. 3 — Some Statistics on Corporations." 2008. *EVE Insider Dev Blog*. CCP. 2 June 2008. <http://myeve.eve-online.com/devblog.asp?a=blog&bid=525>.

Woodcock, Bruce Sterling. "Charts." 2008. *MMOGCHART.COM*. 2 Apr. 2008. <http://www.mmogchart.com/charts/>.

# 21

# A Place to Call Home:
# The Experience of One Guild
# Chat in *World of Warcraft**

*Wendi Jewell*

*World of Warcraft* (*WoW*), as an MMOG (massively multiplayer online game), is distinguished from many console games and computer games by one key feature: social interaction. Within the "synthetic world" of an MMOG, players can meet other people, get acquainted, form friendships and relationships, and in general participate in a community of other players. Of course, the character and tenor of these communities varies, not only from game to game, but even within a single game, as members form alliances frequently known as guilds. In *WoW*, these guilds are semi-permanent groups of players who organize for a variety of reasons. Players must be invited to the guild by a member with the appropriate permissions (most likely an officer of the guild) and can stay as long as they choose to and abide by the guild's rules. Each member of the guild can see and type in "guild chat," a place to discuss whatever they like, but where the focus of the guild often sets the stage for the types of conversations likely to take place within.

Because a player can only be in one guild per character, choosing a guild that matches one's interests is crucial. Many guilds have strict standards and codes of conduct and require applications to join. Guilds might be focused on raiding or pvping (player versus player combat) and strictly regulate attendance and performance. Vorpal Bunnies offers players another type of guild — a family oriented guild. This emphasis governs the character of Bunnies' guild chat as well.

The Guild information for Vorpal Bunnies reads: "We are a family ori-

*A player's associations with a guild in* World of Warcraft *can be short-lived. Some of the players mentioned below have moved on to other guilds, other servers, or even other pastimes.*

ented guild, with lots of wonderful members. We don't turn anyone away based on their age or their commitment — there is no required raid attendance. We want this guild to be a fun place for you to call home." By encouraging a family-friendly guild chat, they create a space where members can relax, seek help in their adventures, and chat about life in general. Wepuenka, a member of Bunnies since she started playing *WoW*, says of the guild chat:

> [Bunnies] are more helpful, less critical. I don't perceive any criticism at all — it's not as competitive. They're not going to beat you down, or make demands on you. It's much more family like. Most people in Bunnies will take the time to get to know you. We know everyone fairly well. I know what they do, what their other hobbies are. You're more like an extended family. Things you wouldn't say in front of your family you won't say here either.

Discussion in this guild chat requires players to transition smoothly through a variety of roles, roles based on their skill and knowledge of the game, as opposed to gender, race, or income. As the transcript from one conversation below demonstrates, players in Bunnies interact with each other in ways that are constantly shifting.

> [Guild][CHEBURASHKA]: that's what collector's do!
> [Guild][WEPUENKA]: yes, we all have pet enby
> [Guild][WEPUENKA]: envy
> [Guild][TASYANA]: it was actually pretty good, the previews sucked
> [Guild][MOJOKHOTNIK]: Where r u.... I haven't seen your new pet yet
> [Guild][CHEBURASHKA]: SW, doing the torch dailies
> GIL says: Where we goin'?
> [OOTKA] has invited you to join a group.
> [Guild][WEPUENKA]: i liked it too, but i know why they kept the series to 30 min
> Looting changed to Group Loot.
> Loot threshold set to Uncommon.
> GIL says: Are we there yet?
> [Guild][CHEBURASHKA]: I thought Get Smart was soo funny
> [Guild][TASYANA]: oh, so you know how I spent 9 hours on the phone w my broken computer?
> [Guild][CHEBURASHKA]: Steve Carrel has done some awful movies, but that one was awesome
> [Guild][WEPUENKA]: it's funny but then starts to get a little predictable/formu-latic (sp?)

In the above selection, players shift through several roles. Through guild chat Cheburashka shows off her "pets," vanity items players can collect and may be difficult to acquire or are rare. Pets are an optional aspect of the game, and though they do not contribute to game mechanics in any way, some require a good deal of persistence or gold to obtain. By showing off her new rare pet to other players, Cheburashka is displaying her accomplishment and receiving validation for her efforts. In addition to discussing accomplishments, many Bunnies use guild chat as a place to organize group activities, or ask for help or advice.

Wepuenka and Tasyana continue a conversation about a new movie, and other players jump in to add their opinions. Thus, they pull in their tastes and opinions on matters outside the game. While such conversation may seem superficial, this discussion brings players together in context that, though facilitated by the game, is at the same time outside the game. Cheburashka's discussion about pets informs others about her identity and values within the confines of the game, but discussions such as this give players insight into each others' "RL" — real life.

Finally, Tasyana mentions an ongoing problem with a broken computer. In doing so she references earlier conversations that at least some of the Bunnies will no doubt remember, and once more these are conversations outside the realm of game play. This underscores Wepuenka's statement "we know everyone fairly well." In addition to relating to each other as hunters, paladins, and warriors (some of the available class or character types), members of Bunnies identify with each other as individuals who exist outside the game.

*World of Warcraft*, and MMOGs in general, create worlds where identity is often a function of language and action, rather than real life wealth or appearance. Noura, an officer in Bunnies, says that "b/c you have the ability to create your own character ... you can't tell by somebody's type, who they are, except by what they're saying, so you're actually basing your opinions on a person based on what they say." Vorpal Bunnies creates a space for members to ask questions and receive help without criticism, to announce their accomplishments and be rewarded, to share their worldviews and talk about their lives. When asked to describe the average Vorpal Bunnies member, Lastofthree answered, "There is such a broad range of ages and everyone can get together, you've got fathers, daughters, mothers, you've got guys that are single and they spend all their time in the game, you've got everything you would see in real life, in Bunnies." This diversity enriches the language and discussion, bringing together people of different experiences and backgrounds in a dynamic, interactive, and ultimately beneficial way. It encourages players to learn to constantly navigate between varying roles. It encourages identification of speech genres and patterns. In short, it encourages active discourse.

# 22

# Magic Canvas: Digital Building Blocks

## *Catherine McDonald*

Why would a successful software engineer, a man who works in a digital environment all day long, come home and choose to inhabit a virtual world for fun? Like many of his thirty-something colleagues, my partner Jay O'Conner spends his free time playing videogames, blogging, or engaging in other electronic amusements. Sherry Turkle hypothesizes that young, middle-class wage-earners, underemployed in subsistence jobs, enjoy gaming for its "psychological compensation" (510). But her explanation falls short for Jay because his position as manager of a product development team not only affords him financial security but a high degree of responsibility and status. So I'm compelled to ask: what do plugged-in professionals get out of their computer-mediated entertainments? Jay's story is common in the networked generation, a tale of complex meaning embedded in digital diversions.

Not all videogames are created equal for Jay, who loves strategy games, especially the type he describes as "find, build, and micro-manage" games (commonly called "4X"). The appeal to him lies in constructing increasingly complicated systems out of relatively basic building blocks. It is not the act of "winning," per se, that pleases him, but rather designing successful and unique systems. Traditional conquest-patterned games don't hold his interest because once the defeat is assured, the rest is mechanical. He prefers games that present a puzzle to solve in the game-world, such as RTS (real-time strategy) games. Jay calls them chess *with a plot*. Players must manipulate specialized resources in order to capture other pieces and position themselves to avoid being captured. Even the role-playing games that Jay only occasionally indulges in intrigue him for their constructive possibilities, not of systems, but of identities. He speculates that the "identity playfulness" of these games reflect a positive aspect of postmodern identity ambiguity. The ability to act out alternative subject positions is akin to what readers of literature experience when they vicariously identify with literary characters. But reading is passive compared to gaming, Jay insists (although he is also a reader). The participatory construction of the gaming narrative allows both imagination and agency that readers of print-based fiction cannot enjoy. Because it is even "more animated," his favorite play is an online session where connected friends collaborate in real-time.

Besides the fictional diversion of gaming, Jay devotes a good amount of time and thought to networked communication. Like an estimated fourteen million other weblog readers and writers, Jay is a blogger. His writing is a rich blend of intellectual prose and confessional meanderings. The inclination that prompts his online expression is a felt-need to record seemingly mundane events or to capture apparently random thoughts and post them to the blogosphere. What accounts for his rhetorical exigence? Carolyn Miller and Dawn Shepherd theorize that blogging, with its curious mix of personal writing and public audience, utilizes new technology to simultaneously satisfy two age-old human projects: knowing self and building community. When I ask my partner why he wants to tell the Internet world about his cats, his feelings, or the odd trivia that he finds humorous, Jay points to the sense of "carte blanche" that blogging affords. The opportunity to address the universe at large is fun, he explains, since he gets to express himself at will but does not have to tailor his expression to known audience expectations. As idle as his blogging may seem, it is to him a productive rhetorical enterprise. I think it's obvious that self-sponsored digital writing is redefining what it means to be literate. Jay's experience is a rich illustration of the rhetorical revolution that is happening via e-discourse.

A portrait of Jay's digital life would be incomplete without a snapshot of his musical creations. He spends hour upon hour with his earphones on, listening to sequences of sound that mean nothing in themselves, but that he builds into a satisfying whole. He collects, combines, and sequences audio samples and synthesized instruments into electronica with a distinctly classical flavor. Like the gaming he loves, the music he creates is organized around finding patterns and developing them into layers of increasing complexity, compositions of beauty and pleasure.

While he is attracted to virtual entertainment, Jay is not unreflective about his mediated hobbies. He confesses a sometimes sense of being "trapped in digitality." To me, his cautious feelings are a sign of a necessary safeguard against overexposure. Indeed, Jay does spend all of his free time immersed in simulation. He paints and gardens too, real life activities that are embodied and tactile, but pursuits that require the same crafting and engineering that his digital pastimes do. Nor does the frequency of his cyber connectivity diminish his skill in face-to-face interactions. I can attest that his interpersonal skills are unaffected by his virtual realities. Amiable and personal, Jay has no trouble relating to people socially or professionally.

The common thread among Jay's interests is a quest for creative possibilities. Digital space is what he calls a "magic canvas." Change is almost effortless, former elements can be erased, and new creations can be designed with the ease of a keystroke. The story of his digital entertainment is not a narrative of mindless consumption, but of tireless — and joyful — re-creation.

## WORKS CITED

Miller, Carolyn, and Dawn Shepherd. "Blogging as Social Action: A Genre Analysis of the Weblog." *Into the Blogosphere: Rhetoric, Community, and Culture of Weblogs*. Ed. Laura Gurnak et al. 2004. <http://blog.lib.umn.edu/blogosphere/blogging_as_social_action_a_genre_analysis_of_the_weblog.html.>.
Turkle, Sherry. "Virtuality and Its Discontents: Searching for Community in Cyberspace." *A Meeting of Minds: Strategies for Academic Inquiry and Writing*. 2d ed. Ed. Patsy Callaghan and Ann Dobyns. New York: Pearson/Longman, 2007. 502–511.

# IV

*Teaching the*
*Digital Generation*

# 23

# Encouraging Feedback: Responding to Fan Fiction at *Different Colored Pens*

## *Juli Parrish*

[Fan fiction] give[s] one access to a community of readers and writers who are generous with support and enthusiasm. It's a good way for a writer to find an audience, and a unique way for a reader to offer interactive feedback.— Ruby, *Different Colored Pens*

Many fan fiction websites provide mechanisms by which readers can offer feedback to writers. At some sites, this may simply be an e-mail address; others, like *Different Colored Pens* (the fan fiction forum hosted by a website devoted to the characters Willow and Tara from the television program *Buffy the Vampire Slayer*), build in ways for readers to post comments publicly, so that both the writer and other readers can see them.[1] At *Pens*, which uses a standard threaded discussion format, each work of fan fiction appears in an individual thread; writers post whole stories or installments, and readers write responses that appear in the same thread directly below. While responses are subordinate to the story in any given thread, the feedback that then accrues can contribute a significant amount of writing to the overall text. In "The Sidestep Chronicle," for example, Katharyn Rosser[2] posted 103 chapters; some of her readers posted nearly as much: Leather Queen commented 73 times, Mollyig 78 times, and Zahir al Daoud 90 times. In all, readers contributed 950 written responses. When we keep in mind that "The Sidestep Chronicle" is one of hundreds of stories archived at this fan fiction website, it quickly becomes clear that these writers and readers are producing vast quantities of text.

Sustained attention to fan fiction has increased significantly in recent years, but we know less about the other kinds of writing that frame and respond to fan fiction, including discussions of craft and critical response. How does feedback function as a form of writing? How does it intersect with the fan fiction to which it responds? And what are the writers of fan fiction and feedback learning from one another about the process? It is worth considering, for example, the projects that fan fiction writers and readers take up, including how they refigure not only the source texts that their fan fiction revises — television shows, movies, books, anime — but also their own roles as readers and writers.

My reading of hundreds of stories and thousands of posts at *Different Colored Pens* suggests that the site functions in important ways as a kind of textually mediated writing group. As Anne Ruggles Gere notes in *Writing Groups: History, Theory, Implications*, writing groups tend to feature the negotiation of standards for reading and writing; attention to the relationships among writer, context, and dialogue; use of metalanguage; and a tendency to provide an encouraging atmosphere for their members. "One of the attributes most frequently credited to writing groups," Gere writes, "is a positive attitude" (123). But this positive attitude takes a variety of forms: encouraging authors to continue writing, mentoring less experienced or less confident writers, and softening the impact of critical analysis.

## Case Study: Feedback for "The Laundry Diaries"

To consider in more detail the work of positive feedback at *Different Colored Pens*, I turn now to a discussion of the feedback to a single story, Trom DeGrey's "Laundry Diaries." When she began the thread, DeGrey was a first-time author but an established reader at *Pens*; she had commented on a range of stories and was familiar to many of her own readers. Her pair of vignettes approaches the same event from first Willow's, and then Tara's, point of view: after weeks of seeing one another in the same all-night launderette, the two finally meet with the help of an overeager community police officer. The vignettes function as character studies, placing the familiar characters in a situation where readers may see them act and react in new ways.

In the notes that introduce her story,[3] DeGrey invites readers to "flail away" in their feedback, but as the excerpts in Figures 1 and 2 indicate, respondents praise the story without exception. Half of the forty readers use a version of the word "love" in their comments, and all use at least one positive word in their feedback (e.g., good, great, amazing, delightful, stunning, absorbing, well-written). Figures 1 and 2 excerpt all the feedback posts, organized here for ease of reading into two categories: statements of assessment and statements of anticipation. The assessment column includes comments indi-

| | Reader | Assessment | Anticipation |
|---|---|---|---|
| 1 | Whisper | Well, let me be the first to congratulate you on such a great fic! I loved it! | I can't wait to see how Willow's obsession will work out. More please? |
| 2 | Babyblue | Lovely writing really sparkles | I look forward to Tara's perspective. |
| 3 | EasierSaid | Loved Willow's quiet, frantic fascination with Tara. | So looking forward to Tara's POV. |
| 4 | Ange04 | I love this! | Can't wait to read tara's pov. Keep up the good work |
| 5 | Wimpy0729 | Totally loved Willow's POV, so engaging. | Can't wait for the next one, and I would really love to see more after that.... |
| 6 | The Rose24 | Great start. | |
| 7 | Meretricious | Love her sense of betrayal there. | Looking forward to part 2. |
| 8 | Silentinformer | Great, very funny and touching. | |
| 9 | Singgirl | That was absolutely adorable! | I wouldn't mind a continuation of this story. Just a suggestion. |
| 10 | BigGayBear | Seriously great | I'll agree with the not minding a continuation of this story. |
| 11 | Sassette | I loved the setup / Adorable, well-written. | |
| 12 | Glendaof0z2004 | Amazing, one of the best stories that I have ... read in a long time. | I hope to be able to read more soon. |
| 13 | Pipsberg | Love the instant chemistry which you make us feel so well. Great job. | Hopefully, you will keep this thread going and give us some more. |
| 14 | MissKittysBall O Yarn | I so totally love this! I love your writing style!! | If I had a million dollars I would soooo give it to you if you'd just ... continue! |
| 15 | Behindhereyes | Really liked seeing the world through Willow's eyes / Beautifully written. | |

**Figure 1. Quoted excerpts of all feedback for part 1 of Trom DeGrey's "Laundry Diaries."**

cating a reader's general appraisal of the story, while the anticipation column includes comments expressing a reader's desire to see more from the writer.

Respondents seem to take seriously their roles in encouraging writers to keep writing. In the case of "The Laundry Diaries," twenty-one of the forty posted responses, as shown in the third column in Figures 1 and 2, anticipate further developments to the story or encourage the author to keep writing, even though DeGrey says in her story notes that she has already made decisions about the scope of the story (two vignettes and no more). There is an understandable shift in the language of these posts between the first and second parts; eleven of the first fifteen posts, which respond to the first vignette,

| Reader | Assessment | Encouragement |
|---|---|---|
| 16  Silentinformer | It was wonderful. | Can't wait to see more soon.... |
| 17  The Rose24 | I love Tara's POV as well. / Lovely | |
| 18  Meretricious | This was so absorbing / you have a wonderful take on both their characters | After this of course I'll gladly read wherever else your muse takes you. |
| 19  EasierSaid | You managed to do that [different POVs] very well. / Great job. | Looking forward to reading future stories from you. |
| 20  Tarawhipped | Love your writing style | I hope you continue with this story. |
| 21  Tempest Duer | I also like the follow-up. | |
| 22  Sassette | This was so nice / I love how mentally spastic Willow is in the first piece / | |
| 23  JustSkipIt | Well done / I love their explanations of their parallel lives / Very well done | |
| 24  Miss Kittys Ball O Yarn | That was totally amazing. | I can't wait for your next short story. |
| 25  Artemis | Absolutely adorable / written with definite flair and sparkle | Could I host this on Looking Glass, please? |
| 26  Behindhereyes | Both parts are really excellent / Loved Tara's POV | |
| 27  Dazed and Confused83 | Can I just say I'm absolutely LOVING this so far! | Can't wait to find out what happens next. |
| 28  Babyblue | I'd love to see this series of vignettes continue. | I'd love to see this series of vignettes continue |
| 29  Washi | I adored this. / It was great | |
| 30  Pipsberg | Great job again / You outdid yourself with this one. | |
| 31  VixenyTarasHot | I loved the ending the most | I hope to read more from you soon! |
| 32  Wimpy0729 | That was just amazingly well written, both parts. | |
| 33  BFR from Paris | Very nice, very funny, very sweet | |
| 34  Tiggrscorpio | How delightful this was to read / well written and entertaining story | I'm eagerly awaiting more. |
| 35  Russ | I love the way they surreptitiously check each other out | I hope we'll see more of your writings. |
| 36  the hero factor | What a great story. | |
| 37  darkmagicwillow | Very nice. | |
| 38  Ressick | I love these vignettes! | |
| 39  Candleshoe | Stunning. | |
| 40  Halo | I simply love it. | |

**Figure 2. Quoted excerpts of all feedback for part 2 of Trom DeGrey's "Laundry Diaries."**

note that the readers are looking forward to reading more of the story, which they already know they will see.

After the second vignette, at least five of the twenty-five posts look forward to reading something else that Trom DeGrey might write; five more suggest that they would like to see more of this particular story (posts 16 and 34, at least, can be read either way). Readers use their posts to encourage DeGrey and she, in turn, responds individually to each post in the same thread. Thus any reader will encounter the story itself, comments to the story, and DeGrey's responses.

In many ways, this set of feedback responses is typical in both generosity and range. While all forty posts include positive assessments of "The Laundry Diaries," they vary in degree, focus, and approach. Some offer an overall assessment: "That was absolutely adorable" (9); "What a great story" (36). Others focus on plot or character: "Loved Willow's quiet frantic fascination with Tara" (3); "I love the way they surreptitiously check each other out" (35). And several address the writing, saying that it is "well-written" or "amazingly written" (11, 15, 32, 34) or admiring style (14, 20), a quality such as "sparkling" writing (2, 15) or humor (8, 33).

While all posts are positive, the degree of praise varies. Miss Kitty's Ball O Yarn (24) writes, "I don't think I've ever read anything so well written in my life! (the great novels included)," but she does not elaborate. On the other hand, Just Skip It (23) writes that the story is "well done," adding, "I must say that I like the Tara vignette better than the Willow one just because it's so funny." This post is representative of an important trend in the feedback to this story. While superlative praise (like that of Miss Kitty) is left to speak for itself, any statement that might be read as "critical" tends to be explained or qualified. So Just Skip It is careful to note that although she likes the second vignette better, it is "*just because* it's so funny" (italics mine). Similarly, Washi's (29) comment that "it's sad that we don't even get an epilogue" is followed immediately with "But it was great." Ange04 (4) comes closest, in my reading, to negative criticism, asking how the police officer could "see the chemistry within a couple of seconds while these girls have been washing clothes 'together' for weeks and still need a [X]ena shirt for a clue." There is an implied suggestion here that this aspect of the story is not quite believable, but again, Ange04 wraps this criticism in praise; the two sentences before this statement are "i love this! this is soooo sweet. love the 'serial killer' cop," and the two sentences after are "can't wait to read tara's pov. keep up the good work."

Interestingly, Trom DeGrey's response to Ange04 takes up only these framing sentences and *not* the potential criticism. "Glad you liked Baxton," she writes. "He actually was the reason these weren't posted sooner. He went through rewrite after rewrite till [beta reader] Shamden made a suggestion and it helped me find my way with him. Thanks so much for reading." In fact, DeGrey's response to each of these criticisms constructs it as positive. To Washi, she writes, "Glad you enjoyed it," and to Just Skip It, she writes,

"Thanks so much! I preferred Tara's too, but just because I let myself write that one more." (And notice that in her response to Just Skip It, DeGrey adopts the turn of phrase "just because" that her reader used first.)

Even a post that is simply less superlative in its praise takes a qualifying approach: the "very nice" of Dark Magic Willow's post (37) stands out amid all the "loves" and "amazings." Dark Magic Willow, however, follows this initial assessment with an apology for having taken so long to post and adds that he "love[s] how much [DeGrey was] able to do with so few words"; it is as if the pressure to love the story trumps his attempt at matter-of-factness. And it is *here* that DeGrey seems to find criticism and respond to it:

> DMW: So good to see your name pop up here. Thanks for taking time I know you don't exactly have to read. I love the Laundry Game and wanted to see what would go through each of their heads as they played it too. The lack of dialog was a total fluke and panicked me a bit when I realized I had done it, but I think it was one of those instances where first person was the best way to do things. Thanks again!

Whereas DeGrey did not respond to the implied criticism in Just Skip It's and Washi's posts or did not read it as criticism, she appears to read Dark Magic Willow's comment about doing so much "with so few words" as a possible criticism of "lack of dialog," but here, too, she reframes it right away as a positive, as "the best way to do things."

There is a tendency in this thread, then, to use positive framing terms, but this is not to say that DeGrey and her readers are invested only in reading for (or to) praise. Indeed, a number of posts analyze or offer a close reading of a specific moment in the text, sometimes quoting language from the story. Of Willow's vignette, Easier Said (3) writes that "you give us so few clues about Tara, just enough of a peek to understand a bit why Willow would be freaking out and fantasizing." Of the pair of stories, Dazed and Confused (27) notes that "the characters are retelling their stories directly to the readers in a very casual manner," and Russ (35) comments that it is "interesting how the two women see the decisive moment so differently."

It is possible that in addition to feedback that explicitly praises a story, comments like these are what people have in mind when they suggest that fan fiction criticism is generally positive and encouraging, and indeed, although Easier Said, Dazed and Confused, and Russ are all essentially summarizing an element of DeGrey's story, itself a neutral type of response, they all frame their summaries in positive terms. But just as the degree and focus of the feedback varies within this particular story thread, so too does the work that positive feedback performs at the site more generally. Particularly compelling is the work fan fiction readers and writers do to help one another learn to improve the writing and reading they do.

## *"This Isn't English Class"*

In "The Art of Leaving Feedback," a discussion thread started by site member Garner, participants discuss what good feedback entails, why writers want it, and why readers might be reluctant to give it. Garner specifically notes that she is not an English teacher, that her goal is not to provide rules but to take some of the guesswork out of the difficult project of crafting feedback. "[T]his isn't English class," Garner writes, "We are all basically friends, and there is no right answer." In this way, she articulates a possible reason that writers and readers at *Pens* need to be encouraged in the first place: they see criticism as negative and they associate this negativity with the critical writing practices they learned in school. Language circulating at the site explicitly casts classroom learning and English teachers in a negative light, one to be avoided whenever possible. For example, Wizpup comments that she is uncomfortable when "a reader decides to offer critical analysis of the writer in the middle of the thread." She sees the value of "helpful, private, constructive criticism" when carried out in private, but "just occasionally, [she's] felt like [she] was watching someone get told off by the teacher in the middle of class" ("Reading").

Not all site members agree with Wizpup's preference that criticism take place off screen, but she names a larger ambivalence at the site about what "critical analysis" is. If her own feedback is any indication, then she does *not* mean breaking a text down into its parts. Consider these two excerpts:

> To **Katharyn:** One of the things I love about this story is the way in which, despite the distance from canon, you have chosen to add familiar storylines into the mix. It would never have occurred to me to think about what had happened to the Initiative. But having read this part, it all makes perfect sense. Of course the government would still have an interest ... and with the Master having risen in Sunnydale, the town would stick out like a sore thumb to anyone who was looking at the death/murder rates.

> To **Mike of the Nancy Tribe:** I agree with the comments made by so many others about the effect of the first person narrative, it brought a real sense of intimacy to the tale — sucking me right in to the unfolding events. That is a real gift, to make the reader care about the events, and the characters, even original ones like John.

In the first response, Wizpup analyzes the effects of a plot choice; in the second, she speaks to narrative perspective. In both cases, she frames these moments of analysis in praise, but it is important to note that according to these posts, Wizpup does see engagement and intellectual analysis as part of her reading experience; it is the idea of people being "told off by the teacher" that she dislikes.

Wizpup is not alone in her aversion to teacherly scolding; even when they disagree with a writer's choices, most *Pens* members studiously avoid seeming teacherly or addressing topics that they see as the province of the English (i.e., writing) classroom. It will not surprise readers that such topics include grammar, mechanics, and other editing concerns. Even in a discussion thread like "Art of Leaving Feedback," where no particular story is under scrutiny, writers are careful to qualify comments that might evoke a classroom setting. The title of the thread alone does not seem to be enough to bracket discussions of sentence-level issues from the fiction; instead, writers tend to mention previous English classes as the origin of their editing suggestions.

In this thread, Garner, who suggests several categories of feedback to help readers formulate responses, introduces verb tense as an issue "that a lot of authors really blow," and suggests that they avoid passive voice. This apparently simple piece of advice sparks a debate over what actually constitutes passive voice, and the language that respondents use is telling (all italics are mine):

> SASSETTE: For those who don't really remember passive voice from *English class* ... passive voice is when the subject of the sentence does not perform the action.[...] *Now that the English lesson for the day is out of the way,* I have to respectfully disagree with Garner's assertion that passive voice should not be used. *Passive voice should definitely not be used in, say, an English paper (English teachers seriously hate it),* but when writing fiction it is a stylistic choice that can serve a very definite and important purpose. Here is an example: "The door opened."

> JUSTSKIPIT: Now to respectfully disagree with both Garner and Sassette ... there is no universal rule against the use of passive voice in writing.... "The door opened" is not actually passive voice. A general rule for recognizing passive voice is that the sentence contains a form of the verb to be....

> SASSETTE: Oh, geeze — yes you're right.

> GARNER: I have had avoid passive *drummed into my head in college* and tend to parrot that back, *unfortunately.*

> STILL WATERS T: I've gotten so used to seeing authors write with mixed tenses like this — that I was starting to get confused about *whether I had missed something in my English Grammar classes* lol.

> UMGAYNOW: I must disagree on the passive voice thing ... unless it is a very bad story, *a story is NOT a term paper* and therefore the same rules do not apply....

Note that five respondents here specifically connect rules for passive voice with writing instruction: college, English classes, term papers. Just Skip It is an exception, although her use of the word "rule" could be read as a reference to school, as well. The narrative of this exchange is interesting; although Sassette attempts to close down her own references to schooled grammar, noting that "the English lesson for the day is out of the way," the other readers maintain a close connection between their discussion of passive voice and their own experience with rules and school. And although several participants finally concur on an acceptable example of passive voice, Umgaynow's final comment renders the consensus irrelevant, not because it is not useful but because it comes from school, and this site is *not* for school writing.

If there is a shared wish not to replicate school structures at *Pens*, there are also several possible reasons that surely do not all come down to negative experiences. After all, a number of comments suggest that participants are still high school, college, or graduate students or work as teachers or professors. Garner, for example, notes that "I am not an English teacher, though I have graded more than my share of exams and term papers." Antigone Unbound and Xita have written about their work as teachers, and Vamp No. 12 mentions writing law school briefs. *Pens*, however, is decidedly *not* school, and even those members who by all accounts are committed to their academic work and its practices seem to set an insistence on those structures aside, at least temporarily, when participating at the site. Garner notes in "The Art of Leaving Feedback" that "one of the problems with critiquing written work is that often English classes ruin the process by making one overly self-conscious, making the process of thinking about what one does unpleasant, or putting too much pressure on us to 'get it.'" At *Pens* overall, participants seem to want to shy away from this critical self-consciousness.

*Different Colored Pens* members are not unique in attempting to distance themselves from academic structures; in her brief study of an online *Lord of the Rings* fan fiction site, *Henneth-Annûn*, Kristie Lee Brobeck observes that while writers at this site are deeply invested in improving their own writing and helping others to do the same, the site is emphatically not "an educational institution" (10).[4] At *Henneth-Annûn*, all stories are reviewed by a nine-member panel of readers before being published, and Brobeck suggests that this peer-review process increases individual writers' desire to revise their work. She concludes that because all writers at this site wish to improve their writing in order to get published, they place a premium on editing and critical suggestions. She argues that because all writers must go through the same vetting process, a sense of friendly rivalry exists, with both the newer and the more experienced writers competing for critical response.

This is not the case at *Pens*, which encourages writers to work with a beta reader (a volunteer amateur editor, usually another site member) but requires no formal review of stories before they are posted. In fact, my study of *Pens* suggests that rather than competition, a sense of camaraderie — all writers are in this project together — contributes to the collaborative learning environment. There may be a certain aversion to recreating academic structures and using language reminiscent of schooling, but site members are committed to learning and to helping one another learn.

Sassette, writing in the "Reading and Writing Fan Fiction" thread, comments that "fanfic writers have a very wide range of basic writing skill, and it's wonderful to see how a writer grows and develops. They'll just get better the more they write, and it's a real kick to watch." But "seeing" and "watching" do not mean that *Pens* members take a hands-off approach. Sassette goes on to say that "the fact that they're also fans means that they're very accessible and approachable, and I've never heard of a writer who didn't want to talk about their story — and in that respect, it's easy to just e-mail an author and ask them things. This kind of interaction can really add to the feel[ing] that the reader is somehow a part of the story." Candace Spigelman has noted, in the context of peer writing groups, that "it does seem 'natural' that readers defer to the writer's intentions and wishes" but that "in principle readers have the freedom to suspend this authoritative distance" (99) to feel some collaborative responsibility. *Pens* readers find subtle and not-so-subtle ways to direct, lead, and shape the work of writers and critics at this site, both by circulating a set of values about what good writing and feedback entail and by celebrating the work of expert readers and writers who are held up as models for others.[5]

Now, the work that "experts" do and the expertise that they have are closely linked; a great deal of that expertise has to do with a writer's negotiations of canon because the expectation is that writers will attend to the intricacies of their canonical texts while still being inventive. To the list of relatively short and sweet feedback posts in "The Laundry Diaries" story thread, for instance, Sassette contributes a 954-word response. Excerpted below, it comments on Trom DeGrey's plot, characterization, use of language, and relationship to the source text of *BtVS:*[6]

> Tara, also, is a great fit for a third-shifter, for so many obvious reasons. Now, the DJ thing at first glance is counter-intuitive for what we know about Tara, but looking deeper and it's great! What we know about our canon Tara is that she's deeply caring, bright, creative, and shy.... A great deal of Tara's canon character stems from spending most of her life believing she's a demon, and her mother's death. That's one of the reasons why she's such a fun character to write AU, because you have to peel back these layers to get at her core and work from there.... This AU ... tones down the shyness — but keeps it present — and reconciles these two conflicting motivations with a job that lets her interact with people but maintain her anonymity.

Sassette makes a move here common in *Pens* feedback, noting how a writer has recontextualized a character, and her response shows how specific the expectation for interpretation can be. As Sassette notes, three seasons of *BtVS* offered relatively little information about Tara, and DeGrey's challenge is to respect the set boundaries of the character while placing her in new situations.

Equally important is the way Sassette implicitly frames her response as authoritative. Her language throughout is confident and assertive; she uses declarative sentences in her feedback (e.g., Tara is a great fit, that's one of the reasons, and so on). Sassette's use of "we" also positions her as an authority in matters of canon: "what we know about our canon Tara is that she's deeply caring, bright, creative, and shy." Referring to her own writing — "she's such a fun character to write" — allows Sassette to support her claims. Her comment has weight not only because she is comfortable making nuanced observations but because she is herself a writer.

In fact, Sassette is the author of a series of vignettes, forty-nine written over a period of four years, and her presence in this story thread is one of expert; certainly, Trom DeGrey receives her as such in her reply:

> I have a confession to make. I squealed when I saw your name in this thread. Yes, squealed, and that is so not me. Then I emailed EasierSaid and said, "Holy shit! The QUEEN of vignettes just left me feedback!" I am so glad you enjoyed my personal challenge to myself here. I've always loved reading your vignettes, but I always thought myself completely incapable of writing anything under 200 pages.

DeGrey's enthusiasm here is typical of the reception that *Pens* participants often give to "star" writers, and what is especially important to note here is that she receives this feedback as exceptional *because* Sassette is "the queen of vignettes." DeGrey may in fact find the response useful, but she does not say so here.

If there are star authors like Sassette at *Pens*, there are also star critics whose feedback is known and celebrated for its craft, its interpretative quality. Near the beginning of "Feedback," Sassette observes that "all the replies on this thread so far are writers" and suggests that readers get into the mix. Each of the site members who most immediately respond to Sassette names herself as a non-expert in her post, as these excerpts indicate:

> STILL WATERS T: I don't have much to say here since I'm no expert on leaving feedback, I try my best though. When I have the time I can use a good long while to try to tell the author what I liked and why. And I, like probably most people here, like fics that are written as grammatically correct as possible, but I'm not very good at saying whatever I didn't really like....
>
> GRIMLOCK72: As a non-writer I try to at least tell the writer (who has spent considerable time writing this story after all) what I liked, while sneakily mixing in some remarks about stuff I didn't like.

Still Waters' claim to be "no expert" and Grimlock's identification as a "non-writer" suggest a tension in the role of reading and response. Note that these two writers are demurring for two different reasons: Still Waters claims that she is not a feedback expert, whereas Grimlock merely claims that she is a "non-writer." Grimlock, at least, constructs feedback as *not* writing, but other readers immediately take issue with her construction.

> JUSTSKIPIT: I'm thrilled to see Grimmy comment in this thread. I'd have to rank Grimmy in the top 1 or 2 feedbackers on the forum (from my stories that is). One piece of advice to people wondering how to write feedback: look at Grimmy's average comments. Incredibly insightful and detailed. You can always count on her ... to tell you what she likes but very definitely what she DOES NOT. I so appreciate that as a writer.

In this post, Just Skip It explicitly offers Grimlock's work as a model, explicitly encouraging readers who seem less sure of their abilities as critical writers to write more "insightful and detailed" commentary by studying the work of their peers. It is perhaps ironic that the "non-writer" writes the best feedback, but this fact is consistent with the deliberate separation of "creative writing" and "criticism" at the site.

Although more experienced critical respondents go out of their way to reassure newer site members that they appreciate even the simplest of feedback, they also hold up writers like Grimlock as models from which newer writers can learn and, as in Just Skip It's post above, explicitly suggest that such models ought to be emulated. At the same time, experienced writers at the site remind others that the writing environment should not be confused with school: there are no assignments here, no grades, no apparently arbitrary rules. Instead, there is a desire to develop as readers and writers, and to help one another to do this as well.

There is much more to say about the processes of informal learning that go on at *Different Colored Pens*. In addition to inviting and encouraging people to write themselves into active roles at the site, experienced *Pens* writers advocate that site members read thoroughly, imitate and emulate the work of more experienced writers, respect the opinions of others, express gratitude for the reading and writing that their peers do, and perhaps most importantly, commit their responses in writing to the developing archive. This website thus makes visible a way of thinking about the work of reading and writing fan fiction that is useful not only for fans but for teachers and students of writing. I have certainly raised more questions than I have answered here, and I hope that further work on fan fiction feedback can take up some of them. If, for example, expert readers and writers model critical writing for newer site members, as I have suggested, then how could we read the work of those newer writers for signs of improvement? Do such attempts to instruct, however informally, have identifiable results? Clearly, the work of fan fiction readers and writers — both those who craft the fiction and those who read it and respond to it — needs more critical attention.

*I would like to extend my sincere thanks to the contributors to* Different Colored Pens *and its host site,* The Kitten, the Witches, and the Bad Wardrobe, *for allowing me to read and quote their work, and to Hannah Dentinger and Jean Grace, who graciously provided feedback.*

## NOTES

1. *Different Colored Pens,* http://thekittenboard.com/board/viewforum.php?f=5. Accessed June 30, 2008.
2. "Katharyn Rosser" and all other names used here are screen names chosen by individual *Different Colored Pens* site members.
3. Fan fiction authors generally include, at the beginning of whole stories or individual chapters, a brief set of notes including story title, premise, major characters, rating, disclaimers, and author contact information.
4. *Henneth Annûn Story Archive,* http://www.henneth-annun.net. Accessed June 30, 2008.
5. Camille Bacon-Smith's early ethnography of a *Star Trek* fan community observed that more experienced fans actively mentor new fans into appropriate standards of behavior while John Tulloch and Henry Jenkins have suggested that more "senior" fans "have discursive power in establishing the 'informed' exegesis for their [group] of fans" (150).
6. Responses in "The Laundry Diaries" average 77 words; the shortest is four words ("Stunning. Absolutely frickin' stunning"), and the longest is Sassette's.

## WORKS CITED

"The Art of Leaving Feedback." *The Kitten, the Witches, and the Bad Wardrobe.* 25 Apr. 2005. 6 Apr. 2009. <http://www.thekittenboard.com/board/viewtopic.php?t=3094>.

Bacon-Smith, Camille. *Enterprising Women: Television, Fandom and the Creation of Popular Myth.* Philadelphia: University of Pennsylvania Press, 1992.

Brobeck, Kristi Lee. "Under the Waterfall: A Fanfiction Community's Analysis of Their Self-Representation and Peer Review." *Refractory* 5 (2004): 12 pp. 25 June 2004. <http://www.refractory.unimelb.edu.au/journalissues/vol5/brobeck.html>.

Gere, Anne Ruggles. *Writing Groups: History, Theory, Implications.* Carbondale: Southern Illinois University Press, 1987.

"The Laundry Diaries." *Different Colored Pens. The Kitten, The Witches, and the Bad Wardrobe.* 30 Nov. 2004. 6 Apr. 2009 <http://thekittenboard.com/board/viewtopic.php?t=2916>.

"Reading and Writing Fan Fiction." *The Kitten, the Witches, and the Bad Wardrobe.* 18 Jul 2002. 6 Apr. 2009 <http://thekittenboard.com/board/viewtopic.php?t=2223&sid=02193c7757cef494207c4c3b35dabe28>.

Spigelman, Candace. *Across Property Lines: Textual Ownership in Writing Groups.* Carbondale: Southern Illinois University Press, 2000.

Tulloch, John, and Henry Jenkins. *Science Fiction Audiences: Watching* Dr. Who *and* Star Trek. London: Routledge, 1995.

# 24

## MetaSpace: Meatspace and Blogging Intersect

### Elizabeth Kleinfeld

At a party recently, a new acquaintance, upon discovering that I teach college writing, said, "My condolences. It must be really hard to teach writing in a culture that doesn't value reading." Others at the party concurred that our culture doesn't value reading, and furthermore, that "no one reads anymore," an assumption that specifically motivated this collection (see the Introduction). I suspect that it may be true that our culture doesn't value the same kind of reading that I value, but I must take issue with the idea that "no one reads anymore."

Although my book and journal article reading has remained steady since I started college in 1987, my overall reading has exploded since 1993, when I got my very first email account and learned about the Internet. Since I began blogging in April 2004, inspired by a Clancy Ratliff conference presentation, I've probably read no fewer than twenty blog entries a week written by others. That translates to about 4320 blog entries, and that's an extremely conservative estimate, considering that for the past three years, I've assigned blogging to my students, which adds about sixty entries a week to my weekly blog reading during the academic year.

But I'm an English professor, so of course I read a lot. Well then, let's look at the reading habits of my students. Anecdotal evidence shared in faculty offices and hallways is that students don't even read what's assigned to them. But every semester, twenty-percent or more of my students read and respond to my personal blog, although I've never assigned those tasks to them. When I ask them why they read my blog, they inevitably tell me "it's entertaining." And why do I read so many blogs? There's some professional development to it, sure — I often learn of conferences through the blogs of other academics, or can commiserate with other faculty across the country about issues germane to college teaching, or read others' grapplings with issues I'm grappling with — but I admit that reading blogs is one of my favorite forms of entertainment. Like my students, I find blogs to be immensely amusing and fun, and reading blogs at the end of the day (or in the middle...) helps me relax, unwind, and often laugh.

Blogging is changing how my students and I interact. Before blogging, my students and I got to know each other before and after class through banter and during class through conversations related to course content. Now that my students and I read each others' blogs hours after class has ended, even on non-class days, we know much more about each others' likes and dislikes, hobbies, job, and activities. A sense of community grows much more quickly and friendships develop with speed. As a writing teacher, I am thrilled to see my students writing more than ever.

In this chapter, I discuss four incidents from April 2008 related to my blog, the blogs I read regularly, including those of my students, and conversations/interactions that grow out of this particular combination of blogs. These incidents illustrate the intersections and juxtapositions of public and private, personal and professional, academic and non-academic, silly and serious that blogs highlight. Paying attention to these juxtapositions can be helpful for compositionists interested in what Jeff Rice terms "cool rhetoric," a rhetoric characterized by interactivity and juxtaposition that can help those concerned about the effects of new media on the literacy practices of today's students better understand the shifts they may be observing.

This chapter takes a form loosely based on the form of blog entries, with comments posted below the entries. Because a blogger wouldn't normally comment on her own entries, but would rather respond to comments posted by readers, my comments here should be read as my fulfilling a different role from the original poster; the comments are more analytical in nature and from the perspective of a researcher rather than that of a blogger and teacher. Although I've structured this chapter as a series of posts and comments, I want to emphasize that these are not blog entries, as they have no hyperlinks. Hyperlinks are not a mere detail of formatting but are actually crucial to how blogs function, working as suggestive and implied connectors, subtle hints, and transitions, as well as allowing readers and writers to circumvent all manner of linearity.[1]

## *Blogging as Roleplaying*

I have been blogging for over four years, using my personal blog, revisionspiral (http://revisionspiral.blog-city.com), as a place to report and reflect on developments in my personal and professional life. I have also maintained several class-related blogs that I use much like a course management system, and I have occasionally blogged pseudonymously. In this chapter, I focus on my blogging at revisionspiral because it has the largest and most varied readership.

I do not actively publicize my blog and it does not have a significant readership. In the technorati ratings, as of June 2008, my blog ranks 264,497, well below many other academics' blogs, such as Clancy Ratliff's *Culture Cat* (ranked at 140,327 by technorati) and the pseudonymous Doctor Crazy's *Reassigned Time* (ranked at 55,120). Most of my readers visit either because they've seen my blog's URL in my email signature line or they read another blog that links to mine. Because I blog about a wide range of topics on revisionspiral, from observations about my six-year-old daughter to critical responses to composition scholarship to griping about receiving bad service, a wide variety of different readers visit my blog. My largest audience is graduate students in composition and rhetoric, who tend to find my blog when another links to mine, and colleagues at other institutions whom I've met at conferences or who learn of my blog when I post a comment to theirs. My blog also attracts readers outside of academia. Several of my posts on parenting issues have been picked up as links on parenting blogs, and when I posted a recipe for mojitos I had concocted, many lovers of cool summer drinks visited my blog.

My students are often regular readers of my blog. I require all my students to blog, and I provide about ten minutes of every class meeting in my Composition 1 and 2 classes for blogging. When I introduce blogging to my students, I tell them that I blog, but I don't mention my blog address. The students who find my blog notice the URL in my email signature or follow the link to it on the class blog (all students' blogs are listed in a blogroll there, and I include mine simply because I consider myself a class member) and visit my blog out of curiosity, I imagine. Occasionally, a student will find my blog by Googling me.

Because I have such a wide readership, I play many different roles on my blog. In one entry, I'm a teacher. In another, I'm a colleague. In others, I'm a *Battlestar Galactica* fan, punctuation buff, parent, citizen, or something else.

## The Difference Between Work and Play

> Work consists of whatever a body is obliged to do. Play consists of whatever a body is not obliged to do. — Mark Twain, *The Adventures of Tom Sawyer*

My job as a writing professor certainly does not oblige me to blog, so although I often blog about work-related topics, such as how to manage work submitted late by students, or coping with meetings with no clear agenda, or celebrating a class activity that goes well, blogging for me is pure play. I mean "play" here both in the sense of "fun" and also in the sense of a practical activity recognized by child development experts and psychologists as one that allows children to rehearse roles and skills. When I read the blog of another writer, part of me is tuning into how the blogger has framed an issue and resolved it. When I blog, I am framing and resolving. Play is active, not passive, and when I read and write blogs, I am actively turning over ideas, the same way a child might examine a block from different angles and try fitting it into differently shaped spaces in play.

Because I require my students to blog, the blogging they do specifically for my class is work. Interestingly, every semester, about 15 percent of my students blog more than necessary to fulfill class requirements.[2] They blog about topics unrelated to class assignments, such as how they spent their weekend, what they are working on in their other classes, and their jobs. However, even when students are blogging only to fulfill class assignments, I find that the nature of blogging encourages a kind of playfulness that does not occur frequently in student work. I want to suggest that blogging, even when done so purely out of obligation, functions like other forms of play that have been studied. While my students are blogging, they are engaged in an inherently rhetorical activity, considering audiences and different ways of articulating their ideas to different audiences. And just as I fulfill different roles in my blogging, students are roleplaying in their blogging as well. Sometimes they play the role of engaged, conscientious student; sometimes student-just-trying-to-get-by; sometimes helpful classmate; sometimes confused classmate in need of help; sometimes confused classmate just venting and not really wanting assistance; and sometimes, roles unrelated to classroom identities, such as parent, worker, spouse or partner, citizen, or coffee connoisseur.

Before 2004, I required my students to journal, keeping private notebooks in which they recorded and responded to their developing ideas about class topics. I often had students exchange journals and write comments in each others' books. In 2004, when I began blogging myself, I recognized that blogs could achieve what those private-but-shared journals achieved, only better. The public nature of blogs, combined with the conventional informality of blog writing, allows my students to blog their developing thoughts and ideas in an imperfect way without feeling pressure to focus on surface errors rather than substantive ideas. But because any class member or, really, any person with an Internet connection, can, theoretically, find and read the student's blog entry, the student also needs to consider how to articulate thoughts in a fashion that makes sense to a reader. Most excitingly, students often realize that those readers can be enticed to post comments that may help the blogger refine the thoughts or figure something out. In this way, students begin to recognize and appreciate the dialogic nature of thinking and writing. Because blogging is pubic, the blogger is always interacting with a reader; in other words, blogging is never a solitary experience, it is a social activity, with a reader who is assumed or hoped for or imagined or anticipated.

Reading and writing blogs also allow students to see writing in terms of the process rather than the product. As much as compositionists argue that we should be teaching process rather than product, the students coming into my classes have learned that that's all just talk. They know perfectly well that their teachers, in English and across the curriculum, will ultimately evaluate them based on their written products. In the informal surveys I've conducted in my composition classes since 2002, a majority of students have admitted that they've avoided trying new writing techniques or avoided formulating their own ideas about class subjects because they are afraid they will lose points if they don't achieve surface perfection within the timeframe of the assignment. In other words, a majority of my students admit that they've glossed over thinking and writing *processes* to spend more time on writing *products* to ensure good grades. Blogging helps counteract the tendency to gloss over the thinking and writing processes by putting those processes on display. When I tell my students that thinking is a messy process, they need only read my own blog entries — or a classmate's — on a particular topic to see how I have revised my thoughts over time, sometimes significantly.

## A Nerd in Good Company

April begins with me reading Professing Mama's blogged confession that she is a nerd, as evidenced by her excitement about the *New York Times* crossword puzzle. She ends the entry with "I'm a nerd who loves her some crossword puzzle. My excitement about tonight's season premiere of *Battlestar Galactica* is probably another tip-off as to the nerd I have become. Oh well. :)." I read Professing Mama's confession and feel a connection. I, too, am a nerd.

I've been reading Professing Mama's pseudonymous blog and her previous blog, ABDMom, for about three years. Although I've never met her — heck, I don't even know her real name, where she lives, what she looks like, or where she teaches — I feel that I know her pretty well. Through her blog, I know her teaching philosophy, what she likes and dislikes about her current university faculty position, and about her struggles to get pregnant. I relate to Professing Mama on many levels beyond the realization that we are both nerds, and as I said, although we've never met, I do feel as if she is a friend.

So her admission that she's a nerd does more than tell me that a stranger is, like me, a nerd. It is more like the feeling of warmth and connection I get when a friend and I realize we have something else in common we didn't realize before. And her specific mention of *Battlestar Galactica* deepens my feeling because I am also a fan of the series. In fact, a month earlier, when I had attended the joint conference of the Popular Culture Association and American Culture Association, I had been thrilled to see several sessions devoted to the series. Immediately after returning from the conference, I mentioned on my blog that I had attended a panel on *Battlestar Galactica* and several bloggers posted comments asking me to elaborate on the panel.

On April 8, I finally posted a full entry to my own blog about that *Battlestar Galactica* panel from the PCA/ACA conference, "Humans in Space: Exploring *Battlestar Galactica*." I focused my blog entry on Cyndi Headley's presentation, "Disabled Cures: Laura Roslin and Illness, Gender, and Power," which examined how one series character's illness was presented on the show.

A few days later, in my Composition 1 class, students and I were discussing membership in groups and subgroups. I explained that fans of particular TV shows can be considered to be members of a group, and I mentioned that I am a member of the *Battlestar Galactica* fan group. None of the students in the class had seen the show and one student, Bryan,[3] made a snide comment about science fiction being an inferior genre. Other students in the class, referring to an earlier class discussion about what makes for valid argumentation, urged Bryan to watch *Battlestar Galactica* before making judgments about it.

Bryan heeded their advice and posted a long entry to his blog about a week later in which he responded to an episode he had watched. Although Bryan states in his blog entry that he is unlikely to watch the show again, he does concede that *Battlestar Galactica* seemed more "matrix-y"—a reference to *The Matrix* films by Andy and Larry Wachowski—than he had realized. He went on to clarify the statement he had made in class about science fiction being an inferior genre, articulating a position that science fiction like *The Matrix* films is not inferior because it's interested in human struggles more than in technology, but that science fiction that is concerned only with technological prowess is inferior. Several students in class read Bryan's blog entry and asked him in class to name a science fiction film or TV show that is "concerned only with technological prowess," but he declined.

Outside of class, my blog entry about the *Battlestar Galactica* conference panel generated conversations with two faculty colleagues. Both were talking in the hall and when I walked by, they called me over and one said, "I didn't know you watched *Battlestar Galactica!*" We talked about the show's current storylines and then discussed the portrayal of cylons, robots who evolved to look, think, and feel like humans, and aliens in popular culture.

On April 12, Clancy Ratliff, whose *Culture Cat* was the very first blog I read, posted her prediction of how one of the big mysteries in the *Battlestar Galactica* series may be resolved. A few days later, I tracked down my two *BSG* fan colleagues and we all theorized about the mystery.

## Comment:

This interaction highlights several different incidents of roleplaying. I shifted among the roles of blog reader, blog writer, teacher, and *Battlestar Galactica* fan, while Bryan shifted from student in the classroom to blogger continuing and refining an argument that began in class, moved online, and then continued back in the classroom. Bryan's entry is an example of thinking processes made visible through blogging. His classmates were able to trace his thought process from original claim made in class to his revision of that claim on his blog.

My discussion of Headley's conference presentation allowed my students to see me as a *Battlestar Galactica* fan, but more importantly, it showed them how one could approach a popular television show more academically. My students often suggest that reading critically is "overanalyzing," looking so deeply at something that you distort the thing you are examining, or that it drains the enjoyment out of reading. My entry about Headley's presentation helped some students see that the analysis can be the fun.

## Mean People Really Do Suck

"Mean People Really Do Suck" is the title of the April 9 blog entry on *Lyings and Tirades and Fears, Oh My!,* the blog of a university faculty member who goes by the pseudonym aerobil. This aerobil post tells of a mean-spirited rejection letter she received: "I know how bitter I sound. And it's not just because I was rejected. It's because I was rejected in a mean-spirited way, and the person who wrote that review cannot be held accountable." I posted a comment to aerobil's blog entry, acting as a sympathetic colleague.

Aerobil's blog entry appeared around the same time that some students in my classes started griping to me about their frustration with getting meaningful response to their drafts from classmates. I emphasize peer response in all of my writing classes, and it is typical for my students around this point in the semester to voice frustration that they are not receiving useful responses from their peers. Aerobil's blog entry gave me an idea for how to address the students' frustration in class. One of aerobil's complaints was that "the person who wrote the review cannot be held accountable," and although my students do sign their responses, they cannot really be held accountable, much like aerobil's anonymous reviewer. The students in my class who only want to pass the course, rather than strive for an A or a B, can decide to write mediocre responses to each others' work. While I try to motivate students to write detailed reviews for their peers by awarding more points for stronger reviews, the students who are aiming only for a passing grade will often write vague and general responses, which earn them few points but they are unconcerned about that. The unintended consequence, for me as a teacher, is that the students who receive those responses don't find them very helpful.

Aerobil's blog entry gave me the simple idea to have students blog about response in general. First, I had students blog in class about the best and worst response they've received all semester. Students accomplished that part of the prompt fairly easily. Next, I asked them to blog about the best and worst response they've given all semester. For a few of the students who had given only lackluster responses to their peers' drafts all semester, the second part of the blog prompt got them to recognize that their behavior was having an adverse effect on their peers.

## Comment:

The "mean people really do suck" interchange demonstrates the spatial aspects of blogging. Aerobil is at another university in another state, and her anonymous reviewer is probably in yet another state. I read her blog and posted a comment, then brought the experience to my students who blogged and posted comments. This interchange also shows me moving among the roles of reader and sympathetic colleague to aerobil, then teacher making an assignment to her students, and finally, as I read and posted comments on my students' blogs, into the role of coach, encouraging students to be more assertive with their readers and pushing them to challenge themselves to respond more critically.

## *The To Do List*

By mid–April, my Composition 2 students were spending every class period workshopping drafts of pieces for their final projects. I spent a few minutes at the beginning of every class talking with them about where they should be, what they were struggling with, and other concerns related to deadline pressure. Just as my students were feeling the deadline pressure at that point in the semester, I was, too. Projects that I needed to finish by the end of the semester weighed on me just as the final projects weighed on my students.

I decided the time was right to introduce the students to a common blog meme, the "To Do List." Many bloggers post bulleted lists of what they need to do in the coming days. Posting such a to do list is helpful in part because articulating to an audience what you need to do often helps you realize exactly *what* you need to do. It also provides a dose of public accountability. After I introduced the "To Do List" meme, I ended each class period with ten minutes of blogging to do lists. These lists were amusing and allowed students a chance to blow off steam. Several mentioned items such as "Complain to friends or co-workers about mean comp teacher," while some began experimenting with ways to elicit help from readers of their to do lists, realizing that posting, "I need to figure out how to conclude my essay" wouldn't inspire readers to help, but "My essay makes points X and Y and I can't figure out how to conclude in a way that gives equal emphasis to both X and Y. Any ideas?" could move classmates to post suggestions.

On April 13, I posted a to do list of items I myself needed to accomplish in the next two days and mentioned, in part for the benefit of any students who might be reading,

> The end of the semester is in sight, which is both a good thing (I'm tired and would love to get caught up on sleep, not to mention I need to get my garden in order, finish Marilyn Krysl's difficult book on post–911 life, which I began a month ago and haven't finished, work on the book with Amy, write an article with a June deadline, finish my PCA/ACA blogging, etc.) and a bad thing (so much to get done before the semester ends). This is the point in the semester when I begin to feel the end of the semester breathing down my neck.

I hoped that by sharing my view of the end of the semester as both a threat and a relief, students would realize that I recognized and appreciated the anxiety they felt. My to do list included a reference to the book my book club is reading, *Dinner with Osama* by Marilyn Krysl, and the stacks of papers I needed to respond to for two different classes. I was careful to mention that I was looking forward to reading the papers. I am always aware that the way I write about students and their work on my blog needs to be consistent with my pedagogy.

The next day on campus, two students stopped me in the hall to talk about the Marilyn Krysl book. Both students had accompanied me to a reading from the book — at the time, none of us had read it — and the students are curious about my impressions.

## Comment:

This interchange highlights the random, playful nature of blogging and how that randomness can actually be quite productive. As students blog about what they need to do, they, like I, often ignore boundaries between personal and school-related to-do items, which can lead to interesting juxtapositions and realizations. In my to do list, for instance, reading student papers is technically "work" and reading the Marilyn Krysl book is technically "personal." But it's the reference to the Krysl book that gets the attention of two students, who want to talk to me about the book during my office hours — that's "work."

The public and dialogic nature of the Web also comes into play with this interchange. Students who post to do lists to their blogs are posting for readers, considering how readers might be able to help them with their tasks.

# R.B.O.C.

The R.B.O.C., or "random bullets of crap," entry is a blogging convention in which the blogger posts a bulleted list of thoughts or ideas. Some R.B.O.C. lists are built around a theme, such as "thoughts that crossed my mind while sitting in a meeting," while others are held together through place ("observations made downtown") or time ("random thoughts I had today").

On April 17, I posted a R.B.O.C. entry about a conference I attended that month. Two items on my list sparked responses. The first included a reference to Krav Maga, which I had recently started. Several students in different classes wanted to chat with me before and after class about different forms of martial arts. A former student whom I had lost contact with stopped by during my office hours to talk about Krav Maga. And finally, a colleague in another department stopped me in the hall to talk about whether I would recommend Krav Maga for his son.

The other list item that inspired conversation was a fairly cranky observation about a behavior I'd noted in several of the conference presentations:

> Nothing kills a presentation for me like the presenter making disparaging remarks about students. Otherwise interesting and helpful presentations are ruined for me when a presenter repeatedly rolls his/her eyes when referring to students or makes sarcastic remarks like, "Students *claim*...." I value and respect my students, and I seem to take it personally when presenters don't.

Another blogger and close colleague, Amy Braziller, posted a response on her own blog in which she discussed her appreciation of students both in and out of the classroom.

On April 18, I posted another R.B.O.C. entry in which I mentioned my Composition 1 students' audio essays and announced that I had opened an account with a free file storing/sharing/hosting service. One of my regular readers, a colleague I've never actually met but who reads and comments on my blog regularly, suggested a different file storing service for me to try. A week later, after my students complained about having trouble downloading files from the first service I tried, I took my colleague's advice and switched to the service she had recommended.

The reference to my students' audio essays caught the eyes of two colleagues in the English department, both of whom came by separately to talk to me about designing audio essay assignments for their classes.

## Comment:

I stated at the beginning of this chapter that I find blogging to be entertaining, and I meant that in several different senses. To entertain is to extend hospitality toward another, and it is also an activity; to entertain a thought is to consider it. I would categorize the interchange between Braziller and me as entertainment in the sense that our blog entries on faculty attitudes toward students invited others to consider their attitudes toward students. My blogged mention of my students' audio essays worked as an invitation to two of my colleagues to consider assigning audio essays. Many blog entries can be seen as invitations to the reader to contemplate an idea from a different perspective.

The differences between the blogged to do list and the R.B.O.C. entry can be minimal, and many blogged to do lists lack any sense of ordering of their items. Urgent and non-urgent items, personal and work-related items, practical and whimsical items bump against each other in unpredictable ways. Furthermore, the ability of the blogger to hyperlink items on the to do list or R.B.O.C. adds another dimension of randomness that has no print analog.

## 5 Random Things

One popular blog meme is the "random things" form in which bloggers post a list of random facts about themselves. The pattern makes its way around the blogosphere periodically with a different number attached, so sometimes it's "16 Random Things," sometimes "25 Random Things," and so on. In an effort to resist essayist closure and in keeping with the never finished nature of blogs, I'm going to close with "5 Random Things" rather than a traditional conclusion.

1. Blogging — both reading and writing blogs — is entertaining in both the sense of being a fun escape and in the sense of offering the opportunity to consider and engage with ideas.

2. Blogging provides an opportunity to rehearse roles and skills. Bloggers often play multiple roles, such as fan, student, expert, and citizen. Each role requires analysis of a different rhetorical situation.

3. Through the posting of and responding to comments and the subsequent revisions of thinking that may be made visible on a blog, blogging makes the dialogic nature of thinking and writing explicit.

4. If we assume that all of our reading and writing, whether it is academic, personal, professional, none of the above, or some combination of the above, affects how we understand reading and writing, we can recognize the blogging activities of students as rhetorical activities worthy of both study and encouragement.

5. In *The Rhetoric of Cool: Composition Studies and New Media*, Jeff Rice argues for a pedagogy of digital writing that honors the nature of digital writing without forcing it to conform to the linear model of writing for print.

The challenge for composition studies is to translate the theoretical principles of juxtaposition to a pedagogy appropriate for digital writing. This kind of writing would not analyze juxtapositions found in either popular media or professional discourse and report on their rhetorical effectiveness but would produce a writing comprised of juxtapositions. It would be, therefore, performative. Previously, I have called this writing "hip-hop pedagogy" not because it is dependent on hip-hop music but rather because of how it borrows the rhetorical strategies centered around juxtaposition.... In hip-hop pedagogy, patterns motivate readers and writers to find unrealized connections among disparate events and material things. (91)

Blogged to do lists, R.B.O.C. blog entries, and other blog memes may be ways for teachers to explore the rhetoric of juxtaposition and non-linearity with students.

## NOTES

1. For a more thorough discussion of the rhetoric of hyperlinks, I recommend Nicholas C. Burbules' essay "The Web as a Rhetorical Place" from *Silicon Literacies*, edited by Ilana Snyder.

2. In the interest of full disclosure, I should point out that every semester, there are also students who blog less than they need to to fulfill class requirements. Perhaps that will be the topic of a future essay.

3. The student asked that he not be identified by name in this essay, so Bryan is a pseudonym.

## WORKS CITED

Aerobil. "Mean People Really Do Suck." *Lyings and Tirades and Fears, Oh My!* 9 Apr. 2008. 9 Apr. 2008. <http://aerobil.blogspot.com/2008/04/mean-people-really-do-suck.html>.

Braziller, Amy. "The Company of Students." *Midgebop.* 29 Apr. 2008. 29 Apr. 2008. <http://midgebop.blog-city.com/?d=29&m=4&y=2008>.

Burbules, Nicholas C. "The Web as a Rhetorical Place." *Silicon Literacies.* Ed. Ilana Snyder. London: Routledge, 2002. 75–84.

Headley, Cyndi. "Disabled Cures: Laura Roslin and Illness, Gender, and Power." Popular Culture Association/American Culture Association 2008 National Conference. San Francisco, 19–22 Mar. 2008.

Krysl, Marilyn. *Dinner with Osama.* Notre Dame: University of Notre Dame Press, 2008.

Professing Mama. "I'm a Nerd." *Professing Mama.* 4 Apr. 2008. 5 Apr. 2008. <http://professingmama.blogspot.com/2008/04/im-nerd.html>.

Ratliff, Clancy. "Two Observations About Nerdy Things I Watched on TV Last Night." *Culture Cat.* 12 Apr. 2008. 12 Apr. 2008. <http://culturecat.net/two-observations-about-nerdy-things-i-wa>.

_____. "Whose Voices Get Heard? Gender Politics in the Blogosphere." Conference on College Composition and Communication Convention. San Antonio, 24–27 Mar. 2004.

Rice, Jeff. *The Rhetoric of Cool: Composition Studies and New Media.* Carbondale: Southern Illinois University Press, 2007.

# 25

# Meeting the Digital
# Generation in the Classroom:
# A Reflection on the Obstacles

*Heather Urbanski*

As a college writing professor interested in the rhetoric of digital media and participatory entertainment, what brings the questions and issues raised this collection to a critical mass, for me, is that the Digital Generation will be, and is, entering college, and thus first-year writing. Many of these students will have had a fundamentally different experience with texts than those who came before because digital media allows them to actively interact with their entertainment in significantly greater ways. These students may have read *Lord of the Rings* or (more likely) have seen the Peter Jackson film trilogy but are even more likely to have been more excited about the variety of video and online computer games based on the narrative, in which they do not merely experience the story but actively construct their own, taking on the roles of their favorite characters and setting off on digital adventures. The Digital Generation see texts as more interactive than perhaps previous generations and are less content to merely receive messages, being intent on participating in the creation of those messages. A common thread among the ideas in this collection is that these students have a non-traditional view of textual interaction and often spend a lot of their out of class time employed in significantly creative, narrative-based activities that do not fit the traditional construction of textual engagement.

From my admittedly limited perspective, I see three potentially significant obstacles for those looking to incorporate the rhetorical activities documented and analyzed in this volume into contemporary writing classrooms, or any other classroom really. The first is at the individual level: the steep learning curve that can be involved in manipulating and navigating these technologies. I experienced this firsthand as I tried (and failed) to join Second Life and tried (and in some ways succeeded) to set up Facebook and Twitter accounts. The first section of this chapter recounts those experiences, in a hopefully humorous but definitely humbling fashion, and speculates on ways we can still encourage and account for digital media even if we don't (can't?) experience them ourselves.

The second obstacle operates at a much more cultural, perhaps even global, stage: questions of access. As Siva Vaidhyanathan argues, talking of a Digital Generation without considering "the needs and perspectives of those young people who are not socially or financially privileged ... presumes a level playing field and equal access" when such things are not the reality. Many other scholars and media critics have addressed this question more eloquently and in more depth than I could hope to here so I will just point to Henry Jenkins's work for a review of these issues for those readers interested in learning more ("Confronting").

Finally, stepping back from such global concerns, but remaining at a cultural level, my third obstacle is perhaps the one that will get me in the most trouble: us, the academics who populate Humanities departments, especially in the field of English Studies. I have observed a persistent inclination toward nostalgia for the printed text among critics of digital media that all too often unreflectively paints all print texts as sacrosanct and all digital as unworthy. Such a perspective seems particularly unproductive and I engage with some of the key reasons in the second half of this chapter.

Underlying these two obstacles (the technological learning curves and print nostalgia), the question seems to be "Are we getting in our own way?"

## Obstacle: Technical Know-How[1]

Setting up my Facebook profile during the spring 2009 semester was enough to make me feel like a Luddite. I had heard so much about it that it seemed I already knew how it worked but sitting there, I felt like my four-year-old nephew looking at the directions for assembling his IKEA bedroom dresser: completely confused. There just seemed to be a lot of buttons to click but not a lot of direction. I know that part of the attraction of such digital media is that they are user-directed and self-sponsored but I couldn't help wishing for a nice wizard or two to help me get started. It didn't have to be Gandalf or Merlin; just a clean dialog box with a few buttons, some options, and enough direction to help me get oriented.

Maybe it was there and I just missed it. That is always a possibility but I don't think so. And the whole process of requesting others to be my friend, which is the real power of Facebook, or so I've been told, was a little intimidating, if not potentially humiliating. Asking people "do you want to be my friend" brings to mind all kinds of childhood fears. But why was I so intimidated by such a popular system? After all, so many people use it that it can't be that difficult. And I have used various other programs over the years that I should have been able to figure it out. I came to realize that I may have been expecting too much all at once. Now that I have become more comfortable with the system, I have settled on some speculations on what can get in our way as writing teachers trying to enter new media:

- Our expectations of the media based on the hype, both local and popular.
- Our expectations of our individual learning curves, and the accompanying frustration when the pace feels too slow.
- The lack of guiding/orientation documents, though this varies depending on the media experienced.
- The feeling we "have" to use it.
- Concerns about getting the settings just right so that the horror stories in the media about social networking *faux pas* do not happen to us.

This last one was particularly puzzling as the tension between private and public became less theory and more reality after actually taking the plunge into Facebook. How much info should I post? Whom should I share it with? Which pictures would be "appropriate"? How do I filter students from friends from colleagues? In that way, Facebook is really a microcosm of identity development and should give rhetoricians much material to chew on for a long time to come, at least until the next big thing comes along and Facebook gets replaced or bought or folds on its own.

But my experiments with Facebook were wildly successful compared to the dismal results of my foray into Second Life (SL) in the spring of 2008, from spending forty-five minutes tweaking the appearance of my avatar to failed attempts to learn to drive a car in the virtual environment (flying was much easier). That experiment was hampered by my lack of skill with manipulating keyboard controls and I wonder whether this could explain why so few instructors may actively engage in such participatory digital media.

After the initial set-up visit, I spent most of my second trip into SL adjusting the appearance my avatar, and I realized as I adjusted all the minor settings (everything from the length of "my" shirt sleeve to the volume of my hair) that nearly all of my changes were made based on my physical appearance in "Real Life" (RL). In other words, I was doing all I could to make my avatar look just like me. And even as I was doing it, it seemed strange in some ways. After all, wasn't one of the draws of a virtual world like SL the freedom to create avatars from scratch, removed from the physical reality that had such a deciding factor on my appearance? The conventional wisdom and urban legends about SL and other similar simulated environments often focus on the fifty-year-old man who "pretends" to be a hot teenage girl, or those cutting edge teens who deliberately play with inherited societal gender codes to craft avatars that more closely reflect who they "really" are.

And yet here I was doing the opposite. I was recreating myself in the virtual world and when I realized this, I wondered why I hadn't even considered making different choices. Was it a lack of creativity? Was I just being lazy? I have to admit, that was a big part of it. I was focusing so much on learning to use the system, on figuring out how to see my avatar without other newbies on Orientation Island literally walking onto the screen and blocking my view (this happened twice), that I just didn't think too much about the choices I was making. In fact, it was only after I had been through several screens that I realized all the choices I was making were about matching the avatar to my mirror in RL. It dawned on me, actually, when I began looking for the setting for curly hair since my "real" curly hair is an important part of my appearance.

But the more I thought about it, I realized it wasn't just laziness. My decisions about the appearance of my avatar were also tied to my purpose for joining SL in the first place. While I had been interested in the virtual world, my decision to actually download the program, and to create an account, was for research purposes. I, therefore, was entering SL primarily as a researcher, and so felt an almost ethical obligation to represent myself as faithfully as possible. Creating an avatar that differed significantly from my RL appearance seemed, at least to me, disingenuous for my research purposes.

On that second visit, I also found a writing contest in SL and joined a college professors group there. I so struggled, however, with the multi-tasking aspects of navigating SL, simply trying to figure out how to move while getting requests for "friendship" or other communication requests, that, honestly, I never went back after those initial two attempts to orient myself. I feel slightly embarrassed that I quit so easily, that I didn't try to stick it out longer, but in addition to the other distractions in my life during those months (finishing a dissertation, going on the job market), I also know that I was too digitally-handicapped to integrate into SL at that time.

So am I a member of the Digital Generation? Do I count? I certainly have sympathies for that "generation" but am not sure if I can consider myself a part of it. I find it all fascinating, and wish to encourage the activities. After all, I wouldn't have put together this collection if I didn't. But I find that every time I try to join the group, I fall short somehow. My Second Life adventures are in some ways understandable since my videogame days ended with Super Mario Bros. Actually, to be completely honest, they ended with that impossible *Empire Strikes Back* Atari game. At least, it was impossible for me. So the fact that I found it so difficult to manipulate an avatar using the keyboard while multi-tasking with communications and everything else in the "world" isn't that surprising. I wonder if my SL difficulty is because I dropped out of the gaming world so early on. I just don't have the muscle memory and habits of a gamer. It doesn't help, of course, that hand-eye coordination and fine motor skills have never been among my strengths.

So, I've accepted that SL may always be beyond my reach (the same with *World of Warcraft* and other such MMORPGs) but that doesn't necessarily exclude me from the Digital Generation. After all, while I didn't "grow up" with the technology, I haven't been afraid of it, and at the risk of dating myself, I did witness the evolution of email accounts from DOS-based systems with hand-coded FTPs to share files, through Lotus Notes, then web-based system interfaces, to the pause where we are now. So making the shift to Facebook and Twitter and the other social networking means of communication shouldn't be as difficult as it seems. Should it?

So what can I learn from this experience about the Digital Generation in the classroom? Part of me thinks that they might have more patience than we typically give them credit for. Learning and internalizing such new technology into daily life may come more easily for some than others (which I certainly can attest to) but it still takes time to learn, to play, to take what is useful and do something with it that makes sense for each individual's life. This observation seems to concur with the findings from the "most extensive U.S. study of youth media use," The Digital Youth Project, where the authors observe, "By exploring new interests, tinkering, and 'messing around' with new forms of media, they [the youth in the study] acquire various forms of technical and media literacy" (Ito, et al.). There is, in some ways, a delayed gratification in the "trial and error" (to use the Digital Youth Project's term) required in learning Facebook. It takes time to build a network of friends. It takes time to figure out what cool stuff is available, and then more time to figure out how to use it. These are not skills and habits conventional wisdom would tell us are in abundance with the Digital Generation.

There is also, though, to argue from the "adult" perspective, a lifestyle element in that many new adopters of technologies like Facebook and Twitter might just have more time in the their days for such pursuits. Many of my own students are very busy with full course loads, extracurriculars, and outside jobs but even still, when I look at the demands on their time with how overloaded my own schedule feels, I can't help but wonder if I might not have an easier time adapting to Facebook if I had a student not a professor's workload. It may then be no coincidence that the first place I saw MOOs, MUDS, and other precursors to today's digital media was in the basement computer lab at Rowan University in the mid–90s. Quite frankly, my fellow Rowan undergrads had the time to learn and incorporate those new technologies into their daily lives. Then, when they left college, they brought those skills and sensibilities with them and thus were among the most well prepared when *World of Warcraft*, Facebook, etc. all came along.

## Obstacle: Nostalgia

In what might be related to some of the technological obstacles I just described, we find the more abstract, but no less real, presence of nostalgia for an era when print texts were unquestionably sacrosanct, an era that may never have existed in the first place. While I grant that technophiles are often over-exuberant and promise much more than the technology can really deliver to the average user (see above), the virulence of the technophobes is disturbing to say the least.

Examples of this nostalgia for the printed text, and its corresponding devaluation of digital media rhetoric, are not difficult to find, even ironically in digital media texts. I have encountered what felt like a brick wall of nostalgia in face-to-face conversations with colleagues for years but recently the perspective crystallized in the postings to the website of *The Chronicle of Higher Education* by Emory University professor Mark Bauerlein. In both articles for the *Chronicle Review* and blog postings to *Brainstorm*, tagged as "*The Chronicle Review*'s team of bloggers on ideas, culture, and the arts," Bauerlein frequently reflects what seems to me an ironic rejection of the very medium in which his ideas are often communicated.

So, for this section, I'd like to take one of those articles as a representative example not of Bauerlein's views *per se* (which I believe are much more complex and nuanced than any set of articles can capture), but instead of a nostalgic inclination within the academy, especially among the Humanities, that may provide a significant obstacle to our ability to recognize and incorporate the rhetorical activities of the Digital Generation within our classrooms.

In "Online Literacy Is a Lesser Kind," Bauerlein applies usability and eye tracking studies performed on general audiences to make claims for all online experiences. Even though this article was published late in 2008, the only date provided for the studies is 2003, and Bauerlein's central thesis, that all "screen reading" is by definition deficient, seems to rest on the belief that all interactions with computers are the same, regardless of the content or situation: "Once again, this is not so much about the content students prefer ... or whether they use the Web for homework or not. It is about the reading styles they employ. They race across the surface, dicing language and ideas into bullets and graphics, seeking what they already want and shunning the rest."

In this article, Bauerlein's broad brush condemns all online experiences and halfway through the argument, a nostalgic, even elitist, reasoning seems to be revealed: "Yes it's a kind of literacy, but it breaks down in the face of a dense argument, a Modernist poem, a long political tract, and other texts that require steady focus and linear attention — in a word, slow reading." The article then becomes, for me, disturbingly thick with a devaluation of the Digital Generation, as in this familiar complaint when describing student response to an internet-free research assignment: "Checking a reference book, asking a librarian, and finding a microfiche didn't occur to them. So many free deliveries through the screen had sapped that initiative." He goes on to attack "a strange flattening of reading," invoking as his standard-bearers the stalwarts of *Madame Bovary* and *Middlemarch* while charging nameless colleagues with "cavalierly violat[ing] their charge as stewards of literacy" for promoting non-print literacy as anything other than a "lesser kind" that "conspires against certain intellectual habits requisite to liberal-arts learning."

Besides the fact that Bauerlein seems to ignore that digital media encompasses so many more experiences than reading, as the preceding chapters in this collection demonstrate, by embracing the gatekeeper function so dramatically, he seems to be endorsing the use of "literacy" as a weapon, in the way that composition scholar Mike Rose has so eloquently critiqued many times. I hope that readers will indulge me in just one more extended quote from Bauerlein because the perceived conflict with students' values seems central to the nostalgia with which I'd like to engage:

> The inclination to read a huge Victorian novel, the capacity to untangle a metaphor in a line of verse, the desire to study and emulate a distant historical figure, the urge to ponder a concept such as Heidegger's ontic-ontological difference over and over and around and around until it breaks through as a transformative insight — those dispositions melt away with every 100 hours of browsing, blogging, IMing, Twittering, and Facebooking.

Yet, as Rose has argued from the perspective of the Basic Writer, and as I would now like to argue for the digital media specialist, just because a rhetorical activity doesn't fit into a familiar *belles lettres* box, does not devalue that activity and Rose's concern for the dangerous consequences that follow from the urge for the "fast quip" are as real today as they were then (409). Rose argues that the word "literacy" and its opposite, "illiteracy," carry so much "semantic baggage" and reveal "deeply held attitudes and beliefs" that they must be used carefully (409). The use of such terms, Rose asserts, is often intended to affirm "the faculty's membership in the society of the literate" (409) and as Bauer-lein directly contrasts "intelligence" with "information-age mores" and urges rebellion against the "imperial force" of digital technology, Rose's critique, originally written in 1985 and for a different educational debate, nevertheless seems directly relevant here.

But this nostalgia is fairly pervasive and as I mentioned, many examples can be found, so here is just one more: the senior editor of *The Washington Post's* Book World "laments," according to Don Troop, that contemporary students' tastes in reading compare so unfavorably to earlier times when "amid the passion of civil rights, Vietnam, and the women's movement — student tastes ran more along the lines of *Howl, Soul on Ice*, and the poetry of Sylvia Plath": "'For the Twitter generation, the new slogan seems to be "Don't trust anyone over 140 characters," [the editor] writes. 'What you see at the next revolution is far more likely to be a well-designed Web site than a radical novel or a poem. Not to be a drag, but that's so uncool.'" While most of the comments to this News Blog item on the *Chronicle* website disagree with the nostalgic condemnation, those echoing the lament are particularly vehement: #4 from "jon" reflects what I would describe as "the Great Books bully":

> the stuff my students read — it's crap about dragons and the like — or, less recently, Harry Potter.... The sixties were full of hope for the future and this was reflected in at least some students reading habits. There is la difference between Dickens, the Brontes, Camus, Sartre, and Nietzsche and the Lust in the Dust writers of today.

The latter part of that comment, I believe, references Stephanie Meyer's vampire novels. And another comment (#6 from "Jeff") to Troop's News Blog item seems to reject all web-based texts: "The problem is not what the 'kids' are reading so much as that they are not reading as much as they should and if they do read beyond requirements for classes (which I have been told by my students is rare) it is something they Googled or Wiki."

Even a commentator who disagrees with the lament does so with a backhanded compliment when #10 from "D," in part, declares, "I acknowledge that the Internet provides masses of useless and sometimes harmful information, but it also sometimes succeeds in making useful information more accessible" (Troop).

In the neighborhood where I grew up right outside of Philadelphia, books were part of our lives and our school communities but they were not perceived with the staid reverence reflected by the articles I've just cited. We were just as likely to get excited about Science Olympiad as an author visit, or to spend the weekend at the Recreation Field watching and playing baseball and softball. In fact, for many of my classmates, and me to a certain extent, the intensive (myopic?) privileging of "proper" literature was a part of our education that more often than not was responsible for turning us away from that line of study. I won't name names (that would be unfair) but the declarations of printed texts, at least those properly sanctioned by professors like Bauerlein, to be sacrosanct, killed the reading impulses of more students than the English professor I am now cares to acknowledge. Rose has made this point so eloquently from the perspective of those students with "non-mainstream" backgrounds and experiences. Now I would like to extend that warning to a new generation of students.

The nostalgia at the root of Bauerlein's critique was itself the target of Siva Vaidhyanathan's (associate professor of media studies and law at the University of Virginia) criticism in the very same issue of *The Chronicle Review*: "I have been hearing some version of the 'kids today' or 'this generation believes' argument for more than a dozen years of studying and teaching about digital culture and technology." Vaidhyanathan even addresses Bauerlein's recent headline-grabbing book, *The Dumbest Generation: How the Digital Age Stupefies Young Americans and Jeopardizes Our Future* with his own pithy response: "Well, if there is one way to ensure that young people do not read more books than necessary, it is to call them dumb in the title of a book. The book is strongly argued, but the voices of those who concern the author are curiously absent." Nostalgia as a malady, to use Vaidhyanathan's word, has long been with us: in 1985, it was Neil Postman blaming television, as Vaidhyanathan reminds us.

At the risk of sounding too vehement, or being accused of "over-reacting," I nevertheless decided to engage in this analysis for several reasons. First, crisis rhetoric such as we see in the articles cited above always brings out my instincts for complexity and inquiry that have been honed by a diverse career and graduate level training, regardless of which "side" is being advanced. I continually emphasize to my first-year writing students that we need to move beyond an "argument culture" where there are only two sides. They are tired, I'm sure, of hearing me say, "Any question worth our time has to have more than two answers." And so when I encounter such polarized, over-simplified thinking in my own field, I find it hard to resist engaging it.

But the more important reason for my response in this chapter has to be my unwavering belief that we betray our students when we expect them to think like us, to value what we value, and to devalue what we reject or degrade, simply because we tell them to do so. I have seen the negative consequences of this betrayal firsthand. Our students know, instinctively, when they or their experiences are not valued or welcome in a classroom or discipline. And so I cannot sit still when I see such rejection reflected in one of our profession's primary media outlets.

## *Now What? Preliminary Conclusions and Discussions*

I had originally envisioned this chapter as documenting my own difficulties with SL, to offer some comfort to readers who find digital media like SL too alien to even consider. Then I came across Professor Bauerlein's posts and knew I had a new mission.

This chapter has come to represent an intersection of my research interests: fandom, digital media, and student writers. In my dissertation research, I studied a group of students I described as Resistant Writers, those who come into a Composition course "hating" writing and believing they can't do it. So many of these Resistant Writers point to "literature" as one of the things they don't like about writing and their laments echo in my mind as I write.

While I was planning this chapter, I wondered about the wisdom of engaging such a high profile figure and perspective and I am still ambivalent about whether this piece is too harsh, or not harsh enough. I do acknowledge, though, that there is a bit of a "straw man" here: I have never met Professor Bauerlein and so am only responding to the missives he publishes on the *Chronicle* website. In that way, then, I am raising concerns not with him personally but rather with the persona he reflects in these postings. Given the role of the *Chronicle* in the halls of higher education, I cannot help but cringe at the unreflective nature of the critiques. We are all incredibly busy and if the only characterizations of digital media many have time for is the *Chronicle* blog while they are having their morning coffee in their offices, then I think we might have a serious problem on our hands.

We cannot continue to reflect, intentionally or not, the mindset that the best (or only) lens with which to view the world is our own. We cannot continue to denigrate those digital texts our students engage in because they look different, because they play a different role than our "beloved" literature. This cannot continue not only because it creates a persona of the English professor as the curmudgeon who complains loudly about "those damn kids" (will we be yelling at them to "get off our lawn" next?) but also because it is ultimately an uninformed, self-justifying mindset. We also run the risk of alienating our students. Sheenagh Pugh's description of the supportive community of fandom as opposite the "sense of isolation from mundanes" that comes from "awareness of baffled disapproval from those outside their own community" points to a matter of concern for instructors: we may not know we have students engaged in the types of digital media described in this collection in our classrooms because of their intense need for self-preservation against the usual reception. We therefore need to be sure we don't perpetuate that disapproval with our own actions. We are all fans of something — sharing that passion with students may open up a safe space for them to reciprocate.

In addition, even a brief investigation into the history of education reveals that the judgments of what is worth studying so unreflectively underpinning the nostalgic approach are fairly recent constructions. The current "canon" that is so critical to articles like that from Bauerlein has been a fixture in the liberal arts for at most the past century. This unequivocal acceptance of the Great Books model has caused more harm than good in my own experience — as a student, an observant friend, a writing teacher, and a scholar.

I am not really arguing for the value of any particular genre or medium; rather, I am trying to cogently articulate my discomfort with the persistent, pervasive efforts at devaluation within the academic point of view. It isn't that "anything goes"; I'm not advocating for an unfiltered, all-encompassing relativity that forbids cultural, aesthetic, or even literary judgments of any kind. Rather, I am expressing my increasing concern that the ways in which we express those judgments too often resort to bullying, to declaring texts, theories, and even scholars, to be the "other" so that we can demonstrate our insider status, to prove our worth, our membership status in the academic world.

I am also concerned that such nostalgia distracts from other, more complex pedagogical and theoretical questions raised by digital participatory media. For example, the rhetorical activities described in this collection can challenge the theoretical apparatuses with which we approach education and pedagogy. As Espen Aarseth argues, "The thought that these complex media can be understood by any existing media theory ... grows more unlikely with every stage of the ongoing computer evolution" (361). Aaresth calls for the construction of "an alternative theory that is native to the field of study" (362). One option could be Chris Bigum's argument that we need to see "information and communication technologies in schools in terms of relationships" among students and schools (136). In addition, Stephanie Gibson invokes Walter Ong's concept of "secondary orality" to describe "contemporary literacy ... [which] does not directly involve reading, yet would be impossible without someone being able to read" (6), calling into question traditional assumptions about literacy (7).

Similarly, the nostalgia may disguise the fact that, as this collection describes, when it comes to how we approach digital media, as both scholars and instructors, the biggest change we will need to make may actually be to reconsider the social nature of that media. For example, Catherine Beavis points to the interactivity and "social nature of game playing" as key elements of the "games world," which "is in marked contrast to the less immediately engaging forms of print text and literacy generally on offer in schools" (47). In her study of using videogames in a high school curriculum, Beavis identifies that "Contrary to popular beliefs, playing games in this situation was intensely social and interactive" (56). Similarly, for Pugh, the defining characteristic of fan fiction is the "canon," the "shared resource that the whole community of that fandom feels it knows and cares about" (26), a key element of the social nature of fandom.

Unfortunately, as many of my colleagues would note, my own response to the nostalgic critiques here is likely only to reach the usual suspects, to "preach to the choir," if I may resort to a cliché. But that potential reality only serves to spur me on, to call on my readers to be ambassadors for the Digital Generation within our own departments. If we are able to provide a counter-narrative to fill in the missing elements of incomplete critiques and to counteract the nostalgia underlying them, perhaps we can smooth the way for our students to learn to integrate the digital and print worlds in ways we cannot even imagine, even if we ourselves can't get our own avatars off Second Life's Orientation Island.

## NOTES

1. There was also going to be a Twitter reflection in this chapter but that experiment ran afoul very quickly and is still too new as of this writing. At some point in the future, I hope to share that experience in an appropriate forum.

## WORKS CITED

Aarseth, Espen. "Quest Games as Post-Narrative Discourse." *Narratives Across Media: The Languages of Storytelling.* Ed. Marie-Laure Ryan. Lincoln: University of Nebraska Press, 2004. 361–76.
Bauerlein, Mark. "Online Literacy Is a Lesser Kind: Slow Reading Counterbalances Web Skimming." *The Chronicle Review.* 19 Sept. 2008: B7. *ChronicleReview.com.* 15 Sept. 2008 <http://chronicle.com/weekly/v55/i04/04b01001.htm>.
Beavis, Catherine. "Reading, Writing, and Role-Playing Computer Games." *Silicon Literacies: Communication, Innovation, and Education in the Electronic Age.* Ed. Ilana Snyder. London: Routledge, 2002. 47–61.
Bigum, Chris. "Design Sensibilities, Schools, and the New Computing and Communication Technologies." *Silicon Literacies: Communication, Innovation, and Education in the Electronic Age.* Ed. Ilana Snyder. London: Routledge, 2002. 130–40.
Gibson, Stephanie B. "Literacy, Paradigm, and Paradox: An Introduction." *Emerging Cyberculture: Literacy, Paradigm, and Paradox.* Ed. Gibson and Ollie O. Ovideo. Cresskill, NJ: Hampton Press, 2000. 1–21.
Ito, Mizuko, et al. *Living and Learning with New Media: Summary of Findings from the Digital Youth Project.* Nov. 2008. MacArthur Foundation. 21 Nov. 2008 <www.digitalyouth.ischool.berkeley.edu/report>.
Jenkins, Henry. "Confronting the Challenges of Participatory Culture: Media Education for the 21st Century (Part Two)." *Confessions of an Aca/Fan* Web log. 23 Oct. 2006. 7 June 2009 <http://henryjenkins.org/2006/10/confronting_the_challenges_of_1.html>.

Pugh, Sheenagh. *The Democratic Genre: Fan Fiction in a Literary Context.* Brigend, Wales: Seren, 2005.

Rose, Mike. "The Language of Exclusion: Writing Instruction at the University." *College English* 47.4 (Apr. 1985): 341–59. Rpt. in *The St. Martin's Guide to Teaching Writing.* Ed. Cheryl Glenn and Melissa A. Goldthwaite. 6th ed. Boston: Bedford/St. Martins, 2008. 397–416.

Troop, Don. "The Undead Soul of Today's College Best-Seller List." *News Blog-The Chronicle of Higher Education.* 7 Mar. 2009. 9 Mar. 2009 <http://chronicle.com/news/article/6088>.

Vaidhyanathan, Siva. "Generational Myth: Not All Young People Are Tech-Savvy." *The Chronicle Review.* 19 Sept. 2008: B7. *ChronicleReview.com.* 15 Sept. 2008 <http://chronicle.com/weekly/v55/i04/04b00701.htm>.

# 26

# Making Dorothy Parker My MySpace Friend: A Classroom Application for Social Networks

*Ashley Andrews*

To this day, Dorothy Parker has refused, or rather ignored, my repeated requests for her to be my friend on the infamous social network, MySpace. I found Dorothy Parker the same way I found most of my MySpace friends: by adding friends I knew and then looking to see who their friends were. I got downright giggly when I saw that my good friend, the husband of my then officemate, had somehow befriended Dorothy Parker. What began as my own frustration at her lack of response to my request for friendship would end up reshaping the way I taught undergraduate literature courses.

Obviously, Dorothy Parker, who died in 1967, did not develop her own MySpace page. And yet, typing her name into a search engine on MySpace produces twenty different entries, over half of which were completed in homage to the beloved writer. While some are transparently created as fan sites, many of them purport to *be* Dorothy Parker. I just so happened to be working through a postdoctoral fellowship that centered on incorporating digital media into the classroom when I discovered Dorothy Parker's MySpace page. The final task for my literature courses needed to be some kind of creative digital media project that my students could create and implement by the end of the semester. I decided to start with the idea of MySpace pages related to personas from the American Literature course I was teaching and see where it would take me.

The first semester I tried out my idea, I drastically underestimated what my students could do with such a site and how involved they would become in the project. They all had MySpace or Facebook pages of their own, and they knew immediately what worked and what didn't work without much instruction. My only requirements for that first semester were that students post a proposal for their project on our own WebCT classroom site early in the semester and that they return to that proposal and amend it with any justifications for choices that may not make sense to the average viewer. For example, one student wanted to justify why he thought Huckleberry Finn would have enjoyed the Foo Fighters had he been living in more contemporary times. I hoped that students would engage differently with the texts and be forced to relate to characters and authors in different ways. The freedom of choice I gave them would let them feel a good deal of ownership for the project as a whole. For this class, they were allowed to choose any character or author from American Literature during the period covered by my class, whether we had read the material or not. The results[1] showed more than my students' ability to think critically about course content. It also showed pieces of their own beliefs and values that had been affected by the readings associated with their projects. One student completing a page on Booker T. Washington included a music video by Common that showcases pieces of Martin Luther King, Jr.'s "I Have a Dream" speech and scenes from the contemporary film *Freedom Writers*. The student connected pieces of Washington's dream for the Tuskegee Institute with the dreams of King and Common to show a thread of connection that made her more deeply consider the history of challenges that she had already seen in her community.

While this first semester exceeded my expectations, there was room for improvement. I needed to more clearly establish criteria for the projects and use those functions that make the network a "social" one. Some of my students had experimented with these functions by making friends with each other. Stephen Crane and Truman Capote had become especially friendly by the end of that first semester. My next attempt at the project took place at Embry-Riddle Aeronautical University, where I began teaching after my fellowship ended. I soon realized that these types of projects have added benefits at technical schools without English majors by allowing students to become involved with literature outside the strict parameters of an academic essay. For the next two semesters at Embry-Riddle, I divided my classes into small groups and had each group compose its own MySpace project. Each group had to decide on a set of characters or authors that would have some reason or purpose for befriending and communicating with one another on the network. Because this project had more required components and was part of a class that covered major literary genres, I limited the students to works read in class or other works by authors whom we had read. The results[2] from these projects indicate that students had intuited connections among literary figures based on the themes of the works and interpreted those connections on their sites. One of the most creative groups chose literary characters that had each challenged fate by asserting their own free wills. Their choices of characters included The Correspondent from Stephen Crane's "The Open Boat," the grandmother from Flannery O'Connor's "A Good Man Is Hard to Find," Montresor from Poe's "The Cask of Amontillado," Oedipus, and Tom Wingfield from Tennessee Williams's *The Glass Menagerie*. Each of these characters ended up challenging the assumptions of the other characters in how fate or free will was being considered, and lively debates ensued in the comment section of each page.

What I realized most from these projects was that students crave outlets other than traditional academic work because their methods of learning new material and integrating that material into their daily lives has changed so radically with the digital media environment in which they work and play. Learning to step back and assess the values of using new classroom activities that will enable our students to access ideas from where they are sitting (most likely, in front of a computer, television, or iPod) will help students and teachers learn from one another.

## NOTES

1. The results from this first semester project may be found online at http://lcc.gate ch.edu/~aandrews6/final_projects_2007.html.

2. The results from the second and third semester projects may be found online at http://webfac.db.erau.edu/~andrewsa/courses.html.

# 27

# Novel Cartographies, New Correspondences

## Jentery Sayers

Let me begin with a speculation: One thing that makes the "digital generation" distinct from others is how, exactly, they perceive where they are. As digital maps, global positioning systems (GPS), and all things GPS-ready become increasingly accessible in the United States, more and more people are getting to know their longitude and latitude. Or at least their mobile technologies are getting to know their location for them. A portable TomTom gives you turn-by-turn directions, a handy iPhone visualizes where you are, and a convenient Family Locator finds your children for you. Orwellian, perhaps. Marketable, most certainly. But for those of us who teach writing, digital maps afford more than an opportunity to simply say "I am here" with some precision. They give us the chance to change what "here" means in the first place.

In 2007, a colleague of mine, Curtis Hisayasu, and I began designing a multi-authored "geoblog" that would allow students to use mobile technologies, such as mobile phones, to collaboratively map the University of Washington's Seattle campus through digital media, including digital photography, video, and audio. With the geoblog, these media could be uploaded to the Internet, time- and author-stamped in individual blog entries, and pinned on a Google map. Once Curtis and I finished testing the geoblog, we published it, together with an article recommending its implementation in English composition courses, in the online journal, *Kairos: A Journal of Rhetoric, Technology, and Pedagogy.* As we mention there, the geoblog helps students acquire, through participatory learning, both technical and critical competencies in digital media.

Part of that participatory learning asks students to decide what about their campus matters to them and to document it, through digital media, on a map. Students can then reflect upon their decisions in writing. This process expands the notion of composition to include a variety of tools and practices, and how to document, with what technology, and through what medium all become rhetorical choices for students to make and explain. With each student participating, these rhetorical choices — these depictions of what about the campus matters — quickly aggregate in a single digital space, and when examined collectively, they start to form relationships and patterns. A series of photos from a bike ride across campus intersects with a number of bird sounds captured at approximately the same time. A video of a building under construction is juxtaposed with postcard-perfect shots of the library. What is initially an abstract snapshot of a campus is manipulated into a novel cartography of specific campus activities to be navigated and potentially revised by future audiences. That is, novel cartographies needn't end with the time and space of a given class or course. Since digital media are read as dynamic somethings to be picked up, built upon, and modified, asking students to anticipate how someone might eventually change their maps alters how they perceive the lifespan, and the importance, of their work. After all, what matters about the campus varies, depending upon who contributes, how, and for what purposes. The next question, then, is how mapping a digital campus can change the actual campus — how representing the campus becomes corresponding with it.

When can a map become more like a letter? More like a dialogue or a conversation? With the help of our colleague, Megan Kelly, Curtis and I produced a curriculum that includes assignments where, toward the end of the course, students are asked to examine the map they collaboratively composed and then write persuasive proposals for new spaces (e.g., a building, a learning commons, or a public event) on campus. Ideally, these proposals are simultaneously acts of imagination and demonstrations of sustained research on a particular campus topic or place. For instance, they require arguing for something that does not yet exist and supporting that argument with a blend of critical thinking, archival research, and interviews. Much like a digital campus map pinned with media, such proposals are a balance between what is and what isn't. As writers like Lewis Carroll, Paul Auster, Jorge Luis Borges, Alfred Korzybski, and Gregory Bateson remind us, the map is not the territory. The digital campus is not the actual campus. Nevertheless, when compared with print, digital maps afford a flexible representation of space. This flexibility is a vehicle for composing through a creative impulse, with practical implications. Indeed, novel cartographies demand thinking both big and small. For students to correspond with their campus and persuasively propose new campus spaces, they must in turn learn more about the ins and outs of their university, use their maps to organize and communicate, and closely attend to people's everyday practices, not to mention their own.

Influenced such as it is by an "imaginary" cartography, the proposal for a new campus space is a way of learning about the university in order to shape it and feed back into it. True, imagination and proposals alone do not make changes. There are always steps after the writing and research, and there are always material constraints to consider as well. However, a proposal for a new campus space — a space that is catalyzed by the malleability of a digital map — is a step toward bridging the digital with the physical, the imaginary with the actual. Otherwise, these domains risk being understood as two detached worlds, devoid of correspondence, with one merely representing the other. In that scenario, the digital map becomes but a guide, telling you where you are and where to go. On the other hand, novel cartographies lead to new correspondences. With some direction, they are negotiations between what "here" is now and what "heres" are possible.

## WORKS CITED

Sayers, Jentery, and Curtis Hisayasu. "Geolocating Compositional Strategies at the Virtual University." *Kairos: A Journal of Rhetoric, Technology, and Pedagogy.* 12.2 (2008). 16 Feb. 2009 <http://kairos.technorhetoric.net/12.2/>.

# About the Contributors

**Melissa Ames** is an assistant professor at Eastern Illinois University specializing in media studies, television scholarship, popular culture, and feminist theory. She teaches courses in these fields, as well as in composition and English education. Her work has been published in a variety of anthologies and journals, ranging in topic from television study, new media, and fandom to American literature and feminist art. Her most recent publications include her book, *Feminism, Postmodernism, and Affect: An Unlikely Love Triangle in Women's Media* (2008), and chapters in *Grace Under Pressure: Grey's Anatomy Uncovered* (2008) and *American Literature After the American Century* (2009).

**Ashley Andrews** is an assistant professor of the humanities at Embry-Riddle Aeronautical University in Daytona Beach, Florida, where she teaches composition, studies in literature, and modern literature. She recently completed her work as a Marion L. Brittain Postdoctoral Fellow at the Georgia Institute of Technology, where she focused on digital pedagogy. Her research interests include digital media in the classroom, American literature, feminist narrative theory, and literature of the American South. She is currently working on a science fiction course that will require students to create hypertext research projects, in lieu of traditional essays.

**Thomas B. Cavanagh**, Ph.D., is assistant vice president of Distributed Learning at the University of Central Florida. His research interests include e-learning, technical communication, and the societal influence of technology on education, training, culture, and commerce. He is also the author of several mystery novels.

**Susanna Coleman** received a master's degree in composition and rhetoric from Auburn University, where she completed a thesis on fan fiction as feminist composition and performed research on feminist aspects of other forms of digital writing and participation. She is currently an instructor at Auburn University–Montgomery. She has written fan fiction for over fifty fandoms in the space of twenty years and has been publishing her fan fiction online for over a decade. More recently, she has added the creation of fan art and music videos to her online participation in fandom.

**Andréa Davis** is a Ph.D. candidate in digital rhetorics and cultural rhetorics at Michigan State University where she studies multimedia and multimodal communications, particularly storytelling, across a variety of cultures and locations.

**Dànielle Nicole DeVoss** is associate professor and director of professional writing at Michigan State University. Her research interests include digital and visual rhetoric, and digital intellectual property issues. DeVoss recently co-edited (with Heidi McKee) *Digital Writing Research* (2007), which won the 2007 Computers and Composition Distinguished Book Award.

**Kimberly DeVries** earned her M.A. and Ph.D. in English (rhetoric and composition) at the University of Massachusetts–Amherst and is now on the faculty at California State University–Stanislaus. Her research interests include transnational literacies, global rhetorics, new/digital media, and Internet culture. Most recently she has been studying the institutionalization of new media in the Netherlands, particularly the involvement of women. She found *Sequential Tart* in 2000, posted a reply, and ever since has been a staff writer for *Tart*. Her professional and personal commitments don't allow her to keep up as regularly with online discussions, and as an academic, she has the habit of interpreting everything. Thus, she sees *Tart* with a sort of double vision: as an observer, but also as a Tart reflecting on her own experiences.

**Julie Flynn** is an independent scholar who received her M.A. in English literature from Drew University in 2005. She is the former secretary of the Graduate Student Caucus of the Northeastern Modern Language Association, a test preparation coordinator, and an adjunct composition instructor. She has written 24 fan fics (seven of which are crossovers), many conference papers, and one thesis.

**Marina Hassapopoulou** holds a B.A. in English from the University of Bristol (U.K.) and a M.A. in English and film studies from the University of Oregon. She is currently a Ph.D. candidate in English with a concentration in film and media studies at the University of Florida. Her academic interests include representations of race and ethnicity in the media, new media and participatory culture, interactive cinema, horror films, and Queer cinema. Her essay "Babel: Pushing and Reaffirming the Boundaries of Mainstream Cinema" was published in *Jump Cut* (Spring 2008), and her research paper "'It's All Greek to Me': Misappropriations of 'Greekness' in the U.S. Mass-Mediated Popular Culture" appeared in the *Journal of the Hellenic Diaspora* (Dec. 2007).

**Karen Hellekson** is an independent scholar in the fields of science fiction and media studies who is active in several fandoms as an archivist and fan fiction writer. She is founding coeditor of the online fan studies journal *Transformative Works and Cultures* (http://journal.transformativeworks.org/). Her coedited volume, *Fan Fiction and Fan Communities in the Age of the Internet,* was published by McFarland in 2006.

**Wendi Jewell** is an avid gamer and graduate of the University of Oklahoma's master's degree program in composition, rhetoric and literacy. She enjoys mixing popular culture and classical rhetoric to invigorate and illuminate both areas of study. She has pioneered several courses in games studies at the undergraduate level, including the first course in the subject taught at the University of Oklahoma. In addition to games and games studies, Jewell explores technology in general, and the impact technology has on writing pedagogy in university education.

**Matthew S. S. Johnson** is a composition/rhetoric specialist and an assistant professor of English at Southern Illinois University–Edwardsville, where he also serves as assistant director of expository writing. His academic interests include composition and rhetorical theory, writing pedagogy, computers and composition, digital/electronic literacies, and technology. He has contributed to the journals *College English* and *Dichtung Digital,* as well as the collections *TechKnowledgies: New Imaginaries in the Humanities, Arts, and Technosciences* and *From Hip-Hop to Hyperlinks: Teaching about Culture in the Composition Classroom.* He also co-guest-edited (with Pilar Lacasa) a special issue of *Computers & Composition,* "Reading Games: Composition, Literacy, and Video Gaming," on gaming and composition studies. He serves as reviews editor for the *Journal of Gaming and Virtual Worlds.*

**Elizabeth Kleinfeld** is an assistant professor of English and Writing Center director at Metropolitan State College of Denver, where she teaches composition and rhetoric. She was on the faculty at Red Rocks Community College in Lakewood, Colorado from 1995 until 2008. She is currently coauthoring with Amy Braziller a composition textbook on researching and composing in multiple genres and media. She presents regularly at national, regional, and local conferences on peer groups, revision theory, New Media/Web 2.0, and writing center theory and practice. She blogs about teaching, writing, and other things at *http://revisionspiral.blog-city.com.*

**Dundee Lackey** is a Ph.D. candidate in Michigan State University's rhetoric and writing program. Her interests are in digital literacy, pedagogy, and activism.

**Kristine Larsen** is a professor of physics and astronomy at Central Connecticut State University. She is the author of two popular-level books, *Stephen Hawking: A Biography* and *Cosmology 101.* Her scholarly work focuses on interdisciplinary applications of science, such as women in the history of science, science pedagogy and public outreach, and scientific motifs in the works of J.R.R. Tolkien. She first forayed into the world of online fandom and fan fiction in 1997 in response to the unpopular death of a major character on the television series *Highlander.*

**Catherine McDonald** holds a Ph.D. in rhetoric and language from the University of Washington (2006). She is the assistant director of composition at Western Washington University, where she mentors the graduate students who teach in the writing program. Cathy teaches classes in rhetoric, language and society, and various composition courses. Her publications and presentations address the transferability of writing instruction, rhetorical genre theory, and self-sponsored digital literacy. She and a graduate student have collaborated on a grant to study the effect of digital writing and they are writing a chapter about joint research in the digital age for a collection on technology and collaboration.

**Kim Middleton** is an associate professor of English and an affiliated faculty member in the American Studies Program at the College of Saint Rose, in Albany, New York. Her courses examine the intersections among contemporary culture, literature and new media. Her work has appeared in the edited collections *Contemporary British Fiction Post-1979: A Critical Introduction* and *High Pop: Making Culture into Popular Entertainment.*

**Georgianna O. Miller** received her Ph.D. in rhetoric, composition, and the teaching of English from the University of Arizona in May 2009; her dissertation is entitled *The Rhetoric of Hysteria in the U.S., 1830–1930: Sirens, Suffragists, Psychoses.* In addition to pursuing her feminist historical research, she has taught lower- and upper-division composition and business writing courses at the university level and worked in various capacities in numerous writing centers. In her "spare" time, Georgianna enjoys almost every television show there is. When she's not trying to revise her dissertation into journal submissions, she's Googling past seasons of various reality TV shows. Currently, she works at Arizona State University.

**Sean Morey** teaches writing and digital media in the Department of English at the University of Florida. His research focuses on Gregory L. Ulmer's theories of *electracy* and addresses the intersection between networks, systems theory, and composition as well as the role of visual rhetoric in constructions of environment. He also designs and maintains the Ichthyology Division's website at the Florida Museum of Natural History, including the website for the International Shark Attack File (ISAF). Along with Sidney I. Dobrin, he is co-editor of the edited collection *Ecosee: Image, Rhetoric, Nature* (2009).

**Juli Parrish** is an assistant professor of writing studies at the University of Minnesota–Duluth. She is particularly interested in exploring the ways that "mini-genres" emerge within specific fandoms and in finding meaningful ways to talk about the relationships between individual works of fan fiction and canonical texts. She studies the work of amateur readers and writers more broadly, as well; other current projects include archival research on the communal dormitory journals written by Bryn Mawr College students between 1977 and 1997.

**Christopher Paul** is an assistant professor in the Communication Department at Seattle University where he teaches courses in rhetoric and digital media studies. He teaches "VideoGames, Communication, and Culture," where students explore the history and context of video games, while using *World of Warcraft* as both a common site for play and research. In addition to raiding in *World of Warcraft* with his spouse and father, Christopher also enjoys experimenting with the economy in *WoW*. He is currently working on projects related to rhetorics of raiding in massively multiplayer online games and using online games as instructional tools.

**Diane Penrod** is a professor of English and director of the University Writing Program at East Carolina University in Greenville, North Carolina. She is the author of several books and articles linking popular cultural issues to writing instruction. Her current research focuses on the place of trust in the college writing classroom and a historical look at the 1970s and that decade's influence on composition.

**Mark Pepper** is currently earning his Ph.D. in rhetoric and composition from Purdue University, where he teaches courses on multimedia writing and online collaboration. His current research interests include popular culture, network/complexity theory, cool study, and virtual worlds. His Second Life avatar is named Rhett Hitchcock and can often be seen working around the Technical Writing center on Purdue's SL island.

**Julie L. Rowse** is a recovering Air Force brat currently living in Nebraska. She holds a B.S. in secondary education from the University of Nebraska–Omaha, and taught high school journalism, English, and speech for six years. She left public education to pursue her graduate studies, and now holds an M.A. in popular culture from Bowling Green State University. Her master's thesis is titled "Trouble Right Here in Digital City: Censorship of Online Student Speech." Her research interests include film and television studies, media literacy, and sports. After completing her graduate studies, Julie returned to the classroom and is teaching American literature at Bellevue West High School in Bellevue, Nebraska.

**Jentery Sayers** is a Ph.D. student in English at the University of Washington, the recipient of the 2008 *Kairos* Teaching Award for Graduate Students and Adjuncts, a 2008-09 HASTAC Scholar, and a 2008-09 University of Washington Huckabay Teaching Fellow. His dissertation is on the influence of sound reproduction technologies on 19th and 20th century Anglo-American literature, and he has taught several undergraduate courses on the intersections of mapping with digital media and composition. With Curtis Hisayasu, he co-authored "Geolocating Compositional Strategies at the Virtual University," published in Issue 12.2 of *Kairos: A Journal of Rhetoric, Technology, and Pedagogy.*

**Michael R. Trice** currently serves as an assistant editor for the web journal *Kairos* and writes for a variety of web outlets. He holds an M.A. in technical communication from Texas State University and is currently pursuing an M.A. in research in communication studies at the Centre for Digital Citizenship at the University of Leeds on a Fulbright grant, studying how wikis might be used as cultural preservation tools.

**Heather Urbanski** is an assistant professor of English and director of composition at Central Connecticut State University. She holds a master of arts in writing from Rowan University and a Ph.D. in English, specializing in composition and rhetoric, from Lehigh University. Her first book, *Plagues, Apocalypses and Bug-Eyed Monsters: How Speculative Fiction Shows Us Our Nightmares*, examines the role of science fiction and fantasy in contemporary culture. Her current work with digital media and popular culture began at the 2006 World Science Fiction Convention and the fandom community continues to remain a source of inspiration for her scholarship.

**Zach Waggoner** received his Ph.D. from Arizona State University. His research interests include videogame rhetoric, computers and writing, technological interfaces and identity construction, and the rhetoric of gender in society. Zach teaches a variety of composition and rhetoric courses for ASU's Writing Programs, including first-year composition, professional writing, and videogame theory. Zach also helps facilitate new TA training and orientation for ASU's English Department.

**Harald Warmelink** has an M.A. (*cum laude*) in new media and digital culture from Utrecht University and a BCom in Communication Systems from Hogeschool Utrecht, both in the Netherlands. He is a Ph.D. candidate at Delft University of Technology where he is researching virtual world organization in online games as well as virtual worlds applied by business and governmental organizations worldwide. His main interests concern how real-life organizations instantiate and sustain organization and institutionalization in the virtual worlds they create.

**Suzanne Webb** is a Ph.D. student at Michigan State University studying rhetoric and writing with a concentration in nonfiction. Her research begins at the crossroads of digital and visual rhetoric, class studies, professional writing, and nonfiction.

# Index